Sharing Our Pathways

Sharing Our Pathways

Native Perspectives on Education in Alaska

Edited by

Ray Barnhardt
Angayuqaq Oscar Kawagley

ALASKA NATIVE KNOWLEDGE NETWORK
UNIVERSITY OF ALASKA FAIRBANKS

Alaska Native Knowledge Network
Center for Cross-Cultural Studies
University of Alaska Fairbanks
PO Box 756730
Fairbanks, AK 99775-6730
www.ankn.uaf.edu

ISBN 978-1-877962-44-8

Library of Congress Cataloging-in-Publication Data

Sharing our pathways : native perspectives on education in Alaska / edited
by Ray Barnhardt, Angayuqaq Oscar Kawagley.
    p. cm.
  ISBN 978-1-877962-44-8 (alk. paper)
  1. Indians of North America—Education—Alaska. 2. Indians of North
America—Science—Alaska. 3. Ethnoscience—Alaska. 4. Education and
state—Alaska. 5. Alaska—Social policy. 6. Alaska—Race relations.
  I. Barnhardt, Ray. II. Kawagley, Angayuqaq Oscar.
  E78.A3S43 2011
  371.829'970798—dc22
                            2010049939

Text and cover design by Paula Elmes, ImageCraft Publications & Design

Contents

Part I Athabascan Pathways to Education

Part II Iñupiaq Pathways to Education

Part III   Tlingit/Haida Pathways to Education

Part IV   Unangan/Alutiiq Pathways to Education

Part V   Yup'ik/Cup'ik Pathways to Education

Appendices

Acknowledgments

It is with a renewed appreciation that we acknowledge the contributions of the many staff and associates of the Alaska Rural Systemic Initiative whose hard work is reflected in the recycled essays that make up this book. These articles, more than anything else, capture the dedication, collaboration and innovation that went into rethinking and reconfiguring the role and make-up of schooling in rural Alaska over the past decade and a half. Special acknowledgment goes to Julie Kitka and the Board of the Alaska Federation of Natives for their unflinching sponsorship of the Alaska RSI, and to Jody Chase, whose support as our Program Officer at the National Science Foundation provided the opportunity to explore innovative strategies for rural school reform. In addition, we acknowledge the leadership provided by our Co-director colleagues Dorothy Larson and Frank Hill, as well as the Regional Coordinators and Elders whose on-site support brought the AKRSI initiatives to bear in each cultural region.

We also owe a special thanks to Lolly Carpluk, Dixie Dayo and Malinda Chase who served as editors of the *Sharing Our Pathways* newsletter (where the essays in this book were originally published), as well as kudos to Paula Elmes who brought her graphic art and layout talents to the preparation of the newsletter, and to Sean Topkok who assisted with its distribution. A complete set of the newsletters can be viewed on the Alaska Native Knowledge Network web site at http://www.ankn.uaf.edu/SOP. The selection of essays included in this book are organized in chronological order by cultural region and represent the range of issues and initiatives that made up the work of the Alaska RSI.

Finally, we dedicate this publication to Frank Hill, Andy Hope, Rachel Craig, Jim Walton and Ruthie Sampson, whose time with us was all too short, but whose contributions to the AKRSI will live on in the generations that follow.

Ray and Oscar

Ray Barnhardt | Introduction

The essays contained in this compendium were assembled from a collection originally published in the *Sharing Our Pathways* newsletter, which was issued bi-monthly over a period of ten years (1996–2005) under the auspices of the Alaska Rural Systemic Initiative. The AKRSI was funded by the National Science Foundation and implemented by the Alaska Federation of Natives in collaboration with the University of Alaska Fairbanks. The purpose of the AKRSI was to implement a set of school reform initiatives that systematically documented the indigenous knowledge systems of Alaska Native people and developed pedagogical practices and school curricula that incorporated indigenous knowledge and ways of knowing into the formal education system. The essays contained in this volume were produced as an outgrowth of the many initiatives implemented by the staff and Elders associated with the AKRSI.

While the NSF funding served as the catalyst for the core reform strategy focusing on math and science education, we were able to acquire substantial supplementary support from other sources to address areas for which the NSF funds were not suitable, such as indigenous curriculum materials development (funded by USDOE), and implementing comparable initiatives to those of AKRSI in the areas of social studies, fine arts and language arts (funded by the Annenberg Rural Challenge/Rural School and Community Trust). All of these initiatives combined to provide an opportunity to address the issues facing schools in Native communities throughout rural Alaska in a truly comprehensive and systemic fashion.

The central focus of the AKRSI reform strategy was the fostering of connectivity and complementarity between two functionally interdependent but historically disconnected and alienated systems—the indigenous knowledge systems rooted in the Native cultures that inhabit rural Alaska, and the formal education systems that were imported to serve the educational needs of rural Native communities. Within each of these evolving systems there exists a rich body of complementary knowledge and skills that serve to strengthen the quality of educational experiences and improve the academic performance of students throughout rural Alaska.

AKRSI Participants

The most salient feature of the context in which this work took place was the vast cultural and geographical diversity of the state of Alaska. The following map outlines the five major cultural regions around which the AKRSI initiatives were organized (Alutiiq and Aleut/Unangan were combined), with twenty participating rural school districts distributed across the five regions:

To take on such a complex endeavor in ways that recognized and

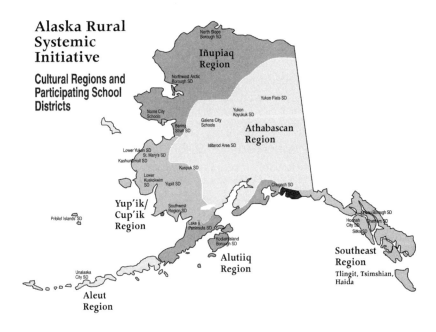

capitalized upon the diversity of cultural conditions throughout the state, a staff of three statewide co-directors and five regional coordinators was assembled to serve as the core team for implementing the initiatives on a rotating cycle over the course of 10 years. Each cultural region took on responsibility for a set of focused activities each year, building upon and contributing to the activities in each of the other regions, as illustrated in the following chart:

NSF/ARC Combined Yearly Cycle of Activities by Cultural Region

NSF						ANNENBERG
Rural Systemic Initiative/ Year	Year 1	Year 2	Year 3	Year 4	Year 5	Rural Challenge Initiative/ Year
Native Ways of Knowing/ Teaching	Yup'ik Region	Iñupiaq Region	Athabascan Region	Aleut/Alut. Region	Southeast Region	ANCSA and the Subsistence Econ.
Culturally Aligned Curriculum	Southeast Region	Yup'ik Region	Iñupiaq Region	Athabascan Region	Aleut/Alut. Region	Language/ Cultural Immersion Camps
Indigenous Science Knowledge Base	Aleut/Alut. Region	Southeast Region	Yup'ik Region	Iñupiaq Region	Athabascan Region	Oral Tradition as Education
Elders and Cultural Camps	Athabascan Region	Aleut/Alut. Region	Southeast Region	Yup'ik Region	Iñupiaq Region	Reclaiming Tribal Histories
Village Science Applications	Iñupiaq Region	Athabascan Region	Aleut/Alut. Region	Southeast Region	Yup'ik Region	Living in Place

Given the persistent high turnover of personnel in the rural schools, the key participants in the cultural adaptation and implementation of the AKRSI initiatives were the Elders and the Native educators in each region. As the Native educators came together to address the needs of their respective region, they began to form into regional associations and sought independent funding to develop initiatives tailored to their regional needs. Following is a list of the Native Educator Associations that emerged in response to the AKRSI initiatives over the ten years of the program:

> Ciulistet Research Association
> Association of Interior Native Educators
> Southeast Native Educators Association
> North Slope Iñupiaq Educators Association
> Association of Native Educators of the Lower Kuskokwim
> Association of Northwest Native Educators

Native Educators of the Alutiiq Region
Association of Unangan/Unangas Educators
Southcentral Alaska Native Education Association
Alaska Native Education Student Association
Alaska Native Education Association
Alaska First Nations Research Network
Honoring Alaska's Indigenous Literature
Consortium for Alaska Native Higher Education
Kuspuk Native Educators Association

As the statewide and regional initiatives unfolded, each region was responsible for submitting material for the *Sharing Our Pathways* newsletter and helping to populate the emerging Alaska Native Knowledge Network web site, so that the lessons learned in each region could be disseminated and shared with others. It is those articles, first published in the *SOP*, that now make up the rich compendium of information and insights shared in this book.

Cultivating Indigenous Knowledge

While developing new strategies for integrating Indigenous knowledge and Native ways of knowing into the formal educational system, the AKRSI staff sought to reach beyond the surface features of Indigenous cultural practices and illustrate the potential for comparative study of deep knowledge drawn from both the Native and Western systems. Examples of topical areas for instruction in which opportunities for linking local knowledge with the textbook curriculum were readily available are illustrated in the lower portion of the following iceberg diagram.

The metaphor used to illustrate the multiple initiatives in which the Native communities and schools were engaged is that of converging streams of knowledge, as illustrated in the streams diagram.

A variety of initiatives were implemented that aimed at documenting the makeup of the Native knowledge stream to make it more accessible to schools, along with parallel initiatives aimed at loosening up the structure of the Western knowledge stream to make room for the local contributions. In addition, initiatives such as the Old Minto Cultural Camp illustrated how both knowledge streams could come together in mutually productive ways. The goal of these efforts was to demonstrate the complementarity and reciprocity that can be achieved by guiding the interaction of these knowledge systems in

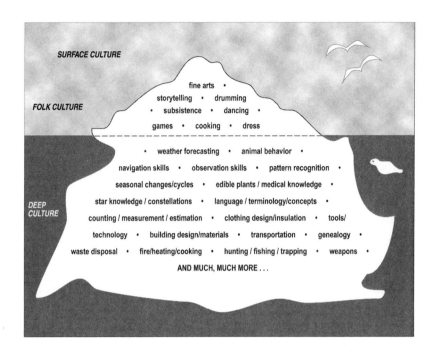

SURFACE CULTURE

FOLK CULTURE

fine arts •
storytelling • drumming
• subsistence • dancing •
games • cooking • dress

DEEP CULTURE

• weather forecasting • animal behavior •

navigation skills • observation skills • pattern recognition •

seasonal changes/cycles • edible plants / medical knowledge •

star knowledge / constellations • language / terminology/concepts •

counting / measurement / estimation • clothing design/insulation • tools/

technology • building design/materials • transportation • genealogy •

waste disposal • fire/heating/cooking • hunting / fishing / trapping • weapons •

AND MUCH, MUCH MORE . . .

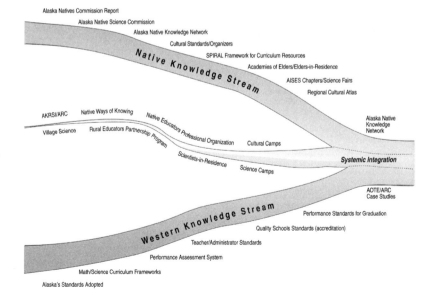

Alaska Natives Commission Report
Alaska Native Science Commission
Alaska Native Knowledge Network
Cultural Standards/Organizers
SPIRAL Framework for Curriculum Resources
Academies of Elders/Elders-in-Residence
AISES Chapters/Science Fairs
Regional Cultural Atlas

Native Knowledge Stream

AKRSI/ARC   Native Ways of Knowing

Village Science   Rural Educators Partnership Program

Native Educators Professional Organization   Cultural Camps

Scientists-in-Residence   Science Camps

Alaska Native Knowledge Network

Systemic Integration

AOTE/ARC Case Studies

Western Knowledge Stream

Performance Standards for Graduation

Quality Schools Standards (accreditation)

Teacher/Administrator Standards

Performance Assessment System

Math/Science Curriculum Frameworks

Alaska's Standards Adopted

ways that increase both the depth and breadth of learning opportunities for all students.

As the Native educators in Alaska (including the Elders) began to examine the curriculum development, staffing and policy issues impacting their schools, they became concerned about the constricting forces that were bearing down on their schools as a result of the nascent standards movement—a school reform process being driven by a national and state agenda in which they had little involvement. As they reviewed the standards that had been developed for the various content areas, they didn't quarrel with what they saw, but were greatly concerned with what they didn't see. From their perspective, neither the state nor the national content standards in all the subject areas added up to a well-rounded education. As one Elder put it, "The schools are more concerned about preparing our children to make a living than they are in preparing them to make a life for themselves." With guidance from the Elders, the Native educators in each cultural region began to document what they thought their children and grandchildren needed to know and be able to do as they went through school, and the strategies by which these life-affirming knowledge, skills and values might be achieved.

A turning point in the AKRSI efforts took place in 1998 when the Native educators from each of the regional associations assembled their collective insights and produced the *Alaska Standards for Culturally Responsive Schools*, which have since been endorsed by the State Board of Education and are now in use in schools throughout the state. The "cultural standards" have provided a template against which schools and communities can examine the extent to which they are attending to the educational and cultural well-being of their students, i.e., preparing them to make a life for themselves. They include standards in five areas: for students, educators, curriculum, schools and communities. The emphasis is on fostering a strong connection between what students experience in school and their lives out of school by promoting opportunities for students to engage in in-depth experiential learning in real world contexts. The cultural standards embodied the cultural and educational restoration strategy of the AKRSI and their implementation has had ripple effects throughout Alaska, in urban as well as rural schools.

Through the *Alaska Standards for Culturally Responsive Schools*, educators and community members are directed toward preparing culturally knowledgeable students who are well grounded in the cultural heritage and traditions of their community and are able to understand and demonstrate how their local knowledge and practices relate to other knowledge systems and cultural beliefs. As articulated by the Native educators, the *Alaska Standards for Culturally-Responsive Schools* point to the need for educators who:

- incorporate local ways of knowing and teaching in their work.
- use the local environment and community resources on a regular basis to link what they are teaching to the everyday lives of the students.
- participate in community events and activities in an appropriate and supportive way.
- work closely with parents to achieve a high level of complementary educational expectations between home and school.
- recognize the full educational potential of each student and provide challenges necessary for them to achieve that potential.

The educational reform strategy implemented through the AKRSI produced an increase in student achievement scores, a decrease in the dropout rate, an increase in the number of rural students attending college, and an increase in the number of Native students choosing to pursue studies in fields of science, math and engineering. The consistent improvement in academic performance of students in AKRSI-affiliated schools over each of the ten years indicated that the cumulative effect of utilizing the Alaska Standards for Culturally Responsive Schools to promote increased connections between what students experience in school and what they experience outside school appears to have a significant impact on their academic performance.

The AKRSI school reform initiatives demonstrated the viability of introducing strategically placed innovations that would serve as catalysts around which a new, self-organizing, integrated educational system could emerge that would produce the quality of learning opportunities that have eluded schools in Native communities for over a century. The substantial realignments that are evident in the increased interest and involvement of Native people in education in rural communities throughout Alaska, as reflected in the various initiatives described in this compendium, point to the applicability of locally driven strategies in shaping reform in Alaska's educational systems.

1

Athabascan Pathways
to Education

Frank Hill, AKRSI co-director and retired superintendent

Rural Alaska School Districts: Who is in Control?

Sharing Our Pathways, Vol. 5, Issue 1, Jan/Feb 2000

Most of rural Alaska's schools and districts are populated by Alaska Native students. School boards are elected by and from residents of the district, resulting in mostly Alaska Native-majority boards. With this fact one would assume that the Alaska Natives of the region would have little to worry about concerning whether their local culture and language would be a strong, if not dominant, facet of the local schools' curriculum and instruction.

Given the fact that few licensed administrators and teachers are Alaska Native, or even Alaskan-born, the assumption above is not a safe one to make. At the present time there is not one Alaska Native school superintendent in Alaska, only a handful of Alaska Native school principals and less than six percent of all teachers are Alaska Native. Over 80% of Alaska's newly-hired teachers continue to come from out of state.

Since so few school district superintendents and administrators are from Alaska, or are Alaska Native, they are often unfamiliar with the cultural and environmental conditions of the districts they administer. To the extent that we tend to teach and administer the way we were taught, in most cases rural Alaska school districts with Alaska Native school boards and student populations are run just like Anywhere, USA. Add to this situation the extremely high turnover rate of teachers and administrators in rural schools, where in some cases you literally have to start all over again every year or two, we often end up repeating the same mistakes over and over again. I don't fault these professional educators alone because lacking strong direction from the local school boards they will do what they think best, even when they know it is not, because they have only their own experience to draw upon. Recent State of Alaska improvements in professional educators' licensure requirements begin to address the cultural relevancy issues noted above. However, the full effect of these improvements will not be realized until all teachers and administrators have been re-licensed under the new system.

If the local school boards do not have definite and strong policy statements concerning budget development and approval processes, relevant curricula, teaching practices and materials, school calendar considerations, teacher/personnel hiring/performance effectiveness reviews and staff development preferences, the administration will often carry out and operate the district with little if any input from the governing body of the district-the school board. It is the professional duty of the administration to make sure that at least the letter of the law is met in school operations. There are few, if any, school laws or regulations that require school administrators to pay attention to the local culture, language or environment in the administration of schools and districts. State laws are designed to allow for variation to take place on the local level. Schools and professional educators have a technical language and jargon of their own that is often confusing and mysterious to the general public. Alaska education laws and regulations are no less technical or confusing.

Many Alaska Native school board members will not dispute policy or personnel recommendations made by their administration, assuming that the administrators are the professionals in these matters. In addition, members of many Alaska Native cultures do not, or will not, publicly disagree with others even if they have other opinions. Yet the school board is ultimately responsible for the academic success of their district's students. Perhaps one of the causes of the lingering fact of low academic achievement of Alaska Native students is due to the lack of assertiveness of local school boards regarding budget, policy, instructional program and personnel matters. Who knows the most about local needs: local members of the school board or the administrator from Outside?

Perhaps a program to train Alaska Native school board members to more fully realize their legal responsibilities and to actually take policy control of their districts should be developed. Of course, not all school boards would need this training. It is my understanding that the Association of Alaska School Boards (AASB) has developed an accountability model for school boards, but I am not sure what level of training or participation rural Alaska Native school boards have had in this accountability model. Maybe a supplementary funding program could be developed to assist AASB and the local boards in implementing this school board accountability program?

As a facet of Alaska Native self-governance, I believe that control of education matters is an area that lends itself well to developing a locally-relevant program of instruction with Alaska Native educators in the classrooms as well as district offices. The long-term effect would reach into many other areas of Alaska Native self-determination. Also, if most of the teachers and administrators in rural schools were Alaska Native, the employment picture of rural Alaska would change considerably. In many villages, the highest paying jobs are held by non-Native, non-Alaskan teachers and administrators. Too often the money earned from those positions goes outside the state with little secondary benefit to the rural economy.

A program could be developed that would train and sensitize new-to-Alaska teachers and administrators to teach and work in Alaska Native villages and schools. Such a program once existed at the University of Alaska Fairbanks where participants were sponsored by their districts to learn about Alaska Native cultures and living and working in small, often remote schools where they would be in the minority. This program was discontinued but I believe that many school districts would pay for their new-to-the-state teachers and administrators to participate in such a program, especially if it were offered on a regional level. Here is another area that could have positive long-term effect on the stability and improved academic performance of Alaska Native students.

Two promising programs are the Rural Educators Preparation Partnerships (REPP) and Native Administrators for Rural Alaska (NARA). These programs sponsored by the University of Alaska have a goal to significantly increase the number of Alaska Native classroom teachers and school administrators. However, they are both small in scope, with limited budget capacity. These are efforts that should be significantly increased with more funds made available.

Without the elected Alaska Native school board members exercising their responsibilities as policy-making bodies, not many of the initiatives discussed here will significantly improve the academic performance of Alaska Native students.

Research and Indigenous Peoples

Nakutluk
Virginia Ned

Sharing Our Pathways, Vol. 6, Issue 1, Jan/Feb 2001

My interest in the issues associated with documenting indigenous knowledge evolved this fall while instructing CCS 601, Documenting Indigenous Knowledge. Research of indigenous peoples has been endured since the first arrival of non-indigenous peoples. Many times the research project and purpose wasn't clearly explained or in some cases not explained at all to individuals or communities involved in the research process. "Informed consent" wasn't a

Johnson Moses and his daughter, Nakut luk Virginia Ned, sit with a model of a soos, created by Virginia.

requirement until recently and often there was no sharing or presentation of results to the individual or community studied after completion of the research project. Little attempt was made to engage the people involved in a continuing knowledge sharing process.

In the past research was often done by amateur botanists, surveyors, government officials, traders, missionaries or anyone able to write and/or illustrate. The purpose of research then was to gather information on the indigenous people to serve the interests of an audience of non-indigenous people. While the books that were written made for interesting reading, they were usually written from the perspective of authors who spent only a limited amount of time living among the people they describe. Their stories have contributed to the general impressions and the myriad of ideas that have informed non-indigenous peoples about Native life in the past. The studies provide interesting details, much of which is now taken for granted as fact and has become entrenched in the language and attitudes of outsiders towards indigenous peoples.

Documenting indigenous knowledge continues to be of interest to many people for a variety of purposes. Indigenous peoples themselves are beginning to contribute to the research, thus providing greater authenticity and control over their own forms of knowledge. Indigenous research today has implications for the survival of peoples, cultures and languages. It is part of the struggle to become self-determining and to take back control of the issues that affect indigenous people.

Indigenous knowledge as intellectual property that can be used by others for financial gain is not something that the indigenous peoples have had to deal with before. It contradicts the way we perceive the knowledge of our Elders, our communities and the tribe. Indigenous knowledge was preserved and retained in the oral tradition through stories, language, songs, beliefs, values and respect for all living things, usually shared overtly by example and demonstration. "The quantity and quality of knowledge varied among community members depending upon gender, age, social stature and profession." (Lore, 1992) There continues to be many specialized fields of knowledge that are known by only a few people. There are expert teachers, sled builders, snowshoe builders, storytellers, trappers, dog mushers, hunters, skin sewers, skin tanners, beaders, leaders, orators, singers, knitters and fishermen. There is sacred knowledge that is shared within families, communities and tribes that teaches the local traditions, values and customs. There are many people who are adept in a number of areas, but very few who are experienced in all of the above.

What is Indigenous Knowledge?

Indigenous or traditional knowledge is the knowledge of the local environment that people have developed to sustain themselves and thus it serves as the basis for cultural identity. It is knowledge built up by a group of people through generations of living in close contact with nature. (Lore, 1992) It is knowledge and skills gained through hands-on experience while interacting with the environment. It is knowledge of plants, animal behavior, weather changes, seasons, community interactions, family genealogy, history, language, stories, land and its resources, values, beliefs, traditional leadership, healing and survival.

The Elders of our communities are the holders of the indigenous knowledge that will show us the way to healing and wellness in our communities. Indigenous knowledge is the key for our survival and sustenance as indigenous peoples. The Elders present the indigenous knowledge in the actions they take, their stories, their display of respect for all things, their role-modeling and their investment in the community. They are the repositories of the language, wisdom and knowledge of the past that is needed to resolve problems that we have today and in the future.

Research Requirements: A Code of Conduct

To help guide and encourage culturally-appropriate indigenous-based research, I have put together a preliminary draft of a research "code of conduct" for discussion and review. This draft is only the beginning of an indigenous research process that can be revised and adapted for each community and/or tribe.

In conclusion, my investigation of issues surrounding documenting indigenous knowledge has raised more questions than answers. It is a topic that is essential to the survival of indigenous peoples and therefore it is imperative that we pay careful attention to what we do.

Even in the 21st century, indigenous peoples will have to defend and protect our indigenous knowledge and cultures.

Further information and guidance on documenting indigenous knowledge can be found in the *Guidelines for Respecting Cultural Knowledge*, available through the ANKN web site at http://www.ankn.uaf.edu/standards/knowledge.html. Another excellent resource on the issues outlined above is the book, *Decolonizing Methodologies: Research and Indigenous Peoples* by Linda Tuhiwai Smith. It can be purchased from Zed Books VHPS, 16365 James Madison Highway, Gordonville, VA 22942. E-mail address: customerservice@VHPS VA.com. Phone: 888-330-8477.

References

Johnson, Martha 1992. *Lore: Capturing Traditional Environmental Knowledge*, Dene Cultural Institute and the International Development Research Centre, Hay River, NWT, Canada

Documenting Indigenous Knowledge and Languages: Research Planning & Protocol

Beth Leonard

Sharing Our Pathways, Vol. 6, Issue 5, Nov/Dec 2001

I have been preparing a research proposal for the Interdisciplinary Ph.D. program at UAF that focuses on "Athabascan Oral Traditions: Deg Hit'an[1] Narratives and Native Ways of Knowing." Much of my current research and language learning centers on kinship and (personal) family histories. Hopefully this research will serve dual purposes in terms of both academic significance and potential value to the Deg Hit'an community.

Research by indigenous researchers for the benefit of indigenous communities also dovetails with political/postmodern movements of self-determination, autonomy and cultural regenesis. Maori researcher, Linda Smith (1999) states: "The cultural and linguistic revitalization movements have tapped into a set of cultural resources that have recentred the roles of indigenous women, of Elders, and of groups who had been marginalized through various colonial practices" (p. 111). Although some Deg Hit'an Elders were recorded during the Alaska Native Literature Project and more recently during the development of Deg Xinag Dindlidik: Deg Xinag Literacy Manual, there remain several Elders who have not had a chance to record traditional stories and/or lend their perspectives to the history of this area. Deg Hit'an narratives will be valuable as language maintenance efforts proceed and more emphasis is placed on integrating Native knowledge and history into the school curriculum through projects such as the Alaska Rural Systemic Initiative.

---

1. The term Deg Hit'an ("local people" or "people from around here") is used to refer to the people of Anvik, Shageluk and Holy Cross. Osgood (1936) and subsequently the 1982 ANLC Native Languages map used "Ingalik" which is not a Deg Hit'an word but a Yupi'k word meaning "lice infested."

Researcher's Background

I grew up in Shageluk, Alaska, an Athabascan village on the Innoko River located in the lower-middle Yukon area. I also spent four years in neighboring Anvik, a village on the Yukon approximately 30 miles from Shageluk. My father is James Dementi of Shageluk, a multilingual speaker of Deg Xinag and Holikachuk Athabascan and English. My mother, Jean Dementi, who died in 1988, was a non-Native

Deg Xinag

Sidithniqay James Dementi, Jean yił xivi'ezre'. Sito' Didlang Tochagg nadheyonh. Vidadr (sivadr) Katherine, Susan, Louise yił xivi'ezre'. Katherine Dzox-tsey dhido. Katherine vichoy Patrick viyix dhido yił. Louise viqing' Richard yił Qay Xuchux xiditl'tth'e. Sito' vichidl (sitoy) Gilbert vi'ezre'. Gilbert vi'ot Eleanor yił Cantwell xiditl'tth'e.

Singonh California nadheyonh. Vichidl (sidhi'a) Keith, Don yił xivi'ezre'. Don vi'ot Lucille yił Santa Barbara California xiditl'tth'e. Vidadr (siq'oy) Yvonne vi'ezre'. Yvonne viqing' Richard yił Redding California xiditl'tth'e.

Sitsiy Charlie Cikal Dementi, Charles Aubrey yił xivi'ezre'. Sitsiy Charlie Dementi Dishkaket nadheyonh. Sitsey Lena Phillips Dementi, Ruth Aubrey yił xivi'ezre'. Sitsey Lena Dementi łeggijitno', Niłteghelinghdi' yił nadheyonh. Sitsey viyił xethdlan Clara, Albert xivi'ezre'.

Beth Dementi-Leonard si'ezre'. Deg Hit'an itlanh. łeggijitno', Dzox-tsey, Qay Xuchux, Gitr'ingithchagg xinasiyonh. University of Alaska Fairbanks School of Education q'u'isineyh. Siqing' Michael Leonard vi'ezre'. Clear AFS q'u'idineyh. Siyotr'a' Samantha vi'ezre'. Fairbanks tr'iditl'tth'e.

English

My parents are James and Jean Dementi. My father grew up in Swiftwater (on the Innoko River). His younger sisters (my aunts, father's side) are Katherine, Susan and Louise. Katherine lives in (new) Shageluk. Her grandson Patrick lives at her house also. Louise and her husband Richard live in Anchorage. My father's younger brother (my uncle, father's side) is Gilbert. Gilbert and his wife Eleanor live in Cantwell.

My mother grew up in California. Her younger brothers (my uncles, mother's side) are Keith and Don. Don and his wife Lucille live in Santa Barbara. Her younger sister (my aunt, mother's side) is Yvonne. Yvonne and her husband Richard live in Redding, California.

My grandfathers are Charlie Cikal Dementi and Charles Aubrey. Charlie Dementi grew up in Dishkaket. My grandmothers are Lena Phillips Dementi and Ruth Aubrey. Lena Dementi grew up in Old Shageluk and Lower Village. Her siblings are Clara and Albert.

My name is Beth Dementi-Leonard. I am Deg Hit'an Athabascan. I grew up in Old Shageluk, New Shageluk, Anchorage and Anvik. I work for the UAF School of Education. My husband's name is Michael Leonard. He works at Clear AFS. My daughter's name is Samantha. We live in Fairbanks.

woman who came to Alaska from California as an Episcopal nurse-evangelist. In 1976 she became Alaska's first woman ordained to the priesthood in the Episcopal church.

Due to a variety of socio-historical influences, most people of my generation did not learn to speak Athabascan. Both the early Episcopal church missionaries and the territorial and Bureau of Indian Affairs schools mandated English and parents had been told not to teach their children the Athabascan language. During the time I lived in Shageluk and Anvik, there were no Athabascan language programs in place in either the school or community. I do, however, remember the first linguists from the Alaska Native Language Center (ANLC) who came to the Shageluk area to work with speakers during the early 1970s. My father and other relatives often worked as consultants in these early language documentation and translation efforts. This contradiction in Native language status, i.e. continuing suppression of local language and culture by churches and schools versus promotion by prestigious outside academic interests, conveyed ambiguous and confusing messages to communities struggling to maintain their local cultures.

Barriers and Challenges in Language Learning

In my current role as language learner—along with other language learners from the Deg Hit'an area—I find myself struggling with the best way to learn the Deg Xinag language and share the knowledge I have documented. Although many of us as language learners work directly with linguists, obvious differences between English and Deg Xinag Athabascan are not articulated and we (the learners) are forced to stumble along as best we can. I believe this is due in part to the lack of knowledge of the deeper Athabascan cultural contexts and constructs and the failure to document language beyond the lexical and grammatical levels.

I was an undergraduate linguistics student when I began my study of Deg Xinag. At that time I had no experience in learning a non-European language and was accustomed to being taught conversational language by experienced teachers using immersion methods. I was also used to having an extensive collection of practical dictionaries and grammars at my disposal to assist in the learning process. Although there is not a published grammar for Deg Xinag, there are materials that can be used for language learning. To date, publications include one set of verb lessons, a language curriculum for elementary students, one literacy manual, two books of traditional stories, several short children's stories and a limited collection of supplemental learning materials. The verb lessons explain the linguistic structures at an elementary level for language learners, however, as stated above, significant cultural constructs and concepts are not addressed.

Through my academic coursework I would often run across barriers to my own self-confidence in being able to someday speak Deg Xinag fluently. For instance, there is a whole body of research on second language acquisition that says if learning begins after adolescence, the learner cannot expect to become fully fluent in the second language. In a similar vein, linguists often describe Athabascan "as one of the most difficult languages in the world to learn," thereby insinuating that one needs to be of above-average intelligence to indeed even attempt such a process. As a learner and student I have been questioned as to the potential for true authenticity (purity) of Athabascan when learned as a second language and whether or not I think the "back velars"2 will drop out of the language.

I began my own language learning by asking for phrases in the languages and listening to taped narratives and literacy exercises. I also would sit down with my father and go through sections of the noun dictionary to find the literal meanings of words. I found that, although writing and studying written language is not considered the best way to learn conversational language, it provided a base for further understanding of the language structure and helped with learning the sound system. I continue my study of conversational language through regular interactions with various members of my immediate and extended family. Sometimes this learning takes place in more formal environments such as the ANL 121/122 audioconferences or Athabaskan Language Development Institute's on-campus classes. On most occasions this learning takes place through informal interaction with speakers through visits or phone conversations. I still use a variety of learning methodologies, including writing the language on a regular basis.

One of the more popular ways to teach/learn language involves a method called Total Physical Response (TPR). In English this would require the use of the imperative mode to give a series of commands which require some action on the part of the learner, e.g. come here, open the window, close the door, etc. In Deg Xinag, however, many of these do not equate to commands but describe instead what the subject is doing. In the case of "wake up" for instance (when speaking to a child), a more appropriate way to express this in Deg Xinag is "*Xejedz tr'aningidhit he'*?" which translates to "Are you waking up good?" Examples such as these reflect the deeper value system, i.e., a gentle way of relating to children as they awake.

I am continually impressed with the Deg Xinag speakers' command of English and Athabascan and their strength and resilience considering the damage that has been done since contact. In the past there was a great deal of travel and intermarriage between the Deg Hit'an and Holikachuk areas, so many speakers have command of at least two Athabascan languages. As multilingual speakers, they are aware of our difficulties in learning these languages and are able to provide the context we often ignore. I have observed that in immersion or partial immersion situations, speakers will adapt their use of language so as to not totally overwhelm, but assist learners through individual levels of learning by varying the complexity of their speech.

Language Learner As Researcher

"Alaska Native worldviews are oriented toward the synthesis of information gathered from interaction with the natural and spiritual worlds so as to accommodate and live in harmony with natural principles and exhibit the values of sharing, cooperation, and respect" (Kawagley, 11).

Kawagley's observations about Alaska Native worldviews are reflected in my initial research with the *Ingalik Noun Dictionary*. In reviewing this dictionary with my father, I found that the literal translations were not included. For a beginning language learner, literal translations provide a great deal of fascinating cultural information and further impetus for investigation into one's own culture. For example, the Deg Xinag words for birds, fish, animals and plants reflect complex and scientific beliefs and observations.

English	Deg Xinag	Literal Translation
black bear	*ggagg gichidl*	animal its/the little brother
otter	*tixet'an (te xut'an?)*	water people (?)
water snipe	*teyeg*	water spirit/shadow (its shadow reflects on the water?)
junco	*legg ney*	"fish" it says (the junco calls when salmon are coming)
yellow pond lilly	*vichingadh ethog*	muskrat's plate
raven	*yixgitsiy*	your (plural) grandfather

English	Deg Xinag	Literal Translation
rusty blackbird	*yixgitsiy vozra*	raven his nephew
puffball mushroom	*yixgitsiy nolchildl*	raven's (sewing) bag

Culturally Appropriate and Respectful Ways of Language Learning

Learners, like myself, who do not have latent knowledge of the language, use a translation approach. Often we inadvertently ask for words or phrases for concepts that do not exist, or concepts that are expressed in very different ways in this cultural context. Learners also tend to provide an incomplete or sometimes total lack of context when requesting words or phrases. As English speakers, we nominalize and decontextualize many concepts, without realizing that Athabascan is a dynamic, verb-based language.

One example of differences between Deg Xinag and English categorization reflects the way one would say "Where are you/where is it?" *Xidanh* is used when referring to people (e.g. *Xidanh si'ot?*—Where is my wife?), whereas *xiday* is used to refer to an animal or object (*Xiday sileg?*—Where is my dog? or *Xiday sigizr?*—Where are my mittens?) The same is true for counting people, animals or objects (*nijtayh/nijtay*). From what Deg Xinag speakers have said, using these words for "where" and "how many" show respect toward animals who might be offended if the wrong reference is used. This reflects a context of care and respect for animal spirits and other non-human spirits present in the environment, as well as the power of the spoken word.

When learners request generic phrases for weather, for instance, it can be difficult for speakers to provide this information when not given a particular context. A more holistic context might provide the following information:

- whether a phenomena is happening now, a little while ago, yesterday, last week, etc.
- if a phenomena is/was happening for the first time during the specified time period, or is/was beginning again
- variations in intensity—a little, very hot/really windy, etc.

These limited examples gathered by members of the language class reflect both major and subtle changes in context (Fig. 2.)

Deg Xinag	English	Literal Translation
Dranh ngi'egh ilyoth.	It's snowing outside today.	Today outside it is snowing.
Getiy ghilyotth.	It really snowed.	Really it snowed.
Chen ititlyotth.	It started to snow again.	Again it started to snow.
Chen nititlyotth.	It's started to snow again.	Again it's started to snow.

These limited examples gathered by members of the language class reflect both major and subtle changes in context

Documenting Oral Sources and Research Issues

I write down new words and phrases gathered from speakers in my family during phone or face-to-face conversations and audioconference classes. I also record speakers (with their permission) when possible and have several tapes of recorded audioconference classes as well as phrase lists. In the past, I had not really thought about the proper way to obtain permission to record information either in writing or with audiovisual equipment. Often I would ask if I could record, but assumed the speakers knew I would use this information for learning purposes. Now I realize that there are a great many issues to deal with when documenting in writing or with audio/visual equipment, including:

- Who should have ownership of audio/visual materials?
- How will the material be used?
- How will the material be cared for?
- Where should materials be stored?
- Who should have access to the materials?

"Just Speak Your Language"

Lately, it seems the endangered languages bandwagon is a popular vehicle for access to "other," providing many opportunities for publication through description and analysis of various Native language revitalization programs. Outside researchers continue to debate the authenticity and effectiveness of projects and programs from non-indigenous perspectives. Language revitalization, instead of being viewed holistically within social and cultural contexts, is often treated as strictly a linguistic venture, i.e. "just speak your language." "Just speaking your language" assumes abilities and resources are available to assist in this process. It involves learning cultural constructs and concepts often hidden in translation along with a myriad of other environmental, ideological and personal factors. Fortunately there are now indigenous educational models providing examples of contextual/situational learning that can be applied at a local grass-roots level.

References

Kawagley, A. O. (1995). *A Yupiaq Worldview: A Pathway to Ecology and Spirit*. Prospect Heights, Illinois: Waveland Press, Inc.

Smith, L. T. (1999). *Decolonizing Methodologies: Research and Indigenous Peoples*. London: Zed Books Ltd

Frank Hill | # Remembering Our Heroes

Sharing Our Pathways, Vol. 7, Issue 5, Nov/Dec 2002

Since 9-11 we have heard much about the heroism of the policemen and firefighters of New York City. Their actions need to be remembered and celebrated. Their actions remind us of the kind of people we could or should be if we had the same dedication to purpose.

Today, if we were to ask our young people who their heroes are, many would say Michael Jordan, Eminem or other sports or entertainment personalities.

The heroes of my childhood have endured for my entire life. I grew up in a time and place rich with opportunity to be among heroes. Besides my Finnish seafaring father and my Dena'ina mother and grandmother, my favorite hero is my Uncle Gabriel Trefon, a Dena'ina from Nondalton and the Lake Clark area. I refer to Uncle Gabriel's life for inspiration and an example for myself as I have transitioned from those days of living with the land to earning a living in the modern world.

Uncle Gabriel was my mother's brother, who was born at the beginning of the last century. As was customary in those times, his life as a true Dena'ina man required him to become an expert hunter, fisher, provider and leader. And that he did for the remainder of his life. After he became chief of the Nondalton people and I was old enough to be aware of Uncle Gabriel's leadership, I began to pay attention to his activities. Many people regarded Uncle Gabriel as a gruff, stern person. At first, I thought so too. But as the years passed I became aware of his other strong traits.

Uncle Gabriel was the local church leader. Active in the church as well as performing the duties of traditional chief, Uncle Gabriel combined Dena'ina cultural values with those of the church. I recall him

counseling a young couple who wanted to get married in the church. He admonished the young man for thinking about marriage and family responsibilities without first demonstrating his independence from his parents by having his own house. Another time, Uncle was asked by a couple to plan a funeral for a newborn baby. I recall watching Uncle carefully examine the dead infant and ask the parents questions about how and when the baby died. When we were building the casket for the tiny baby, I remember his tears and the mourning songs he sang to the child.

After realizing that the cost of store-bought goods was prohibitive for his people when purchased and transported from the nearest store a day's travel away, Uncle Gabriel established a store in the village. Although he lacked formal schooling, he kept the store accounts accurately. He made arrangements with the cannery employers of his people to sign over a portion of their earnings to the local store to ensure that their families could buy what they needed. Among other firsts, Uncle was the first in his village to own an outboard motor and to bring a washing machine to his home. This demonstrated to me that he was continuously thinking of how life for his people could be made better.

Once, when there was a very long cold spell of winter weather, no one could travel in the extreme cold and whiteout blizzards to get needed supplies. Even the younger men were fearful of going out into the weather. As the storm continued and supplies in the village ran low, Uncle Gabriel hitched up his dog team and made the trip by himself. My family was living in the community where the store was located and I remember him returning in that blizzard, to the surprise of everyone. Again he showed the commitment and leadership that a Dena'ina chief should have.

Uncle Gabriel passed on while I was away attending high school. I remember one of the last conversations I had with him, telling me it was good that I was going on to get an education and to remember that I was Dena'ina too. One of my grandsons is named after Uncle Gabriel and I am proud that my daughter also remembers my hero every time she calls her son's name.

We need to remember and honor the heroes that helped us become who we are—whose memories should not be allowed to die. There are heroes in every Alaska Native culture like my Uncle Gabriel. I hope their children and grandchildren will continue their examples. As they do so, they remind us of the strength, knowledge, honor and wisdom of our cultures; characteristics which are needed even more today.

Howard Luke and
Sarah McConnell

An Elder Interview With Howard Luke

Sharing Our Pathways, Vol. 7, Issue 5, Nov/Dec 2002

Sarah McConnell interviewed Howard Luke on April 3, 2002. Below is an excerpt from that interview. Transcription by Jeannie Creamer Dalton

SARAH: It is a sunny April 3, 2002 and Howard, you wanted to talk about respect?

HOWARD: Yeah I like to talk about respect because we're losing it so fast right now it's terrible. Myself I don't care about it because I'm old enough now. The biggest thing right now is I want my young generation to pay attention about respect because down the road they will find out but it will be too late by then.

Respect is the biggest problem: respect is something that you really got to take care of yourself by being clean and when you're skinning moose or cutting fish. Never try to get bloody, get blood on your clothes or nothing.

Many years ago I use to hunt with a lot of old people; my mother used to tell me to go out with them old people so I used to go with them. They give us some meat and stuff. I lost my dad when I was really young so it was just my mother until she got married, married again. So I went out with a lot of old people and I seen them how they do it 'cause my mother say you pay attention now you see how they do it; you see they don't try to get bloody and the first thing they do is clean all the tripe—they clean all the guts—they never throw anything away. The main thing they do right away is they roast meat.

I hunt caribou, there used to be a lot of caribou in Nenana at one time way back in 1934, somewhere around there anyway. I used to go out with them, I seen how they do it, they clean the tripe, they clean it good. They wash it, they use a little water, then they turn it inside out; they put all their stuff in there. They put the kidneys, and heart, and all the stuff they can put in there. They tie it—they put a stick through it—then you can just carry it on your hand. That little bag would hold all that. So I learn all that. This is what I want to teach the kids how to do things because if we don't show respect, our animals are going to disappear. That's what is happening right now, we don't respect, that our fish is disappearing. People, when they were fishing, all they want is eggs, the roe, they just take the roe, and just throw the fish out. That's not respect. That's what I mean, right now, if you were mistreated, you wouldn't go back there, would you? Well, that's the same thing with the animals and the fish and our ducks and everything, you see.

Like I'm saying about the airboats, that they go out in the spring, they run over the eggs and all young ones, they run over them. We don't take care of our animals. We just don't care and that's the reason all our animals are disappearing, especially our ducks. Every year it's getting lesser and lesser. And that's what I mean. They're not coming back. I mean, if I was mistreated, I'm not going to go back too. Well it's the same way with animals.

When I was brought up that's what they tell me about respect.

Right now, just like, you bring moose head in house and there's a bunch of kids in house and the kids look at that moose head, the eye, and they play with that. They play with that, and that was against our nature. We always covered up because if you make fun of that animal, they tell each other, just like humans, same thing, humans that are dead. Their spirit is here and they tell each other and that's what our people used to tell us—not only my mother, but my uncle, people I used to hunt with. People always used to tell us that if you are skinning moose or skinning caribou you always try to stay away from the blood. Don't try to cut the veins they say. When you're skinning moose, you always take the brisket out first. Take the brisket, then you feel your way, you get by the throat, then you take the whole thing, the throat, you just pull it right out. The whole thing will just come right out. That's our way of doing it. That's the reason a lot of people used to lose their luck. But now, right now, we don't respect. They throw the head away. There is a lot of good stuff on that head there.

When I went to New Zealand, them people down there, when they kill a cow, when they're going to have something going on, a potlatch, or something like that, they throw the head away. So when I went down there, I told them, gee, man, I said, there's a lot of good meat on this stuff.

When we kill a moose, we never throw it away, we take the tongue, we dice it up, all the cheek, we dice it up and make a good pot of stew. So I did that. I taught them something and they started doing it. So that way we work with each other. We share with one another. That's my biggest thing right now is that I want to share with people. Especially young people. My big thing right now, when I'm laying down here, I think about these things that, gee my uncle, all my old people I used to go out hunting. I used to go out hunting with big Albert and John Silas and lot of old people down in Nenana. I use to go out with them, a big run of caribou. So I go out hunting with them because they give me some meat when I go out. When I go with them, they give us ribs or something like that. Even the little thing, you were so thankful for it. Right today, I'm so thankful right today, that what I went through, what my Mom taught me and the other people taught me—how to respect, take care of your things and always when you kill moose, they always say, you turn the head towards home and that way, the next moose you kill will be closer to your house, they said. So all them things, it make me think about it. But right now, we're going the other way, we're not going the right way. We always trying to make that cut off, just like we're going against nature. We want to get done with it right away. Just like if we go visit or something like that, we look at the time, well I gotta go, I gotta go, I gotta go, I gotta do this, I gotta do that. And old people figure that oh no, that fellow he thinks I got nothing to say.

That's the reason why right now a lot of our people doesn't want to share with people because they do that and I tell my young people right now that that's not the way to act because people watch how you work—if you show respect.

Components of Culturally-Responsive Schools

Frank Hill

Sharing Our Pathways, Vol. 8, Issue 1, Jan/Feb 2003

Those of us associated with the Alaska Rural Systemic Initiative for the past seven years have been promoting the concept of cultural-ly-responsive schools as a means to create systemic reform in Alaska's rural schools—especially those whose student populations are pre-dominantly Alaska Native. Improved student academic achievement is the ultimate goal. We understand and believe that if we base teach-ing and schools on the local environment and culture, giving respect and credit to students and heritage, we can begin teaching at a higher level. We also understand and believe that students who have healthy self concepts are better learners.

What exactly does a "culturally-responsive school" look like? What would be happening in a culturally-responsive school that will be different?

Alaska Native Knowledge Network publications *Alaska Standards for Culturally-Responsive Schools* and *Guidelines for Developing Culturally-Responsive Teachers for Alaska's Schools* provide guidance for describing what we should find in culturally-responsive schools. Rather than go into all of the sections covered in the referenced pub-lications I will share my version of what constitutes a culturally-re-sponsive school by listing what I believe should be evident if I were visiting that school and the school community:

- Teachers and administrators would be those who were born and raised in the community or region.
- Local community has direct and significant input in the pro-cess and recommendations for hiring all school staff.

- School is named for a local cultural hero or leader and whose picture and contributions to the community and region are detailed in the pictorial presentation.
- Local cultural statement of values and beliefs are prominently displayed throughout the school.
- Behavioral standards for students are based on the values of the local culture and are developed with full participation of local parents, Elders and leaders.
- Classrooms display local cultural events and people
- Local Native Elders are prominent in every classroom and are regulars in the school throughout the day and school year (celebrate Elders, birthdays in school.)
- Elders are accorded "dignitary" seats during important school functions (games, meetings, graduations, etc.)
- Local school's annual goals for students are prominently displayed.
- Teachers teach within the culture, not about the culture. Teachers utilize local environment, language and culture in developing and delivering lessons for students.
- The instructional program and curriculum includes:
  - instruction in the local Native language
  - local cultural history and a correct and complete Alaska history course that details how Alaska Natives have been recognized and treated as well as how they are now organized for cultural, political and economic reasons.
- Flexible/alternative instructional methods including regular field trips outside the school in the local environment.
- Process for reporting student academic progress includes options besides report cards (school academic fairs, highlighting student achievement during student basketball games, etc.)
- School calendar/daily schedule take into account the local community's cultural activities.
- ALL school staff are included in staff meetings and inservices.
- Administrators, teachers and other school staff learn and use local cultural language greetings and words for praise when working with students.
- The school's facilities are readily available to the local community when not in use for instruction or student activities (someone in the community has keys to the school.)

- Local school board meetings include regular reports by all of the classroom teachers, instructional support staff and maintenance personnel.
- Administrators/teachers attend all local village meetings including tribal councils, cultural celebrations, local holiday events, etc.
- Students learn and present plays and performances of local legends spoken in Native language, develop and wear traditional clothing with assistance from local cultural experts.
- Students translate reports and other activities into local language and present to Elders/community.
- Local community develops standards for students that would prepare them for participation in local cultural community, takes responsibility for and delivers instruction both within and outside school day. Students meeting these standards are recognized by village leaders during end-of-year graduation ceremonies.

These observations are really only a beginning of what could be developed for any local school and could be the beginning of a plan for a local school to become culturally responsive. We know, too, that some rural schools have developed their own list of culturally-responsive practices. It would be helpful for all of us if those components were shared with those schools wanting to become more culturally responsive.

Learning Dinaxinag: A Personal Journey Through Higher Education

Beth Leonard

Sharing Our Pathways, Vol. 9, Issue 3, Summer, 2004

Keynote Speech to the 2004 Bilingual Multicultural Education Equity Conference

*D*ogidinh (thank you) for your introduction. Since Deg Xinag is one of the languages honored at this conference, I would like to give the Deg Hit'an Elder teachers the opportunity to introduce themselves as they are the teachers, and the ones who provided the translation of the conference theme: My aunts, Hannah Maillelle of Grayling and Katherine Hamilton of Shageluk and my father, James Dementi of Shageluk.

The Deg Xinag language area has been inappropriately labeled on the Alaska Native Languages Map as "Ingalik." The term Deg Hit'an references the people of the area, while the term Deg Xinag refers to the language. There are currently Deg Xinag speakers living in Anvik, Grayling, Shageluk and Anchorage. The conference theme, "Enriching Student Achievement Through Culturally and Linguistically Responsive Instruction", was difficult to translate. We reworded it in English and the speakers put forward the phrase

Members of the author's family, L to R: James Dementi (father), the late Lena Phillips Dementi (grandmother), Katherine Hamilton (aunt). In front is the late Susan Dutchman (aunt).

Sraqay Xejedz Deg Xiq'i Xidixi Dindli'an' that means "kids learn well/ good through Deg Xinag."

In 1992 I attended this conference for the first time. I was an undergraduate student at the University of Alaska Fairbanks and had recently changed my major from accounting to linguistics. I had become interested in learning my heritage language and contributing to language revitalization efforts. I was very new to the fields of education and bilingual education. I remember being overwhelmed as this was the first conference I had attended, and I didn't know many people. I was so impressed with the keynote speakers, and all the expertise represented at the conference from the different areas of Alaska. If someone had told me that I would one day be chosen to give a keynote address at this conference, I would not have believed it. I have attended this conference fairly regularly for the past seven or eight years. I have learned so much from all the present and past participants through your presentations and workshops. You continue to educate me as I go through the process of writing my dissertation, the final stage of my Ph.D. program. The mentoring and support you have provided has been invaluable. For me, and probably others as well, this conference is a time of renewal and re-energizes us to continue the work that we do.

I have lived in Fairbanks since 1978, and currently work as a language coordinator-instructor for the Interior Athabascan Tribal College (IATC), a post-secondary educational center operated by Tanana Chiefs Conference, a consortium of Interior Athabascan tribal governments. The IATC language program currently has partnership agreements with the Alaska Native Language Center and the Yukon Koyukuk School District. However, I do want to say a few words about a family language program we are trying to promote-a program that involves children and their parents or caregivers. This program started a couple of years ago when Susan Paskvan, who is currently working with the YKSD Athabascan language program, decided to offer a Fairbanks community schools course that was open to 8–12-year-old students with an accompanying parent or guardian. Kathy Sikorski also taught Gwich'in and accepted students at the high school level and above. Kathy and Susan developed a variety of games and other language learning activities and offered their courses once a week. The community really appreciated these courses and they had a great response. Thanks to our current partnership with the YKSD, and funding from the Administration for Native Americans, this program is starting to pick up within some of the TCC region villages. We are also hoping to continue this program in Fairbanks with the help of Velma Schafer and Virginia Ned.

I did not grow up speaking my ancestral language, Deg Xinag. I am currently learning my language as an adult with other adult students from our area. My mother, Jean Dementi, was a non-Native woman from California and English was the primary language used in our home as I grew up. My father grew up in a small community on the Innoko River below Shageluk called Didlang Tochagg, which means spruce slough. His father—my grandfather, Charlie Dementi, was from the Holikachuk language area and his mother from the Deg Hit'an area, so he speaks two Athabascan languages in addition to English. My father has some education within the formal Western system, however is more highly educated in the place-based subsistence educational system that was, and still is, necessary to the survival of the Deg Hit'an people. My grandmother, Lena Phillips Dementi, who had spent time in the Episcopal mission at Anvik, taught my father and his siblings how to read, write and speak English.

I am enrolled in the interdisciplinary Ph.D. program at the University of Alaska Fairbanks. My research focuses on illustrating Deg Hit'an epistemologies and knowledge systems, or Native Ways of Knowing, through analysis of Deg Xinag oral traditions. Through language learning, I am becoming more familiar with cultural beliefs, world views and value systems that sustained the Deg Hit'an people for thousands of years prior to contact with Russians and Europeans. However, there is a certain measure of frustration involved. I find myself struggling with the best way to learn the Deg Xinag language. Many times I am not aware of obvious differences between English and Deg Xinag or do not understand the social and kinship relationships within the culture. Many of the written resources we have access to do not connect the language with the cultural contexts. I believe this is due in part to the lack of knowledge of deeper Athabascan cultural contexts and constructs and the failure to document language beyond the lexical and grammatical levels.

For instance, in the *Deg Xinag Noun Dictionary*, if I was to look up an entry under kinship, I would find the word for "grandfather" is *sitsiy*. If I looked further into the dictionary under birds, I might find a similar word *yixgitsiy* or "raven." In another section under plants, I would find *yixgitsiy nojchidl*, or "puffball mushroom". When you see these words grouped together, you can tell there is some relationship here. For example, *yixgitsiy* literally means "your (pl) grandfather", so there are connections with this bird within the human kinship system. *Yixgitsiy nojchidl*, or the puffball mushroom, literally means "Raven's sewing bag". So within many of our resources, there are all these glimpses into kinship relationships and the whole cultural context that goes unexplained without going beyond a literal translation to some other means of cross-referencing.

This past summer I took my written comprehensive exam. On the exam was a question about a story told by the late Belle Deacon who was honored with a Honoring Alaska's Indigenous Literature (HAIL) posthumous award. In her book, Belle told each story in Deg Xinag, then English. The Deg Xinag is presented in the book with a line by line English translation. Some of the speakers who are here today helped with those translations of her book.

Here is the question from my exam:

> Based on your research, discuss Deg Hit'an symbolic, ontological and epistemological notions of the pike in Belle Deacon's story, "Man and Wife" in *Engithidong Xugixudhoy*. Discuss the cultural implications of transformation, subsistence and hierarchy in this narrative as contrasted to other Athabascan peoples.

I will briefly summarize the parts of the story that relate to the creation of the pike and then address the different components of the question:

> "*Nij'oqay Ni'idaxin*—The Man and Wife" (Deacon, 1987) tells the story of a couple living by themselves at the mouth of a side stream. When fall came, the man spent a lot of time trapping while the wife stayed at home chopping wood, sewing and cooking for her husband. The wife would always make fish ice cream for her husband and after he had eaten he would specifically ask for this. As the man continues to go out hunting and trapping for days at a time, his wife begins to feel lonesome. This cycle of the same activities goes on for a number of years, with the wife making fish ice cream (occasionally snow ice cream) for her husband. One day during falltime she does

not feel well and does not make the ice cream for him. He urges his wife to make the ice cream since he does not get full without it, and sleeps well after eating ice cream. His wife then goes outside for snow to make ice cream and does not return. The man searches for her and finds the bowl and spoon she had taken with her, but finds no tracks beyond the water hole. He mourns for her during the subsequent fall and winter then becomes thin and weak, thinking that he will die.

At mid-winter an old man (whom he later learns is Raven) visits him and tells the husband that his wife was stolen by a giant and taken to "a land deep down in the water" (p.15). Raven tells the man that he will not be able to get his wife back without his [Raven's] help. After the man has eaten and rested, they begin work by cutting down a large spruce tree with a stone axe. They then limb the tree and cut the top off, making it about "12 arm spans long" (p.19). The spruce is then peeled and over the course of at least a month, it is carved into the shape of a pike with the insides and mouth hollowed out. After the pike is complete, they tie a rope to it and drag it to the water hole. The carved pike is then painted with white spots. Belle comments that " . . . *jegg xit'a chenh ngizrenh*," "it was such a beautiful fish" (p.21). The man then goes to the cache and brings "things [beads] that were like eyes" (p.21). Raven uses a medicine song on the beads and then puts them in place, whereupon they begin to wiggle and move. Raven instructs the man to go fetch an ice chisel. They then measure the fish (again) and find it to be 12 arm spans long. The man is instructed to chop a hole in the waterhole big enough to accommodate the fish and fetch other items for his journey. Items include a clay lamp which is to provide light for him while inside the fish. Raven then "blew with his hands and made medicine with a song" (p.25), hitting the fish on the back. The fish sinks to the bottom of the river with the man inside and produces a humming noise that shakes the man.

Upon arriving at the underwater village the man leaves the pike and eventually rescues his wife from the giant and villagers. The husband and wife return and enter the pike, whose head is resting on the shore. The giant and villagers prepare to shoot arrows at the pike, when it swamps their canoe and swims around. Belle says, *"Dij yan' yij yixudz xiti'ihoyh"* (p.29), indicating there is blood all over. The pike then swamps the village with waves, straightens itself out and begins the humming sound again. Upon their return, Raven is waiting and then washes the head and teeth of the pike with a rag. Raven instructs the fish to "stay in a place where there are lakes, where no one will go," and "for people who step there on the ice of the lake, you will shake your little tail," indicating "someone's impending death" (p.31). The fish then "goes to the bottom," however they (man and wife) "don't know where" (p.31). In the English version of the story, Raven strongly reprimands the pike for killing the people in the village.

This is not the end of the story, however, I will end the summary here as there are no more direct or indirect references to the pike.

The Pike's Role in Subsistence Practices

For the Deg Hit'an people, pike or "jackfish" as referenced by Osgood (1940; 1958; 1959) were an important part of the traditional subsistence cycle as they can be harvested year-round from lakes, side streams and rivers. Traditionally, pike were harvested in basket traps—*gidiqoy tidhi'on*. Osgood (1940) indicates that traps were set as part of a fish weir during the fall and winter months and the harvest was most abundant after breakup (p.231). Pike also could be harvested individually, in clear water, using a double-pronged fish spear—*nijq'adz ggik vaxa gindiggad*. Data from a study by Wheeler (1997) done in 1990–1991 indicates that Anvik's pike harvest consisted of 19.5% of its non-salmon harvest; Shageluk, 35.8% and Holy Cross, 28.1%, illustrating the continued importance of this fish in the current subsistence cycle (p.160–162).

Nelson (1983) indicates that pike are aggressive, predatory fish and can grow up to six feet in length and 50 pounds in weight (p. 72–73). Their jaws and gills are laced with thin sharp teeth, so they are picked up by inserting fingers in the eye sockets rather than the gills.

Pike are currently harvested using gill nets and the meat is boiled, roasted or fried. As stated above, it is also used to make *vanhgiq*—fish ice cream—as pike flakes well and is readily available at most times of the year, although other white fish are used as well. Fish ice cream is made by combining fat (Crisco or, traditionally, fish oil) with the boiled meat of the fish. This is an extremely time-intensive process as the fish is de-boned and the liquid is previously squeezed out of the meat by hand so that becomes dry and powdery. Air is whipped into the fish and fat mixture using the hand, until fluffy. Sugar, berries and often milk are added to finish the dish. This is served at potlatches, mask dances, funeral feasts and other important events.

Epistemology and Ontology: Aspects of the Pike

Moore (1998) references the following definition for the term "epistemology": "the study of the cannons and protocols by which human beings acquire, organize, and verify their knowledge about the world" (p.271). In his introduction to the book *Native Science, Leroy Little Bear* (Cajete, 2000) talks about science as a "search for reality" and "knowledge," thereby encompassing both epistemology and ontology within a single term (p.x). Gregory Cajete emphasizes that Native science is a participatory process with the natural world and that the understanding of Native science requires developing the ability to "decode layers of meaning embedded in symbols"; symbols that "are used artistically and linguistically to depict structures and relationships to places" (p.36). Stories, or mythology, according to Cajete "are alternative ways of understanding relationships, creation and the creative process itself . . . how humans obtain knowledge, how they learn responsibility for such knowledge and then how knowledge is applied in the proper context." These mythologies contain "expressions of a worldview in coded form . . . " (p.62).

Reflecting on the epistemology and ontology of the Deg Hit'an, according to Osgood (1959), the name for pike in the Deg Xinag language is *giliqoy*, literally, "a lance" (p. 24). There are several different entries in the *Koyukon Dictionary* (2000) for pike, including a cognate term which means "that which is speared at something" (p.345); another term for a large pike, literally "that which stays on the bottom" (p.527) and term which means "that which floats" (p.416). The *Ahtna Athabaskan Dictionary* (1990) has a single reference that is said to originate from an "obsolete verb theme 'fish swims rapidly'" (p.179).

Creation/Transformation, Symbolism and Hierarchy

The spruce tree, or *didlang*, that was used to create the pike, was one of the most useful plants to the Deg Hit'an people providing, for example, medicine in the form of new shoots in the spring that could be collected and made into tea to treat colds; pitch which was used for bandaging cuts and waterproofing canoes and wood for burning, or the construction of items such as sled runners or household items. This wood burns at a higher temperature than other woods and is softer than birch, making it easier to work with.

The creation of the giant pike takes place through transformation of the spruce tree via the medicine song/breath of Raven. Witherspoon (1977), indicates that the Navajo have established cultural categories or hierarchies that classify the world based on "potential for motion" (p.140) and acknowledge "air as the source of all knowledge and animation" (p.53). Posey (2001) also references the energy stored in inanimate objects that can be transformed into an animate being (p.7). In a similar vein, Gregory Cajete (2000) states that "In many Native myths, plants are acknowledged as the first life, or the grandparents of humans and animals and sources of life and wisdom . . . " (p.108). In the Deg Xinag language, the word *yetr* means "life" or "breath". Deg Hit'an medicine men or shaman were often able to cure using their breath in ritual song or blowing in a person's ear for example to cure an earache. When examining these ontologies that acknowledge the power of air, the role of plants in the environment, and potential for motion, the transformation of the spruce tree into a giant pike becomes a natural process.

The clay lamp referenced in the story also seems to be part of the creative or transformative process, contributing to the ontology of the Deg Hit'an concerning fish in general. In Osgood's (1959) description of the "animal's ceremony" (p.116), he references an "insignia which holds a clay lamp tied to the bottom crosspiece" in recognition "that each kind of fish . . . have their own light which corresponds to a person's clay lamp. When fish pass in the Yukon, the side streams are lighted up by other fish which look like lights in the houses of people. Among human beings of course, only shaman can see them" (p.117).

Summary

The information I covered just scratches the surface in terms of the educational value of one story. In keeping with the conference theme, I guess the point I'm trying to get across is that language learning and research involve core educational processes and content. Bilingual education or heritage language learning are fields of education. Those of us who are struggling to learn our heritage languages are not merely learning another language for the purpose of learning another language, or learning another language so that we can go visit another country and be able to order off the menu. These efforts are not some ephemeral, ivory tower field of study with no real goals or objectives.

Language learning within valid cultural contexts causes us to think about the world we live in and the relationships within this world. Investigation of these questions using both written sources and the expertise of cultural tradition bearers requires rigorous scholarship and involves learning about biological and physical sciences, philosophy, religious/spiritual belief systems, ethics/values and literature that encompasses many, if not all, of the content areas.

This is a small example of what I have learned and what can be learned by following the models and processes many of you, the Native educators participating in this conference, have developed. *Dogidinh* to all of the educators for all that you have taught us and especially the Elders who continue to mentor and support us.

References

Cajete, G. (2000). *Native Science: Natural Laws of Interdependence*. Santa Fe: Clear Light Publishers.

Deacon, B. (1987b). "Niâ'oqay Ni'idaxin: The Man and Wife", *Engithidong Xugixudhoy: Their Stories of Long Ago* (pp. 5–40). Fairbanks: Alaska Native Language Center.

Jette, J., & Jones, E. (2000). *Koyukon Athabaskan Dictionary*. Fairbanks: Alaska Native Language Center: University of Alaska.

Kari, J. (1990). *Ahtna Athabaskan Dictionary*. Fairbanks: Alaska Native Language Center.

Nelson, R. K. (1983). *Make Prayers to the Raven: A Koyukon View of the Northern Forest*. Chicago: University of Chicago Press.

Osgood, C. (1940). *Ingalik Material Culture* (Vol. 22). New Haven: Human Relations Area Files Press.

Osgood, C. (1958). *Ingalik Social Culture* (Vol. 53). New Haven: Yale University Press.

Osgood, C. (1959). *Ingalik Mental Culture* (Vol. 56). New Haven: Department of Anthropology, Yale University.

Posey, D. A. (2001). "Intellectual Property Rights and the Sacred Balance: Some Spiritual Consequences from the Commercialization of Traditional Resources". In J. A. Grim (Ed.), *Indigenous Traditions and Ecology: The Interbeing of Cosmology and Community* (pp. 3–23). Cambridge: Harvard University Press.

Wheeler, P. C. (1997). *The Role of Cash in Northern Economies: A Case Study of Four Alaska Athabascan Villages.* Unpublished Ph.D. Dissertation, University of Alberta.

Witherspoon, G. (1977). *Language and Art in the Navajo Universe.* Ann Arbor: The University of Michigan Press.

The Hills on the Telaquana Trail

Frank Hill

Sharing Our Pathways, Vol. 9, Issue 4, Sept/Oct 2004

There are many aspects of cultural knowledge that form the basis for Alaska Native peoples' ability to thrive in their respective environments, among these are the traditional trails.

Throughout Alaska there are trails which have been used by Native people for generations. These overland trails were often the most efficient and safe route for people to travel. They provided routes to hunting and fishing grounds, seasonal camps, for trading between Native groups or, with the arrival of Europeans, to trade with them.

One of the prominent trails in Dena'ina Athabascan country in southwest Alaska is the Telaquana Trail. It is a 50-mile route through

the mountains and river valleys between the old village on Telaquana Lake and the Dena'ina village of old Kijik on Lake Clark. This trail has been used by the Dena'ina for hundreds of years.

Growing up, my Dena'ina grandmother, Mary Ann Trefon, lived with our family periodically in Iliamna and spoke of walking the Telaquana Trail. She, with others, would travel from the community on Telaquana Lake to Kijik to trade furs for staple goods like flour, sugar, tea and tobacco. Entire families, or groups of families, traveled together. In the summer, they would walk the Telaquana Trail, carrying their supplies on backpacks. Dogs also wore backpacks in summer and in winter were used with sleds and harnesses. The Lake Clark area Dena'ina were aptly called the "Walking Dena'inas," due to their ability to cover long distances on foot. It has been said that my grandmother's husband, Trefon Balluta, would walk the entire length of the 50-mile trail in one day!

In June 2003, I spent nine days with my brothers Pete and Lary Hill and Pete's wife BJ, hiking and camping along the Telaquana Trail. Lake Clark National Park Ranger and Historian John Branson joined us for the last few days. We camped on Turquoise Lake, about half-way along the length of the trail, and spent the days hiking and exploring different parts of the trail. Dena'inas know Turquoise Lake as "Vandaztun Vena," which translates as "caribou hair lake" and the Mulchatna River running out of it, as "Vandaztutnu," or "caribou

hair stream". As is evident in the Dena'ina names, the area is known for the migration and river crossing for the Mulchatna caribou herd, one of Alaska's largest. Our intent was not just to camp and explore, but also to appreciate our Dena'ina ancestors' hardiness and spiritual connection to the land they traversed. Another reason was to discover, for ourselves, the love for this part of the world that our Dena'ina mother shared with our Finnish father during their first years together.

We flew to Telaquana Lake with a float plane from Iliamna that required us to carry no more than a forty-pound pack each, due to the plane's weight restrictions. We had lightweight synthetic clothing and tents, Therma-rest mattresses, freeze dried foods, aluminum and titanium cookware, hand-held GPS, VHF radios, first aid kits and waterproof maps. No, we didn't forget matches!

In contrast to our Dena'ina ancestors' simple and practical traveling and camping gear, we looked like we had supplies and equipment enough for a year-long safari! Unlike our huge backpacks, our ancestors traveled light, thereby allowing them to carry more supplies home. Their shelters were constructed where they camped overnight and their trail food was probably dried salmon and moose meat. A day's walking along the trail ended in places with natural shelters, fresh water and a supply of firewood. As they walked, Dena'inas would collect grass, twigs, birch bark, and dry pieces of wood. When

they arrived at their day's end camp, they would already have dry fire-starting materials.

We found the early June season on the Telaquana Trail could provide food enough for someone to survive. During a spring traverse of the trail, our ancestral Dena'ina had available ducks and geese, ground squirrels, ptarmigan, trout and dried berries. Caribou, mountain sheep and bear were also regulars in the area. We found the same abundance of "survival food" when we were hiking in the area.

When we were finally able to determine that we were actually on the Telaquana Trail, it was easy to follow. There were no trail markers, telling us where we were, what we were looking at, or pointing out traditional animal river crossings or other natural features or activities. The trail followed the natural terrain, keeping to high dry ground, always heading toward a sighting on the horizon.

As we walked along the trail, we imagined our ancestors walking along with us; we were seeing the same sights, hearing the same birds and animals and feeling the same sun and breeze on our faces. We stopped in natural resting places to make tea and have mid-day snacks. In some locations we used the same fire pits originally made by our ancestors. We found remnants of things that fell off packs or broke along the way: a piece of non-native wood, a spent 30.30 cartridge, a piece of a broken cast iron-stove (imagine how that was carried or hauled!)

At the end of each day, beside a clear rocky stream, we cooked on fire fed with wood we collected around camp or during the day's walk. We camped in the same vicinity our ancestors did when they were in the area. We found it by following a stream from its outlet at the lake shore. Waist-deep circular hollows, lined with large tundra-covered stones, became our "conversation pit". A foot below the surface of the pit, we found smoke-covered stones, and piles of charcoal. We were certain that the original users of this fire pit were our Dena'ina ancestors. We each contributed our different dehydrated meals to be cooked in one common pot; in the same manner as the Dena'inas sharing their meals together.

Our usual end-of-day activities prior to heading for our tents and sleeping bags included tea and talk. Conversations around the campfire, teacup in hand, in that sheltered campfire area easily turned into discussions of our ancestors, their stories, legends and knowledge of the area. With only the ptarmigan talking, geese calling and the sound of the nearby creek, it was not difficult to imagine that these birds' ancestors and the creek were making the same sounds for our ancestral Dena'ina as they too fell asleep.

One day we hiked to Spirit Rock, a well-known landmark along the trail. Its imposing black, house-sized 30-foot height could be seen hours before we reached its base on the high upland treeless tundra. Dena'inas used this landmark as a day's-end destination and resting place. An opening on one side was large enough to build cooking fires. Another cave-like opening was large enough to provide shelter for several people. Our friend John showed us a stash of rolled up birch bark in a rock crevice, stored there years before, that was used to start fires. Located near a small lake, Spirit Rock was an ideal landmark and resting place.

The Iditarod, Chilkoot, Nabesna and Telaquana, are trails familiar to some of us in Alaska. Look at a detailed map of Alaska and note the dotted lines. Likely they are trails used first by the Native peoples of the area. They traverse lands from Brevig Mission to Shishmaref, Akiak to Russian Mission, Livengood to Ft. Hamlin, Discoverer Bay to Kazakof Bay on Afognak, the Duncan Canal Portage and Atqasak to Barrow. In many cases, these trails later became routes for European explorers, miners, railroads and highways. These represent only a few of hundreds of trails in traditional Native history. All have stories and many have songs which may still be in use today. In Howard Luke's book, *Howard Luke: My Own Trail*, which is about his life in and around Fairbanks and the Chena River area, there is a detailed map showing all of the places in his ancestral area that are important to him. Each place has a story and is significant.

In sharing this story, it is our hope that it will encourage others to visit with Elders about important trails in their cultural area and hear stories or events associated with those trails. Perhaps you will travel on some of those trails as your ancestors did. Doing so will enrich your lives, honor those who established and used those significant trails and, in the process, reconnect you to your ancestral lands and lifeways.

The last traditional chief of Batzunletas in the Ahtna Region, "Iizin Ta" or Charley Sanford (1876–1945) said: "After I die, burn all my material wealth; the only thing of true value to pass to future generations is a trail, a song and a story".

2

Iñupiaq Pathways
to Education

Rachel Craig | # Challenges in Alaska Native Education Today

Sharing Our Pathways, Vol. 1, Issue 1, Jan/Feb 1996

The following is a presentation given by Rachel Craig to the Alaska Native Education Council, October 16, 1995

Ladies and Gentlemen:

Thank you for inviting me to speak to you today. It is a real honor to stand before an assemblage such as yourselves—a group that is involved in molding the lives of our children through education, a group expected to set wise priorities and do the right thing in the face of dwindling available monetary resources.

We fondly look back on the days of our grandparents and great grandparents, and time and distance make their time seem an idyllic life. In some ways it was; but every generation has their challenges. Theirs was physical survival. Always gathering and hunting for food for themselves and their dogs to amass enough storage to last them another year to sustain life. They taught and lived the subsistence way of life which was their sole way of living. They had no other options. They celebrated their good fortunes with feasts and dancing, sharing the good times and helping to temper the bad.

The inventive mind of mankind has given our generation new technologies to make our day-to-day life easier with more leisure time to pursue our interests. If that's all it was, we'd really have it made. But our challenges in life are varied and have drastically increased since our great-grandparents' days. Alcohol and drugs and the abuse of them is prevalent in our society, influencing the making of sound judgments. Child and sexual abuse of minors fill the court calendars—children that we adults are responsible to protect and raise to upstanding adulthood. Very young adolescents are having children that they don't quite know how to raise, adding more responsibilities to the grandparents, not to mention the psychological burden placed on these children. Better jobs require training and education and stick-to-it-iveness, and the percentage of our own people in positions of responsibility and trust seem nil or absent. I know we were blessed with just as much intelligence as any other people, and I think it is worth examining what we are doing today.

Let me direct your attention to our federal and state governments. The federal debt is much larger than some of us can count to. In trying to address solving that issue, many familiar programs are being questioned, down-sized, or not funded. The state revenues are dwindling, following falling prices of crude oil. In order to keep some of our own regional projects viable, we in the NANA region have had to get innovative with our own fund raising efforts because funding from the state legislature is no longer reliable. The economic belt is getting tighter and tighter all around.

Let me tell you a little of what we are doing in the NANA region. We are by no means perfect, but we are trying to do something about our problems together.

We have a program in our region that addresses the one-sided education system. All of the studies in our schools were of the Western culture as they are in most of our State. In order to balance the curriculum and to send a message to our youth that our own culture is OK, that to identify with us older generations is honorable, we have done several things.

We developed curriculum and are teaching our language and culture in the schools. I don't know that it has helped the Native language fluency of the students, but at least it is there. We have also instituted five Iñupiaq Days during the school year—in September, October, January, February, and April. Our Iñupiaq experts are all volunteers from the community. This program is so good for our youth; they are so proud to have their grandmothers and grandfathers teaching in the classroom. After Iñupiaq Day, the students have more pride in themselves, their family, and their community. There is less truancy and vandalism, and the grades go up. Our elders are so proud to volunteer their knowledge and pass it on to the youth. They love the elementary grades because the students are so open and interested.

These Iñupiaq Days are then fortified with a camp experience of a week in the summer. We did not get funding for this camp from the state last year, so our coordinators held biathlons and sock hops to make enough money to buy T-shirts that our children love to wear. All the instructors at the camp are elders and they volunteer their time and skills, from the camp director on down. I love their commitment! Organizations and businesses donate what they could in response to solicitations.

Children from ages seven through high school are given the privilege to experience summer camp at Camp Sivunniugvik along the Northern delta of the Kobuk River, and we are now requesting payment of a camp fee from the parents to help defray expenses. For families who cannot pay the camp fee, we seek donations from the local businesses.

The Upper Kobuk people have also established Camp llisagvik for the Upper Kobuk villages. This will free up more space for the other children at Camp Sivu. We share our camping manual with the Upper Kobuk people so they could be thinking about all the personnel who will work at the camp and also about the topics that will be taught to the youth.

The Kotzebue Elders Council is also working with our local IRA to establish a coastal camp where seal hunting and food preservation and preparation will be taught to young people who never had an opportunity to learn these skills because their parents had to work in town. We are also sponsoring a skin-sewing class once a week this year for the benefit of the community and our elder women are the instructors. We also will offer to teach fishnet making and mending. Even some of our elders say that is one skill that they would like to learn, too. I would also like us to respond to the need of our middle generation to learn the nuances of the culture and have some place to go at least one night a month. But we feel that the middle generation has to make a commitment if that's what they want. The elders will respond, as they say, whatever good thing the younger generation wants to know of us we are duty-bound to teach them.

This economic squeeze has caused our regional organizations to cooperate more closely and pool their resources and do what they have to do in their realm of influence and responsibility. This means the NANA Regional Corporation, Maniilaq Association, the Northwest Arctic Borough, and the School District all work together. It's really great to see our bosses cooperating and those of us who do the actual work don't have to tread the floors hesitantly or lightly when we are on their premises. We feel more confident because we see our bosses working with each other and we are enjoying working with each other, too, pooling our skills together and sharing our outside contacts.

Many times the community expects the school to teach everything, including our Native language and culture, to the students. I personally think that the school needs to reinforce these subjects in school because our students feel anything taught in school is culturally accepted. But those subjects are best taught by the parents and the community if they still know how. We have all experienced the attack of our language and culture by well-meaning teachers in our growing up years. Some regions almost lost the language and really do need help.

In our region, I feel that the only way that the language will stay with the people is for the community to become involved. Those who know the language must speak it publicly, make it an accepted cultural practice. I know how difficult it is to raise a child when the parents of the child's peers have not made a commitment to do otherwise. It is easier for our children to bow to group peer pressure. We are so lenient with the TV programs that our children watch that we don't take them to church or week-day religious classes like our grandparents did with their children. For us, group teaching is strong. Then the other children know the expectations of the parent generation upon their children. There is nothing as strong as peer pressure. I think parents know this.

In my observation of each succeeding generation, there is a marked influence toward the westernization of each succeeding generation. Western civilization is swallowing us up, and more so our grandchildren. Those generations that have not benefited from the wise and continuous counseling of their grandparent generations are preoccupied with the here and now. They want expediency. They have not learned to care about tomorrow, or next week, or next month, or next year, and much less about their connections with the eternities. I think they are ignorant about individual sacrifices for the benefit of the group and want their individual benefits right now because that's what they are being taught in school. I think our educators need to bone up on the philosophies of their Native heritage so they can teach about the contrasting cultures. Neither is bad, but they are markedly different. Teach correct principles and let the individual learn to think and make his own choices as he matures. Then he will be responsible for his choices.

Today, I am supposed to be talking about the Wisdom of the Elders, Power of the Parents and Strength of the Students. If the elders or parents don't exert their prerogatives early and strongly, we will have raised a generation of spoiled children. In the western culture, you let your children go when they are eighteen or twenty-one. My son is thirty and occasionally I still have to exert my influence over him to do the right thing in the strongest possible ways. Maybe that's the Native way. We never stop caring or loving. We always expect the best. We give the best. When we find that the youth are listening to us and are doing the right thing, it is worth it. It makes us so proud we wonder why other people can't see our wings.

My title in the Northwest Arctic Borough is the Iñupiat Ilitqusiat Coordinator. As some of you know, Iñupiat is our collective name for ourselves as Native people in North and Northwest Alaska. *Ilitqusiat* has to do with our spirit—that power which motivates us. Some mistake the program to mean that we are trying to get them back to using the old Iñupiaq technologies and clothing. If that's what they want to do, more power to them. There's nothing wrong with learning to use them. But when you learn the spirit of our forefathers, you have to learn the philosophy—why they tell us not to make fun of others, why they help the helpless, why they share, why they don't boast about animals, why they live the way they do, why the mothers make sure we know our family trees, etc. It is the spiritual part of you that becomes the daily lifetime habit of your attitude toward others and the environment around you.

Thank you for asking me to speak to you today. May God bless you and yours as you strive to do your best.

Rachel Craig is the Iñupiat Ilitqusiat coordinator for the Northwest Arctic Borough in Kotzebue, Alaska. In that position, she is centrally involved with the culture and language of the Iñupiat in her region. She was president of the Kotzebue Elders' Council for the past five years and vice president and secretary for the NANA Regional Elders' Council. She currently is president of the Inuit Elders' International Conference within the international body of the Inuit Circumpolar Conference .

Alaska Native Cultural Integration into the Curriculum

Martha Stackhouse

Sharing Our Pathways, Vol. 1, Issue 2, Apr/May 1996

This paper will cover the integration of the Alaska Native cultures as part of the curriculum within the K–12 school systems throughout the state. The Alaska Native cultural integration had been identified as a need approximately twenty years ago and it is time it is implemented. There have been scores of people who wrote on the subject and many more who have given lectures about the integration of the Alaska Native culture into the school curriculum. It is high time to do something about the actual implementation.

The teaching of culture can range from the traditional past, legends and stories, first contact with the Western world, introduction of foreign diseases, starvation and how these problems were eventually solved, influences left by BIA schools and church, land claim struggles and the passage of ANCSA, how the present regional and village corporations have placed an impact in our lives, how an ordinary Alaska Native family leads a subsistence way of life and survives the impact of the Western world, cultural values and biographies of leaders and elders for our students to read. Since most ethnic studies are portrayed as if they were in a past tense, it is very important to also present ourselves as living cultures which we are presently experiencing. Therefore, it is important to include the different kinds of lifestyles the Alaska Natives are leading today. Scientific studies about wildlife living in our Arctic environment need to be brought into the school curriculum. There has been a tremendous amount of information given by the Alaska Native elders to the scientists who have conducted their studies in our Arctic environment. These topics are only a fraction of what can be incorporated into the school systems in Alaska.

One may ask how this will be implemented. First of all, the Alaska Native individuals who are concerned need to make a commitment and start writing down their cultural experiences rather than stating time and time again that this needs to be done. If we all took the time to write down how we grew up with our grandparents, parents, short biographies of extended families such as uncles and aunts, our cultural values, our legends and stories we heard, traditional medicine, expressive art, our experiences in the boarding schools and how we hunt and fish for our subsistence needs. Even if these experiences are not published, they may get a chance some day. If nothing else, they can be a gift to grandchildren. Most of all, share them with the students within your own community. To insure your writing from possible theft, contact the Copyright Office, Library of Congress, Washington D.C. 20559-6000 for information on copyrighting your work.

The ideal scenario would be to have a team of concerned Alaska Native people from each region gather information about their culture and the biographies of their elders and leaders. They can transcribe them on to computers, input them into computer programming as part of their Alaska Native language study, and publish these writings into books with the assistance of their school districts. Perhaps the regional corporations can help supplement the finances with the school districts. The biographies of the elders and leaders can be used as role models for leadership study.

As indigenous people of Alaska, we have the right to implement our way of life into our school districts. The majority of our rural schools are populated with Alaska Native students. Our urban schools also have Alaska Native students and they will gain self esteem through learning about their culture that has so much to offer to the Western society. The study can bridge the gap between cultural differences and generations. Within the school system itself, it can bridge the gap as interdisciplinary courses. For instance, it can go cross curricular from social studies and Alaska Native language into science, mathematics, computers and even English classes. The Alaska Native studies can be carried out to other areas of curricula. This concept will bridge the gap between the non-Native teachers and the Alaska Native teachers.

I believe that the school systems are trying to implement ethnic studies. As mentioned by Joan Metge from New Zealand, one needs to be careful in the implementation of ethnic studies as indigenous people throughout the world may be kept at the same latitude as other ethnic groups who have made recent migrations into our lands. There are those ethnic cultures who come from other countries or states that make statements about their right to present their cultures as much as Alaska Natives in our school systems. The whole United States is into multicultural approaches. It is good to have multicultural classes so that we can prepare our students to communicate effectively with the rest of the world. Our regional corporations are starting to go into international business with other countries so it would be an asset for Alaska Natives to know about other ethnic groups throughout the world. It is also true that Alaska is part of the United States where there is a big "melting pot" with many different ethnic cultures meshing together. However, the American Indians and Alaskan Natives are the indigenous people of the United States and should have special priorities as we have been under suppression too long. It is time we exercise the freedom to teach our own children and the general population about our culture. We have no other country to protect our cultures and languages.

There are Alaska Native language classes which may have been in existence for about twenty years. However, there is a need to record our lifestyles to go hand in hand with the language studies. I believe the two should go together to be used as effective teaching tools. The books should be as appealing to the student as any other book. They should have lots of colorful pictures, with much of the art work done by Alaska Natives. The writing should also be done by Alaska Natives. In the past, many of the books written about Alaska Natives have been written by non-Natives. The majority of their work might be true, but they are often slightly off balance in their accuracy. A few have been completely off balance. Perhaps what is lacking is the fact that cultural values are often missing or are not communicated very well by the non-Natives. Therefore, it makes sense for Alaska Natives to write about their lifestyles since they are the ones who grew up with the cultural values which were learned from their elders in their communities. They are also the ones who can communicate effectively with the living elders. Indirect communication is often used by elders and they may not be picked up by non-Natives who are used to speaking directly. For instance there are many non-verbal communication gestures which may be missed by those who did not grow up learning how to recognize them.

If books were to be written about Alaska Native lifestyles, I believe it would greatly enhance the reading levels of student populations throughout our rural communities. Most student populations in the villages have reading levels far below the national reading level. If the books were more relevant, they may have more interest in reading. At the same time, they would pick up the cultural values which have been drastically falling in the modern world. They can become adults with contributions to the world and become responsible citizens.

Another idea is to have students write about their cultural experiences and then share them with their peers and younger students. They can write about their camping and hunting experiences. Their work can be used to substitute work that they missed at school while they were out camping. They need to start building their self esteem and feel proud about their culture. Too often we hear our own elementary children talk about who is popular in school. They are often those who are outspoken and economically well off. They are usually those who are non-Native and are often the ones who are most likely encouraged by their teachers to continue on to college. Because of their popularity, they are frequently elected into student council. Our Alaska Native students deserve a chance to acquire these positions. They can acquire them if they are to realize they can pursue them like anyone else and set goals for their future at a very young age. They can practice public speaking. They can read about Native leaders in school and some may make a connection that, they too, can make a difference.

We cannot ignore the fact that many Americans throughout our country are experiencing cultural deprivation, no matter what race they represent. According to the electronic Native American Talking Circle, there are young American Indians who are becoming gang members because of family breakdowns. Some of them are third or fourth generation alcohol abusers who may be using other street drugs as well as alcohol. These young Native Americans may not be articulate in speaking the English language, therefore, not able to land meaningful jobs. They may not be able to speak their own Native language or know about their cultural heritage and values, therefore, do not have self esteem. They turn to street drugs and are placed in jails where they learn how to become better criminals from older inmates. The vicious cycle of going in and out of jail begins at this point. There needs to be counseling provided rather than placing our young people in jail. There needs to be prevention programs taught to the elementary school children about effects of drug and alcohol addiction. Along with these prevention programs, the Native

American traditional values need to be implemented. Cultural pride and dignity can replace cultural deprivation. Our own people can start counseling those who are trying to quit drinking and using street drugs. Spiritual healing and success can become more common.

As Native leaders we need to make a choice to develop Native American/Alaska Native curriculum materials to teach our children. Such a task can greatly enhance young minds to think of their cultural values as an asset, rather than a hindrance. The Native American/Alaska Native cultural heritage has something to offer to the pluralistic society throughout the world. In the Arctic Slope and Northwest Alaska, we have developed a list of Iñupiaq values. To a young Alaska Native, a list may have little or no effect unless they are explained in written form. Examples need to be written and thought provoking questions need to be asked at the end of each lesson. These can generate discussion groups. They may provide a vehicle to do problem solving simulation questions.

There are many traditional community ceremonial dances which are still being practiced today. There are some that are starting to be revived again after many years of absence. In the North Slope Borough, we have revived Kivgiq, a Messenger Feast, or sometimes referred to as the Trade Fair. It was first mentioned by the elders in the late 1970s during the Elders' Conference. Little by little, information about the feast was gathered and was finally revived in 1988. In my research about Kivgiq, I found that it existed all up and down the coast of Alaska from the north to southwest Yup'ik region. We need to start writing about these ceremonies before the elders who are most knowledgeable about them pass away. There were some elders who had not witnessed Kivgiq but had heard their parents reminisce about the great gathering of the people and described it in detail to them.

After writing about the culture, there can be a few questions made at the end for reading comprehension. They can be short answer essay questions for the most part but there should also be two or three questions where they have to write whole paragraphs for each question. Too often, our Alaska Native children write fragmented sentences and the only way they will overcome this phobia for writing is to keep practicing. Paragraph answers should also be included in the tests. Most teachers usually have true or false questions, multiple choice and matching to save time in correcting them. It would be more fair for the student to also include at least a couple of essay questions as part of the exam. Another point is to have final exams at the end of each semester. They are usually implemented in the urban schools but are virtually nonexistent in the rural schools. When the rural students go to college, they experience test phobia when they realize they have to take semester exams.

In closing, I want to reiterate that Alaska Native studies be placed in our school curricula throughout our state. It is time we are recognized as a living people who have something to offer the society. In spite of the fact that we, as Alaska Natives, are becoming a minority within our own lands, we need to make a stance to make our beliefs and values known through teaching our young about our historical past. These need to be included in the Alaska Native language studies which are presently being taught. Furthermore, there needs to be a conscious effort to support the curriculum development in Alaska Native Studies by ensuring financial support from those who can provide it.

Rachel Craig | # What's in a Name?

Sharing Our Pathways, Vol. 1, Issue 5, Nov/Dec 1996

The Recycling of Iñupiaq Names and Implications for Kinship: A Personal and Cultural Account

Naming of our children is something that we as Iñupiat have taken for granted. Everybody has to have a name, right? If we run out of Iñupiaq names of people we like, then we ask our mothers or grandmothers or other close relatives for names that they would recommend from earlier generations or other kinfolk that we were not aware of. It pleased them to know that we would turn to them for assistance in something as important as the naming of our child. This is one of the times that they rehearsed our family trees to us and wonder why certain names did not get used from either side of the family.

As prospective parents of the new namesake in the family, we also got a glimpse of the depth of feeling that our grandparents had for those early forebears and what some of our ancestors' characteristic traits were. This lesson in our ongoing genealogy brought the generations closer together. It gave our generations thoughts and glimpses of our forebears that we knew nothing about. It gave our informers the opportunity to remember their relatives that they had not thought about in a long time, plus giving them a time for a "teaching moment" to the next generation.

Another custom of some of our people is that some elders single out a young child as their future mother or father. *Aakaksrautiin* (my future mother) or *aapaksrautiin* (my future father), the old people would call the child. Somehow they appreciated the qualities of that child with whom they wished their namesake to live. We didn't pay much attention to the words of the old people when we were in our primary ages, but those endearments are remembered at the time of childbearing age.

Take, for instance, my maternal grandfather. I don't remember the exact circumstances one day when he let me know that he didn't want me to name any of my children for him because he said I was impatient. His namesake might be subjected to too much scolding, he said. It didn't matter to me at the time because I was too young to be thinking of children. Years later, I cared for my nephew when his mother was ill in the hospital. Unbeknownst to me, apparently my grandfather observed my "mothering." He said to me then, that if I should have any children, even an adopted one, that I should name one for him. His mother died while my grandfather was young and his father raised him and his two older brothers. Therefore, he would like to call her namesake his "mother."

When the elders hear that so-and-so's name was bestowed on a newborn baby, the attitude of our elders then was that the person had "come home" through the new namesake. Even though I have worked with our elders for many years, I haven't yet figured out if the Iñupiat believed in reincarnation when they made comments like this. Perhaps it's just a figure of speech that, in essence, the person has "come home" as a namesake in a new person.

There are some individuals that our grandparents say do not merit naming our children after. From my understanding, it's not so much the discarding of the name but because of the negative character traits that the person had. If the baby is given that person's name anyway, words are spoken to the baby to the effect that the previous namesake used up all those negative qualities and for the new baby to pattern his life just the opposite way—the specific qualities that the baby was supposed to seek after were spoken to him.

The thing that goes along with naming is that when you talk to a newborn baby, the child hears the words spoken to it and unconsciously internalizes them. Later on you see those traits just naturally exhibited by the child as he is growing up. To give the newborn child words of wisdom of the character traits in its first few days of life that you want him to live by the rest of his life is an important custom among the Iñupiat. In later years, as the good qualities become evident in that person's life, sometimes the only explanation is that so-and-so had spoken to the baby in his infancy. That's why he is the way he is. Very strong medicine.

Perhaps I'm the only Eskimo that many of you have seen, or will ever see. We very seldom call ourselves Eskimo, but because of the power of the printed word, that's how the world knows us. It was the Cree Indians of Canada that the explorers heard call us Eskimo meaning "eaters of raw meat" in their Cree language. Of course the printed word spread that name all over the world. But from time immemorial, the relationship between the Iñupiat and the Indians has been pretty much like the Hatfields and McCoys, although there were some exceptions which ended in marriage. That is hardly the case now for us in Alaska since we have been thrown together and educated by the good old U.S. Bureau of Indian Affairs in boarding schools. We found out that some members of the other tribes weren't so bad after all. But our name for ourselves has always been Iñupiaq which translates to an "authentic human being" or a "real person." In other words, a local Native person, one whose bloodlines are not mixed with other human groups. This does not implicate dislike for other ethnic groups. A Native mixed with Caucasian bloodlines would be *Naluagmiuyaaq* (mixed with people with bleached skin), one who is part black would be *Taaqsipaiyaaq* (one sired by a person having dark skin). We Iñupiat have become notorious for marrying into all ethnic groups of the world.

Back to naming. For most of my young years, I thought I was named for my maternal great-grandmother. My grandfather always called me *aakaan*—meaning "my mother." It was much later when I was doing our family genealogy that I began to realize that my mother's younger sister had died in May and I was born the following December, so I was actually named for my aunt. My maternal grandmother used the same crooning words to me that she had used for her deceased daughter—my namesake. Our word in Iñupiaq is *nuniaq* when you say all those sweet endearing words to the babies. It makes the baby smile and become coy and not know what to do. In Iñupiaq, we say that the baby *una*.

My great-grandmother, for whom we were named, was the favorite niece of one of her uncles. Whenever the uncle hunted, he would save his niece the choice piece of meat from the breast of ptarmigan or other fowl—*savigutchaurat*, we call them because they are in the shape of a knife. So my great-grandmother, whose name was Piquk, actually became known as Savigummuaq, a fractured Iñupiaq word that was intended to mean "somewhat like a shape of a knife." Some members of my family sometimes call me "Savik" for short, meaning "knife." When they ask me how I am, I tell them that I'm sharp as ever. Actually, I have had some dull days, too.

So as names go, Savigummuaq is actually Piquk, like Peggy is Margaret or Bill is William. I also have other namesakes like Quunnignaq (one who calms the waters), Kayuqtuana (root word is fox) and Kaluuraq (has something to do with a drumbeat.) These are the names that my grandfather, Piquk's son, told me about. Later on, I found out from other people that my *atiins* were also Sapiqsuaq, Taapsuk and possibly others. All my namesakes have treated me with the utmost kindness and best regard and I know that anyone of them would have helped me in any way they could as I would do for them. Being *atiin* with someone gives you a special relationship that makes you proud to be with them and uplift them as really good exceptional people. Our expectations from our namesakes are high and we would do any good thing for them and stick up for them.

Two beautiful girls have been named for me. One is a beautiful teenager of Irish descent with beautiful blue eyes who has grown taller than me. She is the eldest of eight children. Another girl, from my extended family, is about four years old. She has a black father and she is equally beautiful in her personality and very much loved by her brothers. I have a special bond with these my namesakes. We really don't know how old our names are or how many generations have used them. There's no way we can do literature research, either, because all our history was oral until an orthography was developed for our Iñupiaq language in the late 1940s.

Iñupiaq names are given to us regardless of gender. I have a friend who has a family of boys. She named one of them for her grandmother who raised her. One of my uncles named one of his sons for his mother. It is our understanding that if a male person is given a known female's name that somehow that person becomes a good hunter. My own mother bore her uncle's Iñupiaq name. I hardly knew her since she died when I was five years old. However, she was known as a sharpshooter among her family. She could take a -25.35 rifle without an attached scope and the geese that are flying high that she aimed at would one by one fall to the ground. Her father used to take her seal hunting with him because of her shooting skills. And yet she was just as feminine as any woman who loved good clothes and was conscious of her femininity at other times. She also had a sister who was named for their grandfather. This sister was strong and drove a dog team , brought home logs to burn for fuel, blocks of ice to melt for drinking water and did village-to-village freighting by dogteam like any man. But still she raised a large family of her own.

My mother's siblings that survived consisted of a brother (the oldest in the family), five sisters in the middle and, finally, another brother (the youngest.) The oldest brother was chosen by a local old woman to be her new namesake because my uncle's three eldest siblings had died in infancy and they wanted this baby boy to live. In her day, the old woman was a known shaman and her instructions were that he should not be called her name while she lived. So one of his names became Atqiluaraq (one without a name) and he became Qinugan upon the elderly lady's death. To *qinu* is to desire something, so I imagine his name became your desired one. When we were growing up we just accepted people's names without wondering what they meant. It is only when we were exposed to the Western culture and began to be asked all kinds of questions including what our names meant that we started to think about our Iñupiaq names in terms of meaning.

Another custom of our people is that when one of the children dies, the parents bestow the same Iñupiaq name on one of their younger newborn children. Then, for the record, two individuals bear the same name in the same family, except that one of them was born earlier but is deceased. My understanding of that situation is that whoever bestowed that name on the child loved the original namesake so much that they want to keep his name alive in the family. I don't think the Christian concept of resurrection of two members in the same family having the same name even figured into the practice. This is a practice that pre-dates the introduction of the Christian religion to the Iñupiat and it is still practiced today even among people who have become good Christians.

Another custom that is prevalent is that when an adult is recently deceased, a new baby is given that deceased person's name. It doesn't really matter that the deceased is not a blood relative. I believe it is considered an honor to have the privilege to name your child for that person to perpetuate his name and memory.

I have given you real examples of how we are given our names. These are not theories, but situations which have developed in families and happened in real life. I hope they mean something to you. They certainly do to us Iñupiat.

Elmer Jackson

Integrating Indigenous Knowledge into Education

Sharing Our Pathways, Vol. 2, Issue 2, Mar/Apr 1997

The Northwest Arctic Borough School District (NWABSD) Iñupiaq Language and Culture Curriculum Review committee is in their second year of reviewing and creating new curriculum. My report will be on the subsistence calendar for all seasons. This indigenous way of life will be incorporated into the curriculum. Another important part of many Iñupiat efforts is to teach our Iñupiat language to the young. Although the future looks grim, it is hoped that one day our Kobuk river Iñupiat dialect will not be forgotten by the young, leaving only our elders knowing how to speak Iñupiaq. With the help of technology, elders and linguists, we might be able to keep our dialect alive.

Last year, the bilingual curriculum committee began the task of restructuring the bilingual curriculum program. We changed our mission statement and began revising the curriculum by creating the Iñupiat subsistence calendar beginning with:

A. *Upingaksraq*: Early Spring (March and April)

1. Food gathering. Caribou, moose, reindeer, bear, rabbits, porcupine and muskrat provide food for the Iñupiat. A variety of seals and whales are a gift from the sea. Edible plants and berries are harvested during the summer and fall. Fish are abundant in the Arctic.

2. It is important to learn about the environment and to respect it. Safety on ice and learning survival skills is important.

3. Arts & Crafts. Waterproof *maklaks*, parkas, mittens and other warm clothing are made by women. Men are creating tools,

sleds, harpoons and other household utensils. The men are usually trapping and snaring rabbits for fur and food.

4. Games that require physical activity are *aqsraaq*—Iñupiaq football, Norwegian ball game, *manna manna, maq, anakitaq* and Native Youth Olympic games.

5. The Northwest Arctic Native Association (NANA) have listed the following Iñupiaq values: knowledge of language, sharing, respect for elders, love for children, hard work, knowledge of family tree, avoiding conflict, hunter success, humor, spirituality, family roles, learning domestic skills, responsibility to tribe, love for children and respect for nature.

B. Upingaksaq: Spring (May)

1. Migrating ducks and geese, whales and beluga provide a welcome change in the diet. The rivers and streams are free from ice. Other food harvested are various types of fish such as sheefish, whitefish, trout and pike. Many people follow the river ice, hunting for waterfowl and muskrats.

2. An Iñupiaq value that is alive is sharing. When a young hunter catches his first game it is given to an elder. A person who lives the subsistence way of life must learn the skill of skinning and dissecting game animals such as bear, moose and caribou. A hunter is a person who when subsistence hunting, treats them with respect. It is important to learn the anatomy of the animals that are hunted for food.

3. The cultural skills practiced are net making, sewing, beading, berry basket making and other arts and crafts.

C. Auraq-upingaaq: Summer (June–August)

1. Berries begin to ripen in July. Blueberries, salmonberries and raspberries are picked. Fresh greens such as rhubarb, sourdock, willow greens, fireweed shoots and beach greens are harvested and some are mixed with berries. Eggs from ducks, geese and other waterfowl are also in season. Ducks and geese molt this time of the season. They are at their heaviest, having fattened themselves. Many Iñupiat are involved in different methods of fishing. Caribou frequent the tundra and river. People of the coast are hunting seals, beluga, walrus and whale. People inland have nets out to catch whitefish, trout, pike and salmon. Another method of fishing is by seining.

2. Summer is a very busy time for many Iñupiat. Many women on the Kobuk river are out gathering birch bark and tree roots for the art of making baskets. Other summer projects are ulu-making, beading, parka-making, carving oars and countless arts and crafts items.

3. There are many plants and herbs that are harvested for medicinal purposes. The stinkweed is best harvested when the plant has a strong odor. This is when the plant curing strength is at its strongest. This plant is used to help cure chest colds and help cure the body of other ailments. Crushed willow leaves are used to relieve bee stings. The food contents of the porcupine are dried for curing loose stools or an upset stomach. There are many other plants that need to be researched for their medicinal purposes.

4. There are many indigenous games that need to be brought back and taught to the young. The Native Youth Olympics and the World Eskimo/Indian Olympics are held every year. Many schools in the Bering Straits, the NWABSD and the North Slope Borough School District involve their students in the Native Youth Olympics.

D. *Ukiaksraq*: Early Fall

1. Bear, moose and caribou are hunted and put away for winter. Many different kinds of fish are cut, cleaned and dried. *Masru* or wild potatoes are gathered and put in seal oil. *Tinniks* or bearberries are picked and mixed with seal oil or bear fat.

2. By observation, Iñupiat people have learned to predict weather through weather and geographical indicators. Elders teach traditional beliefs about weather. It is important to learn place names, camping grounds and geographical places. It is wise to let someone know where you are traveling to. Elders need to teach survival techniques. Learn where hunting and gathering places are. Know whose camps belong to whom and to show respect for the property.

E. *Ukiaksraq*: Fall

1. Mother nature in the fall is generous in terms of food gathering. The Western Arctic caribou herd migrates through the Noatak and Kobuk river valleys. Other food gathering activities include berrypicking, hunting and fishing. Hunting

of seals, walrus and whale occur in the coastal parts of the Iñupiaq region. Many Iñupiat people are skin-sewing, carving, ice-fishing and making and mending nets.

2. Iñupiat of the northern regions celebrate and give thanks on Thanksgiving day. Many have harvested from the bounty of Mother Earth. Many gather at the local church for the Thanksgiving feast. Throughout the day and night there are activities for the people in the community. Spirituality is alive within the Iñupiat culture; we give thanks to our Creator for giving us everything to survive in our environment.

F. *Ukiuq*: Winter

1. Many Iñupiat are busy with their daily lives; some are hunting and trapping; women are sewing warm clothing for the cold winter months. Other projects are net making, carving, creating implements, tanning furs and celebrating birthdays. Many people attend important community and school functions. Christmas celebrations are held with Eskimo dancing and giving gifts at the church. A feast at the community building or at the church is held celebrating our Creator's birthday.

In January, the Iñupiat Curriculum Committee worked on developing K–6 curriculum. Our work on the curriculum is continuing with the hope of keeping our language and culture alive.

Florence B.
Kuzuguk

New Pathways to Excellence

Sharing Our Pathways, Vol. 2, Issue 3, Summer 1997

The following article won first place in the 1997 Bilingual Multicultural Education Equity Conference student speech contest. Ms. Kuzuguk is from Shishmaref. The bilingual instructor is John Sinnok.

Students who succeed in practicing the arts of their culture are those who have a role model from a member of their family, an outstanding citizen of the community or an inspirational teacher. Just as you make up a part of your family, school and community, they are a part of you. Your ability to become a better part of your family, school and community is limited to your motivation to succeed. With a little encouragement, skills, talents and knowledge can become treasured possessions.

As a member of the community, people develop culture that is shared by the students. From the hunting skills passed on from generation to generation, students are taught how to live off the land. The skills students learn are important to the community because they preserve the culture as well as make the community stronger. By learning the skills from the elders of the community, students develop their own individual ways of doing things. Our cultural beliefs become a very important part of the community and these beliefs go on through the community's history. The key to passing along our culture is in the family. Without our culture people would have a hard time functioning in the community. We live in a community that has a culture of its own. And its own unique way of doing things. Our culture is a source of pride for many families and communities. Every family's cultural heritage is valued.

Whether a student decides to give up or not is his/her choice. And many things affect that choice. Communities are made up of families and neighbors who help each other out. Once a student has been honored for any achievement, the community does many things to show how proud they are of that student. Once one student achieves excellence, more students are eager to participate.

Until children are 16 years old, they are forced by the law to go to school. But the next two years of school are optional. And when a student stays in that last two years of school, it indicates that the family and the community have made the student what they are.

What drives students to get up every morning to get to school is their family's encouragement and their own desire to learn. When children do badly in school, the family encourages them to do better. When the community sees a family who doesn't care, the community can guide that family and do its best to help the family out.

The opportunity to achieve excellence is also provided by the school. What you are to become is thought of long before you grow up. Many students in the Native study classes offered throughout their preschool to senior years became great sewers and carvers and are able to speak their language and learn more about their cultural traditions. When you graduate the next thing you want to do is go to a good college or become involved in some program. After that you want to go into a line of work that you enjoy. You make this happen by first graduating from school.

The knowledge and skills you gain transfer to the larger part of the world. In time you will be able to take all that you have learned about where you come from and use it when you are on your own. Within the family you grow and develop and discover the kind of person that you are and that you need and want to be.

Students who know family togetherness, community involvement, school participation and their cultural tradition are the ones who will excel in whatever they want to. To find the new pathways to excellence you have to want to look. Don't expect anyone to look for the pathway for you. You make who you are and who you want to be. Find yourself, and when you look back, you will have achieved excellence. You will also have found new pathways to look forward to.

Martha Aiken

Learning the Iñupiaq Language

Sharing Our Pathways, Vol. 3, Issue 5, Nov/Dec 1998

Keynote Address to the North Slope Iñupiat Educators' Association Quarterly Membership Meeting, April 24, 1998

On behalf of the North Slope Iñupiat Education Association, welcome everyone. I will address what I say to everyone who is with the educational system of today, and that means everyone!

First, I would like to greet all the Iñupiaq language teachers wherever they may be, and encourage them to keep it up. You are very important to us to be leaders of our classrooms. Natives of today are experiencing difficulties concerning our Iñupiaq language, it being the very essence of our Iñupiaq cultural heritage. We claim it as our own and it needs to be utilized at home, school, churches, and at play. We have learned from experience 60 years ago that the Native students were intelligent enough to learn the hardest language in the world to master. But can you imagine how much better it would have been for everyone if those students were allowed to speak their language at home?

One thing for sure is the fact that we need to support our present Iñupiaq language teachers. I know we do, but we all need more action to help them to press on more, and replace anyone retiring as soon as they are out. We need to make a combined effort for our leaders and support our bilingual programs within the North Slope Borough School District. As parents, school boards, school advisory committee members and English language teachers, all of us need to have one voice to protect our language at all costs.

Today almost all of us, here and there, are involved to make education better for our students and we acknowledge the fact that a child's intelligence is not limited to one language. Parents are learning back their mother tongue with their children. Anyone can become literate in their own language as well as in English, if they are really determined to do so; we've seen proof here in Barrow. We may think it's too late for some—maybe so—but it sure does not hurt to try and try again and again. We should encourage our students to be fluent in two languages. Would it not be wonderful to start speaking in Iñupiaq with that beloved grandmother, who is making every effort to speak to you in her sometimes misunderstood conversations with her grandchildren?

The North Slope Borough School District (NSBSD) finally found a way to improve the bilingualism through immersion, but we are watching it teetering because others do not feel our Native language is that important. If we do not do anything and just lay around and watch, what will happen? If we do not fight the never-ending battle, in fact, we may be too late to protect the birthright that our forefathers passed on to us. We have to seek help from all sources and even from our other Alaska Native speakers. We have to seek help from our degreed teachers, lawyers, governments and churches to help us.

We also have to educate the outside world on how crucial it is to keep alive our way of life. This is the time to forgive and forget the wrongs of others so they may help us in this important effort, because not everyone is perfect and we will need their wisdom.

The language we have been trying to revive for the last 20 years or so is having problems as it is. It scares me like heck when legislative bills start appearing concerning our language, especially about having only the English language to teach in schools. There are other legislative bills that we need the public to understand, because even our own Alaskan neighbors are hinting that bilingualism is just a waste of money. And here it is the very heartbeat of most Alaska Natives. The language we are trying hard to revive for the last 20 years or so will start crumbling unless we make every effort to protect it.

But the most important fact we seriously need to ask our school board to do is to employ more fluent speakers to be teacher aides and become Iñupiat teachers. Entice the speakers to join Iñupiat teachers because they sure need help.

The school district has to attract more bilingual teachers and aides even if they have to pay them a little more than most employees. We know for a fact that the teacher's aides can take over a certified teacher's classroom, but an Iñupiaq teacher's classroom cannot be taken over by a degreed teacher, unless an Iñupiaq aide helps him or her.

Again I encourage everyone to become involved in encouraging young people to keep on keeping on. There are young adults out there. We know we need them desperately to teach our eager-to-learn bilingual students. How many times have your young ones begged you to speak to them only in Iñupiaq? We need to help them learn back their language, and not get mad when someone laughs at them. Do not let them forget it was difficult to try to start speaking English too. We, the little Eskimos back 60 years ago, had problems too, as I recall. But we laughed about each other and helped each other to resolve the important situation at that time. Even our peers told on us so we had to suffer the consequences, but we never gave up. English educators say that the English language is the hardest to master, but not for the little Iñupiat. I say there were smart ones and dummies like me—I barely made it to the game activity parties held for the students that could say ten Iñupiaq words. That was hard for me but my determination pulled me through as did others.

Today tables are turned and I want to encourage all the little Iñupiat or Tanik: you can learn to speak our language if you really want to.

Lastly, I want to thank the present efforts the school teachers have done for our North Slope Borough School District. Your love for teaching is more valuable than any effort in life. Sometimes you feel "Is it worth it?" It is; you will see enough in just a few years from now when you retire. But right now you have to evaluate the way you teach your students because they are not all little angels. They will remember how you had been when you were their teacher. Seek help from parents when your students are getting out of hand. Don't just listen in aone-sided way; recognize those little tykes who are having a difficult time understanding that certain little problem. Once they learn to do it, their appreciation will have a great impact between you and that not-so-smart student.

This last comment includes everyone from the certified teachers and aides, to the principals, school board and parents. If you feel you have to leave our schools, do it with pride for all your contributions and involvement with the students, difficult as they may be. Help us help our bilingual programs of today. Share with us what you feel instead of keeping it in yourself. We may be able to help you if you come halfway to meet us. Thank you and may God bless!

I leave you with a poem given to me by a friend:

Prayer for Teachers

Lord, thank you for teachers that have:

WISDOM
To teach principles as well as facts;

COURAGE
To stand firm when challenged by parent or child;

PERSISTENCE
To teach again and again, then again;

VISION
To know what results will show far down the years;

LOVE
For the unlovable as well as the lovely child;

PATIENCE
Lord, patience, forever and unending.

—Author Unknown

Elmer Jackson

Minnie Aliitchak Qapviatchialuk Gray, Ambler

Sharing Our Pathways, Vol. 4, Issue 2, Mar/Apr 1999

Minnie is one of the most well-known and beloved Elders in the NANA region. She has been actively involved with the Alaska Rural Systemic Initiative since the first consortium meetings began. At that time, she was one of the main advisors for the Northwest Arctic Borough School District's Iñupiaq Language and Culture Curriculum Committee. In addition she was active in teaching traditional skin-sewing skills to the young people in the village of Ambler.

Minnie has been an advocate for Iñupiaq language and culture training for as many years as she has lived the culture. She was born in 1924 in Kobuk, Alaska. She was one of three surviving children of the late Robert and Flora Cleveland. She is the widow of the late Friends Church pastor, Arthur Gray. Minnie attended school for six years as a child in the village of Shungnak. After being a pastor with her husband in two villages, she became a bilingual teacher in August, 1973 and retired in 1994. She helped to produce many books to help teach the Iñupiaq language and culture. One of the early books published by Maniilaq Association was *Timimun Mamirrutit*, which is a book about Iñupiaq medicine. Minnie contributed to this publication because of her knowledge of traditional ways of healing, especially in the use of plants and herbs. She later worked at the National Bilingual Materials Development Center to work on other publications. One of the most extensive books she worked on was titled *Black River Stories*—a book of stories told by her late father, Robert Cleveland. She also has written two books titled *Birch bark Basket Making* and *Net Making*. Other contributions included the *Kobuk River Junior Dictionary, How Stories, More How Stories, Atuugaurat* (translated children's songs) and *Taimmaknaqtat*, a book

about traditional Iñupiaq Eskimo beliefs. There are more publications; I have listed a few.

Minnie's beautiful looks, traditional clothing, wonderful friendly smile and graceful stature have been photographed by friends she has made over the years. Her photograph is on the cover jacket of A Place Beyond by Nick Jans. He wrote a wonderful story of Minnie and her friend, Sarah Tickett, seining for whitefish. Minnie is known for her hospitality; she has been a hostess to visitors and friends who have graced her home over the years.

Whenever Minnie travels to AKRSI meetings, she shares her knowledge of the Iñupiat Culture, through hands-on demonstrations and songs. At curriculum meetings, she taught how to make snares using salmon skin and gave demonstrations of various traditional tools. She told the mudshark bone story, using actual bones, to Iñupiaq immersion students at Barrow. They enjoyed this story demonstration very much.

Here are some of her own thoughts about bilingual education. She voiced them in Iñupiaq and they were translated into English:

> Iñupiaq should be taught at an early age. I have seen that the younger students are responsive, the more they learn. It is fun to teach these young people. As an Iñupiaq language instructor, I realize that children need motivation to learn. I motivated my students by offering them a variety of ways of learning. They cannot learn by only writing, so I took them out for field trips and taught them about the plants that grow. In the spring, when they got tired of writing, I took them outside and taught them the name of

the many different birds that migrate north. This motivated them tremendously.

I had projects for them such as skin sewing and making other crafts like birch bark baskets. I allowed them to play Iñupiaq games when they became restless. Sometimes, I even took them home and taught them how to prepare an Iñupiaq dish, such as cranberry or blueberry pudding. Other times I taught them how to make *akutuq*, Eskimo ice cream. I also boiled the head of the mudshark, which has many bones; I told them the individual names of the bones. This is an interesting project and the students think it is fun. For added variety, I sang songs and told them Iñupiaq stories and legends.

Students should learn about life in school. They should learn practical skills such as skin sewing and cooking. Many students need these basic skills. They should know the names of our Native foods and know how to prepare them. It is practical to learn these skills because our environment is going to be the same in spite of the changes in our lifestyles. We still need warm clothing and we need to gather food. Students should know about the weather because we cannot predict what the coming seasons' weather will be. They should also know their regional geography. They should know their local subsistence areas, their trails and place names of creeks, rivers and other landmarks. They should be able to know where they are and be able to communicate exactly where they are as they travel out in the country for it is a matter of survival.

Last summer, Minnie instructed students at the Ilisagvik Camp, a camp between Ambler and Shungnak. They were taught about camping and fishing, everything about the Iñupiat *illitqusrait*, the way of life of the Iñupiat.

Minnie continues to share her knowledge of the Iñupiat culture. Those who have been taught by her have been blessed, her love for her people is immense. Thank you, Minnie, for being a great role model for us all.

Taikuu.

Traditional Knowledge, Environmental Assessment, and the Clash of Two Cultures

Richard Glenn

Sharing Our Pathways, Vol. 4, Issue 5, Nov/Dec 1999

The following paper was presented to the Minerals Management Service, Western Region Meeting, Park City, Utah, August 1999

Native American people have, since the time of the first European contact, struggled with the idea of sharing a storehouse of raw information, truisms, philosophies and ways of life with the outside world. This storehouse, wrapped in a big blanket and named by the outside world as "traditional knowledge", has been obtained (as in any culture) over time by observations of nature, trial and error, dogged persistence and flashes of inspiration. In cultures without a written history, such as North Slope Iñupiat culture in Alaska, knowledge is passed person to person through social organizations and individual training, as well as through stories and legends.

The Iñupiat culture is based on knowledge of the natural environment and its resources. Our foundation is knowledge of the arctic tundra, rivers, lakes, lagoons, oceans and food resources. Knowledge of snow and ice conditions, ocean currents and weather patterns and their effects on natural systems are necessary for navigation, finding game and locating shelter and each other. This knowledge has value. First, to share with each other and pass on to our children and second, (if desired) to pass on to those outside of the Iñupiat culture.

To someone unfamiliar with the Iñupiat culture or the Arctic environment (such as a youngster or an outsider), the storehouse of information must seem infinite and inaccessible. In addition, stereotypes abound among ourselves and in the eyes of outsiders. Legends of the "hundred different terms for snow or ice" perpetuate the mystery. Most importantly, those wishing to learn the Iñupiat culture or environment, there is a stigma: bad experiences too numerous to count begin by good-faith sharing of traditional knowledge with outsiders. These range from simple plagiarism to exploitation and thievery. Legends and stereotypes abound. Such experiences have led many Iñupiat people to first ask "Why share?" And, even if this challenge has been answered sufficiently, an equally difficult challenge remains for both sides: "How to share?"

Why Share?

Why do Iñupiat share traditional knowledge? Despite the stigma, our community is proud of a long history of productive, cooperative efforts with visiting researchers, hunters, travelers, scientists, map makers and others. We share when we consider others close enough to be part of Iñupiat culture and share when it is in the best interest of a greater cultural struggle.

Experts Sharing With Each Other

The question of "why" is always easy to answer when two individuals are sharing equally and the joy of discovery takes place on both sides. Examples of the Iñupiat hundred-year history of cooperation serve as good models: the wildlife biologist and the whaler, the nomadic traveler and geologist, the archeologist and the village Elders. This two-way exchange has often worked when a given researcher has been around long enough to be considered "one of us" or at least has displayed to the community that he possesses some common values.

Sharing for the Greater Good

For a more locally important reason, we share traditional knowledge when we believe it will lead to preserving the land, its resources or the Iñupiat way of life. This reason has prodded us to work hard with regulatory agencies and other organizations to develop policies, draft environmental impact statements or offer specific knowledge of the environment, wildlife or cultural practice.

Sharing as a Part of Education

A third reason exists: pure instruction. Like a teacher to a student, our Elders and experts teach the rest of our community in all facets of traditional knowledge. We share to perpetuate our culture. How does one become involved in this kind of sharing? The answer is simple: become a student. However, this can take a lifetime-pairing with a given expert through years of learning. Chances are that the teacher is learning, too. This is the method most commonly used by Iñupiat people to transfer knowledge with each other. Iñupiat culture has many vehicles to allow this kind of instruction to take place. However, this method faces challenges due to changing culture, loss of language and other factors.

How to Share?

How can an outsider partake in vehicles of sharing traditional knowledge? Choose one or all of the criteria: an exchange among experts, become part of an effort that is of value to the Iñupiat or remain in the community and become a real student. Any other method risks lack of context, data gaps from abbreviated efforts and other problems.

Funding exists in many agencies for programs that elicit traditional knowledge. These programs can be found from NSF, NOAA and MMS. Recently this has drawn praise from outside quarters, as it demonstrates that the government has validated traditional knowledge. Even so, we are still struggling with the very agencies that have given traditional knowledge some credibility. Why is this? In many instances the goal of eliciting traditional knowledge is a short-term project for an effort that might necessarily take a lifetime. A common problem many agencies face is they try to gather traditional knowledge in non-traditional ways. They hold public meetings, offer copies of documents for comment or rely on whatever political leadership happens to be in place.

Another vehicle in vogue for government agencies is contracting with Native organizations. Native tribal organizations, profit and non-profit corporations and rural and local governments all represent some aspect of a Native constituency. So, because the groups have some legitimacy in attempting to be the bridge between traditional knowledge and the outside world, a contract is developed. The contractor must somehow assimilate, document and contribute traditional knowledge. Thus, what should take years of heart-to-heart collaboration between experts, a whole army of local energy focused on a single issue or years of tutelage under a suite of instructors must now be completed before the contract deadline (usually a period of weeks to months). Here, the government can wash its hands of the issue. It looks appropriate; it's in the Natives' hands. Consequently, the Native organization, hungry as it should be for grants and contracts from the "feds", offers to carry the obligation. Again, contract and project timelines become the targets, and we collect what we can while we can. Quality may suffer, content and context as well.

Knowing that change happens slowly and that agencies can only do so much, it is reasonable to assume that what is presently occurring will continue. Meetings to assess traditional knowledge will undoubtedly go on. Knowing this, there are a few more cautions to those interested in documenting traditional knowledge, learning about the environment without reinventing the wheel and working with Native communities on regionally important issues.

Choose the Forum with Care

A meeting's attendees must be matched to the issue. When expertise is really needed, it should be stated. Stereotypes will allow any agency to assume the expertise is there. There is a scene from the movie On Deadly Ground where the leading actress (an Asian woman playing a Yup'ik) jumps on a horse to the surprise of Steven Seagal's character. He asks, "You can ride a horse?" to which she answers, "Of course, I'm Native American!" A comical analogy, but not far from the mark.

Don't Put Your Eggs in One Basket

Check sources. Stated another way, the most talkative person may not be the most knowledgeable. Ours is a culture of consensus. Agreement is mandatory on nearly every item passed as traditional knowledge. If one person stands alone, he may be an expert or he may be wrong.

Given the size of the task, it is easy to run away from documenting traditional knowledge for use by others, even for our own reasons. For many like me, it can be an intensely personal endeavor. Still, such documentation will continue—by Iñupiat as well as by outside groups. Our culture is changing and some day we may be learning traditional knowledge using the same techniques employed by those who are outside looking in. We may be learning of Iñupiat traditional knowledge as if it belonged to others. Just as today, in many places, we are learning Iñupiat language as if it were a foreign language. As long as we are pledged to the task, we should look past the requirements of this contract or that mandate and remember the quality of information—time-tested and true. With everything changing, it is a valuable reference plane. If it is not where we are going, at least it is where we are coming from.

The Time is Right to Write

Dorothy M. Larson

Sharing Our Pathways, Vol. 5, Issue 1, Jan/Feb 2000

Have you checked out the local bookstore shelves lately? How many Alaska Native authors did you find? Not an over-abundance. But for those who have been writing and publishing, I applaud them. We often find stories written about Alaska Natives by others—stories with qualifiers like "as told to me by . . . " It's not that these books aren't well done, it is just time for us to write our own stories—to write the stories of our Elders, our families, our lifestyles, our areas and our recollections. Unique voices will appear among the established voices as more Alaska Natives begin to write and publish.

An Alaska Native writer doesn't have to write about culture to be valid, even though that is how we are often first identified. Alaska Natives can write on par with other writers, including creative non-fiction, fiction, poetry, technical, memoir, biography and autobiography, journalistic, historical, mystery, drama, spiritual and all other categories of writing styles and genres.

This isn't meant to be critical of those writers who use their skills to tell another's story. If it weren't for them, some stories might not have been told or read. This is meant to encourage and support Alaska Native writers who want to write their own stories.

A recent Anchorage Daily News article about Alaska Native writers Diane Benson, Anna Smith, Jeane Breinig and Susie Silook was very enlightening and refreshing. They took the risk in the literary and art world to share their experiences. Their experiences living in two worlds make their writing insightful, powerful and poignant. They bring a special presence through their writing that is not reflected when told through another.

It hasn't been that long ago since Alaska Natives had their own newspaper, Tundra Times, with Howard Rock at the helm. How we looked forward to the weekly edition of the statewide Alaska Native newspaper with a fervent purpose—one of the finest small newspapers ever published. Though we now have several rural newspapers in most regions of Alaska, these papers are more local in nature and often reprint outside news from other sources. Wouldn't it be wonderful if there was a paper modeled after the old Tundra Times with an Alaska Native editor, columnists and reporters devoted to news important to Alaska Native people?

Recently, I read excerpts from a fiction book written by a former long-time Alaskan. Note "former" long-time Alaskan. Though the book was fiction, there were characters in the book that seemed familiar; one had the same nickname as a person I remembered from my childhood. I felt hurt for the person and their family should they happen to read the book. I chose not to finish the book.

Since I am from the area, I skimmed another book about Bristol Bay on a local bookstore shelf. I leafed through it and got the gist in just a few minutes. It was a feeble attempt by the author to depict the Bristol Bay fishery as the "Wild West" of southwest Alaska. Who wants to read about the antics and parties of "Indians" as this college professor called some of his subjects. It was another book of the recent past that was purported to be fact but disgusted old timers of the area because it was filled with errors. It, too, was written by a former "long-time Alaskan" now living elsewhere. If his book were fact, he should be locked up in some penitentiary this very moment.

A year ago I attended the Sitka Symposium which is considered a writers' conference. The symposium isn't a true writers' conference, but people do write and discuss provocative issues. Authors are present to critique and review manuscripts of participants.

The Mesa Refuge Program asked the Sitka Symposium for their list of past participants in order to solicit applicants for their unique writers' retreat. The Mesa Refuge Program is a new writers' retreat in northern California established to provide a place where individuals can come to pay undivided attention to their writing. The program is for established and emerging writers as stipulated by the generous founders.

After much thought, I applied for the retreat on the last day the application could be postmarked for consideration. A few weeks later, I was notified by a public radio message from my daughter (I was out at fish camp) that I had been accepted. In my wildest dreams, I never believed I would be chosen for this opportunity—two weeks by a national seashore with two other writers—a gift of time and space. It was a dream come true.

In the bio they put together, I was called a Native poet and activist in the Native community because of my past involvement and experiences. The word "activist" was not what caught my eye in my bio; it was that I was called a poet. Since 1971 when I first began writing, I called my writing a hobby. When I was a junior-high student, I secretly dreamed of becoming a writer, but never pursued it until I took a course at Anchorage Community College many years later. Over the years I attended a number of university classes and workshops with a couple of renowned poets and university professors. I participated in a number of loosely formed writing groups off and on, more off than on. I continued to call my writing a hobby even though I had a few poems published and read a short story I wrote over the public radio station at home in Dillingham.

When friends read my work, I never knew if they were just being kind to me by telling me they liked it. I returned to writing about a year and a half ago. This class saved my sanity and helped me through a very difficult time in my life. It was then I began to think seriously about writing. I'm not getting any younger and I figured that if I am going to write, I should get serious about it—write more, improve what I have written, study writing and write more.

In September I left for the two-week retreat at Mesa Refuge not quite knowing what to expect. I was introduced as a writer/poet to the other two writers in residence. One resident was writing a book as a result of his work with the *Audubon* magazine. He had four to five publishers waiting for his overdue book. The other was a recent graduate student who started a college geography magazine and became editor and writer. I was the novice, for sure.

A retreat is meant to renew, rejuvenate and inspire. There was no pressure to produce; it was a gift of time. However, past residents have completed books or began new ones at the Mesa Refuge. This retreat forced me to focus. It wasn't difficult to do because the surroundings were tranquil and close to nature. At first, I thought, too close. I was only a few hundred yards from the San Andreas Fault! Once I put that out of my mind, the environment, the setting and the ambiance was perfect—so conducive to writing. I came home with a preliminary draft of my book with new and old work to complete and a dream to publish a book of poetry, prose and a few short stories. I am hoping to convince a very talented artist friend to illustrate my book for me. I want to continue work on another project: a cookbook I began collecting recipes for last year. I hope to be able to find a writers' group where I will feel comfortable in order to share my work and to read the work of others.

Many questions arose for me: How would I get an agent? How would I get published? I still don't have the answers to those questions but I did revisit my dream of some day becoming a poet, a writer and an author. And to those of you with a similar dream, I hope you pursue it.

The discovery at the Mesa Refuge that I could allow myself the gift of time (without guilt) to write was a revelation. We must give ourselves precious time and space to devote to our writing. It can apply to any craft we pursue. Learning to discipline oneself is a challenge. We must rid ourselves of the distractions and allow the garbage to escape and the new material to take shape in our minds and hearts. There are Alaska Native writers who write wonderful poetry, children's stories and who have novels waiting to emerge. These talented writers can and should create their niche in the Alaska and the global literary world.

As Alaska Native writers enter the new millennium, we can denounce the invisibility we have often encountered. Alaska Native's are a very visible, proud people. We are more than capable of creating a significant imprint—the time is right.

Traditional Methods of Healing & Medicines for Science Fair Projects

Elmer Jackson

Sharing Our Pathways, Vol. 5, Issue 3, Summer 2000

The Iñupiaq people living in the Arctic have knowledge of healing utilizing natural products from the land and waters. Plants and other natural products are used in prepared remedies that have healing effects on the human body. Students can research the remedies used in traditional medicine and healing for science fair projects. Elders, tribal doctors and community health practitioners have knowledge of plants and animal remedies that are used for healthy living. The following is some background information on ways Iñupiat have utilized plants and parts of animals for medicines and healing.

In the springtime, willow leaves (*sura*) are harvested and preserved in seal oil for food. *Sura's* high Vitamin C content hastens the healing process. *Sura*, mixed with seal or whale oil and a small amount of sugar, complements many Native foods. Crushed *sura* leaves are applied to wasp or hornet stings. This stops the swelling and removes the poison.

Bear fat and other animal tallow help heal sores, boils and other infections. Eating a well-balanced diet of Native foods aids healing. These foods are meat, fish, berries, sour dock, wild rhubarb, *sura* seal and fish oil.

The intestinal tract is saved from porcupine (*iluqutaq*). This long intestinal tract is stretched and hung to completely dry. Once dried it is ready to be used as a medicine. It is a cure for stomach ailments and diarrhea. The dried, digested food is crushed and water is added, then taken internally. This herbivore feeds on grasses, willow leaves in summer and tree bark during the winter. The *iluqutaq* is a subsistence food of the Iñupiat.

Qaluum uqsrau is fish oil. Fishing for whitefish on calm days seems to make work easier. The fish are scaled, washed, cut and hung on poles to dry. The edible stomach organ and eggs are washed and boiled. The fish oil rises to the surface. The cooked contents are removed, leaving the oil on the surface. The oil is saved, cooled and then used to dip the fish, eggs and stomach before eating.

Qaluum uqsrau can be used as medicine. When young children have a common cold with coughing, sore throat or the flu, they are given fish oil. The soothing oil moisturizes dry sore throats and hastens the healing process. The oils, rich in iron and protein, are essential for healthy living.

You can also massage heated fish oil onto a child's chest when they have a chest cold and congestion.

The cottonwood tree (*ninfuq*) produces buds that can be used as cough syrup in early summer. These sticky buds are used for making cough syrup not only for sore throats, but also for colds and congestion.

Like fish oil, cranberries have healing properties for the human body. Cranberries are rich in Vitamin C and can be used as medicine for sore throats, the common cold, congestion, chest colds and sores. They help the body's organs get rid of the body wastes. Cranberries cooked the traditional way are delicious.

Another home remedy for sore throats is to mix pure honey, lemon juice and stinkweed leaves (*sargiq*). Bring the mixture to a boil, reduce heat and simmer 10 to 20 minutes. Cool and store for preservation. Taking this internally will help heal sore throat and common cold ailments.

The stinkweed plant (*sargiq*) is a common medicinal plant that grows in the Arctic. The 24-hour sunlight nourishes *sargiq*, along with other plants in the ecosystem. In midsummer, when the buds begin to appear, is the time to harvest *sargiq*. Harvest the entire plant: the stems, leaves and bulbs. This is when the plant is most potent. Bundles of *sargiq* are gathered and preserved. Fresh *sargiq* is prepared into medicinal salves or taken internally. Prepare salve for applying on the chest for chest colds, head cold and congestion.

Another salve is made by frying cut onions or wild chives (*paatitaat*) and garlic using shortening or lard. Fry until the onion becomes transparent. Cool and preserve. Apply to the chest for congestion from chest and head colds. Add salve to hot water for steaming. Place the steaming hot salve on the floor. While holding a child on your padded legs, cover with a bed sheet and let the child breathe the medicinal steam. It will help the lungs and nasal passages get rid of the mucus and congestion. Cut and mince *sargiq* stems, leaves and bulbs. Pan fry with lard, shortening or bear fat. Reduce heat and cook until stems and leaves release their medicinal contents. The stems and leaves will resemble cooked spinach. Cool entire contents and preserve. When needed for colds or congestion apply on the chest and neck. For steaming, apply salve to boiling hot water and cover with a bed sheet—breathe the soothing moisturizing cure.

Sargiq can be taken internally for most body ailments. *Sargiq* can also be made into a hot drink prepared like tea. A warm or hot bath with *sargiq* is healing to the skin and body. It helps heal sores and is used for a treatment for arthritis. Students should research other medicinal uses of *sargiq* and discover new medicines and remedies for healthful living.

Crowberry (*tullukam asrait*) has medicine in the berry that benefits the urinary tract, intestines, liver and stomach. The berry is especially effective on urinary tract problems.

Natural clay can soothe arthritis and bone ache. The heated clay relieves aches and helps the healing process. This natural resource also has other uses. For example, this material is put between the logs of the log cabin. The clay hardens, making the log cabin draft proof. Clay can be found at or just below the shoreline where there are large boulders of rocks and sand.

Medicinal greens grow all year long near natural hot springs. Natural hot springs have been visited by the Iñupiat and the

The stinkweed plant (*sargiq*), pictured above, is a common medicinal plant that grows in the Arctic. The 24-hour sunlight nourishes *sargiq*, along with other plants in the ecosystem. (Photo by Dixie Masak Dayo who is studying traditional healing and herbology.)

Athabascan people for generations. They knew about the medicinal greens and the soothing spring waters. Before submerging into the hot springs, one must drink spring water and consume medicinal plants. These two steps help people get their bodies ready for the hot spring water. The medicinal greens that grow near the springs are medicine for ulcers, stomach problems and sores. Water and greens are taken from the springs for home use.

Every so often a tree swallow (*tulugabnauraq*) is taken for medicinal purposes. The feathered bird is split in half and dried completely. When it dries, it is preserved for future use. *Tulugabnauraq* is one of the most effective medicine for sores, cold sores and mouth sores. Part of the dried bird is soaked in pure water and applied to the sores. This application is repeated until the sores heal. The sores heal quickly with this method. Proper diet helps the body's immune system heal sores or body infections. Proper diet includes berries, *sura*, sour dock, wild rhubarb, fish oil and meat that are rich in Vitamin C, iron and protein.

Teachers and students should plan to visit Elders and interview them about traditional healing and medicines. Before the interview it is important that the Elders understand what they are going to be asked to talk about. Get permission to record and to document the interview. They have much knowledge about the Iñupiat *illitqusrait* (way of life). Students can incorporate this information in their science fair projects through video, charts and samples of plants and animal products used in traditional medicine and healing.

Tribal doctors are gifted people who have knowledge of human anatomy. They know about plants and other natural products that promote healing. Students can send samples of medicine plants to be analyzed. There are cures yet to be discovered. Find where medicinal plants and natural products can be analyzed through scientific research for possible new medicines. Make sure you follow the *Guidelines for Respecting Cultural Knowledge* when you do so (the guidelines are available on the ANKN website.)

Finally, when you visit an Elder, bring them a fruit basket or gift to show your appreciation for sharing their indigenous knowledge.

References

Aana (Grandma) Clara Jackson. These traditional remedies are common knowledge and shared with each generation of Iñupiat since time immemorial.

Aspects of Traditional Iñupiat Education

Paul Ongtooguk

Sharing Our Pathways, Vol. 5, Issue 4, Sept/Oct 2000

Iñupiat Society: The Myth

Traditional Alaska Natives are often thought of as a common, no-madic culture that moved almost randomly with little more than hope to guide decisions about where to seek the next meal and where to set up the next shelter. The Hollywood image of Alaska and Alaska Natives reinforces this stereotype, as the film image is one of fur-clad people living in blinding blizzards of constant snow. Imagine the camera, as it pans up to a thin line of specks on the horizon. The camera slowly closes in and the specks become visible as people walking into the blizzard. (I don't know why we always walk into the blizzards, but in films we always seem to.) Then, the narrator, in a low, serious tone announces "In a ceaseless quest for survival, the hearty Eskimo are in search of the caribou." The image is an important one, as it represents most people's only visual encounter with the traditional life of the Eskimo. It is also false, as it portrays the Eskimo as playing survival roulette, wandering about hoping to chance upon some caribou.

Iñupiat Society: Some Realities

It is true that most Alaska Native groups often moved, but it is also true that the locations and times of these moves were not in any way random. A culture would not long survive in the Arctic, much less develop over several thousand years, if it were dependent on such random luck. Rather the Iñupiat cycle of life developed through a careful consideration of the environment. Among traditional foods were caribou, marmot, seal, walrus, several variety of whale, many kinds of fish, bear, rabbit, ptarmigan and a variety of roots, eggs, seeds and berries. The Iñupiat also gathered resources, such as ivory, jade in some regions, copper in others, slate, driftwood, baleen and bones. Sometimes the materials sought included grasses for insulation and baskets or animals and birds for clothing and shelter. Hunting and fishing were planned based on the knowledge of where animals and fish had been found in the past, knowledge about weather conditions and the changing patterns of climate.

Camps were carefully chosen locations. The camp, or living area, was selected, because it was perceived as the most likely location of a concentration of food. Adequate fresh water and relative safety were, and are today, carefully considered. There were also settled communities. Over a thousand people lived in the traditional communities now commonly called Pt. Hope and Wales. These communities were established long before the Roman era of Western Europe.

Iñupiat societies developed unique equipment and tools that were relevant for the area in which that society lived. The invention and refinement over thousands of years of how to design and construct the right equipment was a crucial aspect of traditional life. As William Oquilluk, an Iñupiat author, pointed out in *People of Kauwerak*, the invention of tools and shelter for living in the Arctic was inspired through careful observation of the world: the spider web for the net, not only the fish net, but also nets for birds and seals; the leaf floating on the water for the first boats that were gradually refined into the *qayaq*—one of the more graceful and efficient boat designs. There are many others: the ulu, the harpoon, the reinforced bow, the throwing dart and the *gutskin* parka. The development of tools and equipment is one example that Iñupiat society was not static in traditional times and that change was not a consequence of contact with outsiders.

Thus it was not mere hope and persistence that allowed Iñupiat society to develop in the North. Traditional Iñupiat society was, and is, about knowing the right time to be in the right place, with the right tools to take advantage of a temporary abundance of resources. Such a cycle of life was, and is, based on a foundation of knowledge about and insight into the natural world. Such a cycle of life was, and is, dependent upon a people's careful observations of the environment and their dynamic response to changes and circumstances. Developing this cycle of life was critical to the continuance of traditional Iñupiat society. Also critical was a system to share this knowledge and insight with the next generation.

Traditional Education: a Myth

Many educators today stereotype the traditional education-al system of Alaska Natives in a manner that is reminiscent of the Hollywood blizzard portrayal of traditional Iñupiat society. A prevalent belief, for example, of many educators is that American indigenous people "learn by doing." In schools the application of this belief often results in activities where students are provided a minimum amount of information and a maximum amount of activities that allow for random experimentation and hands-on discovery. Such a simplified view of teaching and learning imposed on a diversified group of people is as foolish as the image of the northern Iñupiat randomly searching for food in the Arctic.

Two common sense observations should immediately lead educators to question this belief. First, the traditional life of the Iñupiat demanded knowledge and perceptiveness about the world. Consider hunting. The successful hunter had to have knowledge about the particular area, the species being hunted and the appropriate technology. Further, he had to be skilled in the application of that knowledge. The Iñupiat were not successful hunters because they threw themselves into "learning by doing" situations. To learn about sea ice conditions and safe travel "by doing" alone would be suicidal. In fact "doing" is the back end of the educational experience in traditional life. Second, it is naive to think that any group of people can be categorized as preferring one learning style. Learning style inventories are popularly administered in schools today in order to determine student preferences and student patterns of insight. Teachers believe that the information revealed about individual students from learning style inventories is important. Teachers often intend to apply that information as they plan, deliver and evaluate lessons. Caucasian students are expected to exhibit a range of learning behavior. (By the way I often think this whole issue is confused in how much it ignores the demands of the subject being learned. Hands-on learning alone of chess? Ignoring the conceptual issues of small engines is partly to blame for all those so-called mechanics trading old parts for new ones without repairing vehicles.) Why would Alaska Natives be expected to perform any differently?

Traditional Education: Some Realities

Then how were people prepared to live in traditional times? Probably no one alive today can answer that question completely.

Decades of changes in society coupled with the demands of compulsory education mean that traditional learning and ways of learning have been obscured and many pieces have been lost. While there are some obvious elements still in place, they tend to be fragmented and are seldom recognized as portions of an entire way of learning. While these fragments can be gathered from a variety of sources, one of the most credible is the personal story. The examples that follow are personal and illustrate how the role of the male hunter was learned by some of the boys in a contemporary Iñupiat community.

Observation

Observation is a critical element of the traditional educational system. The first knowledge about hunting comes from boys watching how hunters prepare their equipment, their clothing and themselves. Observation begins at a very early age and continues for years. At first the boy observes how relatively easy it seems to load a boat. Then, another year, the boy sees more than the work and starts to notice the balance of the load. He sees what will be readily needed, what must not be allowed to sit under the load, what knots should be used to properly tie things down in the various parts. What had appeared simple at the first observation gradually becomes extremely complicated as the issues are understood. The sophisticated observer finally extracts the principles that become the threads by which what has been "seen and done" is understood.

The young boy, through observation, also learns about the value system associated with hunting. As hunters return from a successful trip, goods are shared. In Iñupiat society, it is through participation that a person becomes a part of the community. In contrast to the Robinson Crusoe drama, in the Arctic, if a person is alone, the odds of survival are undermined. In fact, in Iñupiat society higher status is acquired through sharing. Boys learn to prove themselves through helping others.

Immersion in the Stories and Customs

As the child is immersed in the stories and customs of the communities, he learns more about the traditions, values and beliefs associated with hunting in an Iñupiat community. Before his first hunt, he has listened to hunting stories for years. These were both entertaining and informative. As a result of these stories told by Elders and veteran hunters, the young child constructs a mental image of all that is required and some sense of the important aspects of preparing and engaging in the hunt.

Many of the stories he listens to as a child were stories that emphasized the disposition—the attitude—of the hunter. In these stories bragging and pride in personal accomplishment would be condemned. In the stories, animals can read the mind of the hunter and either give themselves or not, in part based on an appreciation of the giving of the physical body. Even after the animal gives up the body, respect should be shown in definite ways according to the stories and traditions. This is why some hunters who are deacons and respected members of churches still pour fresh water in the mouth of a seal after it has been shot. The belief is that the seal likes fresh water and that the undying nature of the seal will remember the gesture and bring another body for the hunters later.

The stories about animals giving themselves to hunters might not seem to make sense to outsiders, but it is difficult to imagine anything else if a person has hunted very long. There are times, when in spite of careful planning and preparation, cautious stalking and quiet approaches, no animal will allow a hunter to even remotely approach. At other times a person will be setting up camp and a caribou or moose will walk within a stone's throw and then patiently wait for the hunter to take advantage of their good fortune. How else to account for these turns of events that have so little to do with skill and more to do with the disposition of the animal? Today some Westerners might deride such practices and beliefs. But perhaps the stories are actually about protecting and helping the hunter. Respect for the animal being hunted may prevent the hunter from becoming overly confident or prideful. Pride often produces carelessness and may prevent learning and observation from occurring. In fact, pride and arrogance can be fatal in the Arctic where the best lesson to keep in mind is how little we actually know and how easily we can be swept from the world.

Showing respect for the animals also ensures that better care will be taken of the physical remains of the animal. The importance of such a disposition for the Iñupiat hunter is obvious. Often the stories children hear will emphasize how clever, thoughtful and ingenious a person has been in becoming successful as a hunter and a provider to the community.

Apprenticeship

Apprenticeship is another aspect of traditional education. Often a young hunter is guided in the apprenticeship by an uncle. The uncle's role may be familiar to some parents in urban life who face the task of teaching their children to drive. For while the young person may be capable of learning to drive, the parents are often so deeply attached and concerned that it is difficult to keep the teaching role in mind. Parents can all too readily imagine that this future driver of over a ton of steel is the same child who broke objects and fumbled through life as a toddler. On the other hand an uncle is close enough in relationship to carry the burden of keeping a youngster alive, while at the same time distant enough to keep things in perspective. Hunting in the Arctic is difficult enough. Hunting while keeping an eye on a young person is just that much more so.

The apprenticeship begins on the day that the uncle chooses to take the future hunter out. In contrast to Western systems of education there is no predetermined beginning and ending schedule for the apprenticeship. The age at which this happens depends upon the maturity of the youngster. The uncle has been watching the young hunter and one day, with almost a casual air, the uncle and his hunting partner agree to take the youngster out.

The young hunter has been trying to show, in numerous ways, that he is ready for this. The youngster may have been hunting ptarmigan, usually with a bow and arrows that he and his friends have made. Why is this hunting so important to the young man? Observation has demonstrated to the boys that hunting is valued in many ways. As a child he has seen the appreciation and admiration shown to hunters returning to the community. As a child, when he got his first ptarmigan or rabbit, he was required to give it to his oldest female relative—grandmother, great-grandmother or an aunt. The female relative made a great deal of the event—praising the fine size of the catch and noting how long it had been since they had seen one as good as this. The boy was then instructed to run to the homes of many relatives and friends inviting them over for a feast. The women prepared a great many foods, but the center of the feast was a stew in which the little bird or rabbit was transformed into a meal for many people. All would eat and praise the stew and note how clever and hard working the young hunter had been in acquiring this meal for the community. All the conversation praising the hunter would take place as though he were invisible and yet he would feel a mixture of pride and embarrassment at all the attention. The lesson of the importance of hard work and persistence in hunting would not be lost.

Apprentice hunters might not actually hunt the first time they go out to a hunting camp. The youngest person sets up the tent, hauls water, perhaps prepares sleeping bags, collects firewood, cooks and certainly cleans. But is this only dreary labor? First, keep in mind that these chores are being done out at camp and so everything is edged with excitement for the young apprentice. But, the real lesson, as a young person, is to learn to deal with the long and hard labor without giving in to fatigue.

While out at camp, the young boy learns about good locations for certain animals, fish or materials during certain seasons. The boy also learns about how to select the location for the hunting camp, what equipment to bring for certain areas and for different kinds of hunting, fishing or trapping. A person would certainly be expected to learn about terrain, travel routes and hazards. A young hunter would also learn something about local weather and about basic weather prediction. Sometimes the significant event is learning about the location of good water and, always, hunting is about maintaining hunting equipment. From these early experiences a person begins a lifetime of learning about animals, fish, various other foods, habitats and animal behaviors.

If the hunt went well a boy would also begin to observe the techniques and skills used by hunters in locating and stalking an animal. The apprentice hears the male hunters discuss the nature of the hunt and anything learned, anything unusual or notable. Often the discussion revolves around how and why things turned out the way they did. They may even tease about the lack of success. But if there is success, the young apprentice helps in packing and hauling the catch. He learns how to pack and store and how to move from one place to another, efficiently and intelligently. The room for error is very slim at times. The apprentice is taught to think about what he is going to do and to ask himself: What can go wrong? What are the dangers? Then he is taught to think again and not to take unnecessary risks, because the necessary ones are dangerous enough. The boy learns that taking risks is for people whose lives are very different than his. Caution and appreciation for life are the dispositions of the hunters who know that life cannot be taken for granted.

The Community as a School

In contrast to the system of modern Western education, in traditional Iñupiat society the community is a school. The observations that a young boy makes are not scheduled in classes or confined to a school building or other restricted environment. The immersion of the young hunter in the stories and customs of the community are likewise an integral part of the child's life. Older men tell stories about everything and the stories are the lessons. When, where and what lessons occur are dependent upon the time, the place and the season. The lessons are tied to the traditional cycle of life.

The apprenticeship, while perhaps seemingly familiar as a model used in Western education, is best understood in traditional Iñupiat education, as one more piece of an educational system that is integral to the notion of the community as a school. Why a particular uncle steps forward to guide a young hunter is dependent upon complex family, social, psychological and community relationships. It is also within the context of a community of hunters that the apprenticeship occurs. Preservation of the communities and societies depends on the cooperation of its members and the apprenticeship occurs within this hunting community. While the apprentice might focus on a particular task, there is no separation of the task from the larger context. Traditional Iñupiat hunters must learn to do several things at the same time. For example, the hunters may discuss how exceptional circumstances in the hunt will be met while they are, at the same time, cleaning their equipment. For the apprentice there is no isolation from the realities of the hunting community.

Within this context traditional education is a highly disciplined education. There is a need to pay attention to the stories that told about right and wrong attitudes and behavior. There is a need for the young hunter to develop both the physical and mental dispositions of a mature hunter, including understanding why something is being done in a particular way. When hunting in the Arctic, things often do not go as planned and skilled hunters must know how to solve problems. An educational goal of traditional Iñupiat society is a careful preparation of the young for the roles of adults. This goal is shared by the community and the children are both attended to and expected to be attentive. The values of traditional Iñupiat education include cooperation and intense effort. These values are rewarded in many ways, including the satisfaction that the hunter feels when people are fed and he knows that he has contributed to the effort that has provided some of the food.

A Cautionary Tale

This description is only a fraction of the traditional educational system. Hunting skills and conditioning were, and are, learned through traditional games and competition such as wrestling, weight lifting and the one- and two-foot high kick. In addition to hunting, traditional education has provided and is continuing to provide a way for children to learn and accept other adult roles that are essential to survival. Further, Iñupiat society has developed many art forms including sculpture, music, dance and story. Celebrations and ceremonies were a part of Iñupiat communities as were people who were philosophers and historians. Despite the challenge of the environment, the Iñupiat survived and developed a complex society. The traditional Iñupiat system of education worked well within the framework in which it developed.

There are many factors that have contributed to the erosion of the traditional educational system. The relocation of Native people and the establishment of boarding schools had devastating effects, as children were separated from the traditional educational system that taught them how to participate in the community. As Western culture collided with Alaska Native cultures, some practices associated with traditional education, such as the telling of stories by the hunters, were condemned by some as "Satanic." As the Western educational system was imposed in Alaska Native communities, those arriving concluded that Native people were primitive and backward and thus no advice was sought in the kind and direction of the education system formed. When missions were established, the choice of location was often unfortunate. Bethel, Alaska was located at its present site simply because it was as far up the river as the boat could travel given the limited knowledge that the missionaries had about the river channels. If they had sought advice, they might have ended a bit farther up the river at the present day site of Aniak with a better source of water, some trees for construction and higher ground for a foundation. One story tells that when the missionaries arrived in Kivalina in the summer they set the school building on a sand spit, not considering that their school would be held primarily in the winter and that the winter locations for the Alaska Native people in that region would have been by fresh water, in the tree line across the lagoon.

Today, teachers and other educators often ask, "Why don't Native parents care about the education of their kids?" This question demonstrates an ignorance that is pervasive in our educational system. Imagine an entire community of adults who do not care about the ability of their children to meet the future. This is so unlikely that it is ludicrous. Also, it seems obvious that any culture that has survived thousands of years must have had a successful system of education. But many people remain ignorant and unconcerned with the complex and successful aspects of traditional Native education. Why does this estrangement between school and community continue? Some parents may have questions about the goals of the school. The parents may not care about the school or they don't equate it with education. Many parents see lots of papers passed back and forth but do not see their children being prepared for anything that they value. Some parents believe that learning about traditional life is the most valuable knowledge that can be taught to their children. Many parents still participate in the more traditional Native educational system as they prepare their children to contribute to the community. Whatever the reasons for estrangement, the school does not have a monopoly on education in an Alaska Native community and is seen by some as a competing system of learning.

The stories told here are repeated all over Alaska. In a sense they might be considered as cautionary tales. Tales about how good intentions may produce mixed results when they are not combined with thoughtful discussions with local people. A little advice from the people who were thought "too primitive or backward" might have resulted in communities that were located in more desirable geographic locations. Knowledge about the traditional educational system of Alaska Natives might, even today, result in schools that are more completely integrated into our communities. This essay is an attempt to break some of the stereotypes about the Iñupiat that persist in American society and by doing so to promote better opportunities for Alaska Native students.

Bernice Tetpon

Community Values and Beliefs

Sharing Our Pathways, Vol. 6, Issue 1, Jan/Feb 2001

L oddie Jones, in a keynote speech to the Alaska Native Education Council in October of 1998, spoke about what it means for the community values and beliefs to be central to effective teaching practices. Her parents were her first teachers and enabled her to become knowledgeable in her Yup'ik culture. Similarly, in my own Iñupiaq upbringing, my parents were my first teachers and taught us values and beliefs that are well articulated in a poster published in 1996 by the North Slope Borough, Ilisagvik College.

These values and beliefs are:

Qiksiksrautiqagniq, which means respect for *Utuqqanaanun* or Elders, respect for *allanun* or others and respect for *inuuniagvigmun* or nature. We also learned the importance of respect for ilagiigniq or family kinship and roles, and respect for *signatainniq* or sharing. Other values and beliefs include knowledge of language, cooperation, love and respect for one another, humor, hunting traditions, compassion, humility, avoidance of conflict and spirituality. How do we go about this?

The Life Cycle: From Infancy to Elder

When children are taught by example within the everyday life of growing up from infancy through the Elder stage, these values and beliefs stay with them for the rest of their lives. Looking at the circle with the community values and beliefs in the center and the cycle of life extending from infancy to the Elder stage, we can see how important it is for these values to be built upon as we enter Western-oriented elementary and secondary schooling. It wasn't until I was in my teacher preparation years and in graduate school that I was taught anything related to my own culture, language or environment. When instruction does not relate to the students' community values and beliefs, or is taught out of context, they cannot relate to what is being taught and lose interest in school.

The Alaska Standards for Culturally Responsive Schools includes standards for students, educators, schools, curriculum and communities. Our students need a strong sense of self-identity and that can only come from our students being strongly grounded in the values and beliefs and traditions of their communities. Our students also need to learn about their local environment so that they can gain a better understanding of where they fit in the world in a global sense. Everyone in the community is a teacher and all teachers must also be learners. As we learn from one another, we can strengthen the sense of well being in our communities.

What Can We Learn?

Educators who come to our communities from outside must make an effort to become part of the community so they can incorporate the local knowledge system into their teaching. How do educators find out about the community's values and beliefs? Many educators have learned that their survival depends on becoming acquainted with a knowledgeable Native person in the community to help guide them in their everyday lives as they join in community activities and informally visit community members to develop a sense of how the community functions. There are many survival skills that have to be learned when educators move to a community they are not familiar with. Most of us growing up learned to understand the world around us through patient observation and practice in hands-on activities. Similarly, educators will have to take the time to observe and figure out how to communicate and actively participate in their new communities.

In the same manner, it is our responsibility as community members to give our children (and the teachers) time to observe and participate in hands-on activities and learn the values and beliefs while actively engaging in the community. We need to ensure that they learn well in their Native ways of knowing and are able to succeed in the Western world. As we return to the circle with the community at the center, let us identify our community's values and beliefs. How can we incorporate these values and beliefs into our school? How can we integrate the school into the community and not see it as a separate entity?

First of all, everyone in the community is a teacher. Some of us are licensed and have credentials in certain subject areas, but many others are experts in language, dancing, singing, hunting, outdoor survival, mediating, reading the weather, preparing traditional foods and so on. Everyone has something to contribute. Secondly, incorporating the Native language into instruction gives students advantages in their ability to understand the content that is required in exams and statewide tests. When a child is taught in their heritage language first, whatever the content may be, the child can then learn that content in the English language and succeed equally with students whose first language is English. Being bilingual is a benefit, not a deficit. Students who are bilingual have cognitive skills that surpass monolingual students who can relate to concepts in only one modality, while bilingual students can relate to concepts through their own culture and make the transition to the English language. Elders can be very helpful in this endeavor. Even when they are unable to speak in the Native language, the Elders can provide a wealth of resources for educators to learn how to integrate local knowledge into the curriculum.

Finally, knowledge of language is an important value within the Native community. From knowing your language, the rest of the values and beliefs come into place. Within the circle we want our children to grow from infancy to Elder status and to fulfill the cycle of life without barriers. Without these strong values we leave our children with a lack of self-identity that often results in the loss of a sense of community. As educators and community members, we will all benefit from helping the children learn the community's values and beliefs. Through the Alaska Standards for Culturally Responsive Schools, we can find ways to make sure these values and beliefs are incorporated into the teaching of our children.

Igxubuq Dianne Schaeffer

Nikaitchuat Ixisabviat: An Iñupiaq Immersion School

Sharing Our Pathways, Vol. 7, Issue 1, Jan/Feb 2002

Nikaitchuat translated into Iñupiaq means "anything is possible" and *ixisabviat* means "the place to learn." Nikaitchuat Ixisabviat is an Iñupiaq Immersion school. The teachers conduct all classes in Iñupiaq. Nikaitchuat was started by interested parents and community members who felt that a cultural approach to education was needed if our children were to thrive.

Tarruq Pete Schaeffer served on the regional school board for about four years and found out that it would be very difficult to have

Ivik Kunuyaq Henry along with Igluguq and Agnik Schaeffer pour uqsruq (seal oil) into containers for their parents.

the school he and his wife envisioned installed in the current school system. Abnik Polly Schaeffer worked for eight years at the elementary school as an Iñupiaq teacher; she taught seven classes a day with 25 minutes for each class. The students had fun, but they never retained anything because of the short amount of time given to each class. Tarruq and Abnik had a vision of a school—of students being taught in Iñupiaq and learning the cycles of the Iñupiaq year.

In the spring of 1998, Tarruq and Abnik Schaeffer sat down with interested community members and said that they were opening up a school in the fall. We didn't have a building, curriculum or staff. We formed committees and each committee had a chairperson. I was on the enrollment committee and we came up with the enrollment process for Nikaitchuat. There was also the finance committee and a couple others. Sandra Erlich Kowalski was hired for the summer to find out what we needed in order to open up as a school.

On September 10, 1998, Nikaitchuat opened with 20 students, three teachers and one director. We had very little furniture and the school supplies hadn't arrived yet. Tarruq Schaeffer gave $100 to Abnik and Aana Taiyaaq to buy school supplies like pencils and paper. We had the determination and will to teach our children what we feel is important: the Iñupiaq language.

Nikaitchuat Ilisagviat 2001–2002 visit the NANA Museum of the Arctic.

Nikaitchuat Ixisabviat is formed under the umbrella of the tribal government, the Native Village of Kotzebue also known as Kotzebue IRA. We have an agreement with NANA to give us some money and lease the building to us for one dollar a month. We get a grant from Maniilaq and from the Department of Education (we are in the second year of a three-year curriculum development grant) and we also get the Johnson O'Malley money from Kotzebue IRA and parents pay a monthly tuition for their child to attend our school.

Parent involvement and education are a vital part of school functioning. Parents help out by volunteering during and after school hours in tasks as varied as reading to children, serving snacks, cleaning, curriculum development and support, providing transportation to the Senior Center, learning and teaching cultural activities and the list goes on. It is not uncommon to see grandparents, aunts, uncles and siblings enter the school to volunteer as well. We ask parents to put in at least four hours of volunteer time a month. There are a few parents that put in eight hours or more a week. We have a bimonthly parent meeting where the parents catch up on what their child is learning. We have a potluck once a month where all parents and relatives are invited to attend.

Nikaitchuat Ixisabviat is in its fourth school year. We have five older students (two are in second grade, two in first grade, four

Qikiqtaq Walker, Aana Taiyaaq Biesemeier, Qignak Atoruk and Urralik Gregg pick asriaviich (blueberries) this last fall on one of our many field trips.

kindergartners and ten pre-kindergartners for a total of 19 students. We have four teachers, one director and one curriculum development specialist.

This year, the first graders have been working on their writing skills along with learning more math. Instead of taking a nap, they do school work, like writing and reading in Iñupiaq. Abnik Polly Schaeffer has been busy teaching them the different subjects. Aana Taiyaaq Ida Biesemeier has been helping Abnik with the first graders, along with teaching the younger students the basics.

Isan Diana Sours and Suuyuk Lena Hanna are kept busy with the younger students (the three and four year olds), teaching them the basics of how to get along and to respect other students. The two biggest things that are reinforced daily is *Kamaksrixutin* and *Naalabnixutin*—to be respectful and to listen! They also learn the colors in Iñupiaq, numbers and their Iñupiaq names. Each student is called by their Iñupiaq name; some teachers don't know the children's English name. The students are learning how to write their name.

We have staff to develop the curriculum for the first graders. Kavlaq Andrea Gregg is the curriculum development specialist. She has been working on developing a curriculum based on the seasons of the year, building upon what Nikaitchuat has done the past three years. We are still looking for an assistant for Kavlaq, who will help in coming up with new and exciting curriculum for our older students.

We make lessons planned by the week and this week's topic is *niksiksuq* (fishing); this week's color is *tufuaqtaaq* (purple); the Iñupiaq value being reinforced this week is respect for nature and the shape of the week is *aqvaluqtaaq* (circle).

My name is Igxubuq Dianne Schaeffer and my title is Director. This is my second year as director—before that, I was on the Parent Governance Committee and a parent of one of the students. I've been working along with the Parent Governance Committee on how Nikaitchuat can expand next year. We would like to continue to grow with the oldest students, hopefully into the fifth grade.

We are looking for a new building as we are at full capacity in the building we are in now. There is a possibility of obtaining a building with our tribal government, the Kotzebue IRA. We continue to grow and hope to share what we have learned with other communities. If you are here during the school year, we invite you to our school; we are located behind the Pizza House in Kotzebue. Come on over and check us out!

Ruthie Sampson

Native Languages in Alaska

Sharing Our Pathways, Vol. 7, Issues 2 and 3, Mar/Apr, Summer 2002

Keynote address to the 2002 Bilingual Multicultural Education and Equity Conference

Good Morning respected Elders, honored guests, educators and parents! *Uummatitchauraqtuami nuna ixiqsraqtiqman nakuqsixiqtufa.* My heart was really beating fast earlier but I feel calmer after the earthquake. I worked in Anchorage in 1978 with Tupou Pulu and attended the BMEEC over the years for a total of 10 to 15 times. I was thinking that if you attend often enough, sooner or later they will ask you to be the keynote speaker—I think this was Mike's way of making sure I get here early. Actually, last night I set my alarm clock to 6:30 am. I didn't want to be late. During the night, I woke up at 4:30 am and went back to sleep. I woke up again and it was still 4:30 am! I went back to sleep again and this time when I woke up it was 2:30 am and then I realized I had been dreaming that I was waking up at 4:30 am!

It is an honor for me to be here today. I thank the BMEEC planning committee, Bernice Tetpon and also Mike Travis, for convincing me that I had something to say to you today. I am here representing the Iñupiaq language, meaning the people who live in Northwest Alaska and the North Slope. I am from Selawik, Alaska and I work in Kotzebue for the Northwest Arctic Borough School District.

I am also here on behalf of our Elder, Minnie Qapviatchialuk Aliitchak Gray of Ambler, Alaska. She is not here due to a mild stroke she experienced this winter.

Minnie is representative of the first Iñupiaq language teachers who began to teach in the schools in 1972 when the bilingual programs were first implemented in Alaska schools. She was part of a wonderful group of enthusiastic, fun Iñupiaq language and culture teachers who took great pride and delight in learning to read and write in their native language. They actually sacrificed several summers while others were gathering food to attend workshops in Barrow, Nome and Kotzebue. They were fortunate to have people such as Martha Aiken, Edna McLean, Larry Kaplan, Hannah Loon and Tupou Pulu to teach them Iñupiaq literacy, grammar and to help them develop materials for classroom use. In those days, sufficient funds allowed all the staff to attend the BMEEC and what fun they had. They have recounted story after story about their cross-cultural experiences when they traveled to Anchorage. Some were afraid to answer the phone in their rooms. When they went to the restaurant, they would often order chicken-fried steak thinking it was chicken. When they went to the stores, one lady said she often grinned at the store dummies thinking it was someone standing. One time, a whole bunch of them were crossing the street and walking when the sign said walk. When it said "don't walk" guess what they did? They ran across the street! Even though they experienced all this, they were always so willing to try things out and paid close attention to learn as much as they could in the workshops they attended.

Several years ago, we nominated Minnie Gray to be the bilingual educator of the year. This was her philosophy of education. She said it in Iñupiaq and we translated it into English (listen very carefully because in this, you can hear everything that needs to be included in a curriculum to teach about a language and culture):

"Iñupiaq should be taught at an early age. I have seen that the younger students are, the more they learn. It is fun to teach these young children. As an Iñupiaq language instructor, I realized that children need motivation to learn. I motivated my students by offering them variety. They cannot learn by only writing, so I took them out for field trips and taught them about the things that grow. Same thing in the spring. When they got tired of writing, I took them outside and taught them the names of the many different birds that migrate north. This motivated them tremendously. I had projects for them such as skin sewing and other crafts, including making birch bark basket. I allowed them to play Iñupiaq games when they became restless. Sometimes, I even took them home and prepared an Iñupiaq dish for them to sample, such as cranberry pudding or some other dish. Other times, I taught them how to make Eskimo ice cream. I also boiled the head of mudshark, which has many bones and, as we ate it, I told them the individual names of the bones. This is an interesting project and the students think it is fun. For added variety, I told them Iñupiaq stories and legends.

Elder Minnie Gray of Ambler

"Students should learn about life in school. They should learn practical skills such as skin sewing and cooking. Many students need these basic skills. They should know the names of our Native foods and know how to prepare them. It is practical to learn these skills because our environment is going to be the same in spite of the changes in our lifestyles. We will still need warm clothing and we will still need to gather food. Students should know about the weather because we cannot predict what the coming seasons' weather will be like. They should also know their regional geography. They should know their local subsistence areas, their trails and place names of creeks, rivers and other landmarks. They should be able to know where they are and be able to communicate exactly where they are as they travel out in the country for it is a matter of survival."

So there you have it. Everything you need to write a Native language and culture curriculum. Minnie was one of this great group of Iñupiaq language and culture instructors who taught what they knew to the students and I give them all tribute today. Over the years, most of this core group retired and we have been struggling to replace them as fewer and fewer candidates who speak Iñupiaq fluently fill their positions.

During the next three days, our BMEEC theme will be "Bilingual and Cross Cultural Education: Tools for Community Empowerment and Academic Success." That's a mouthful and has so much to say to us. We also have so much to say to each other because we come here with our collective knowledge and each and every one of you has something valuable to share with another person. As I thought of what to say to you today I had titled it "Living in a Modern World Without Losing Our Native Identity."

I wanted to talk about how we as Natives need to continue to share our heritage and history to our students so that they can cope in this modern world and still have a good sense of who they are and feel that same comfort of being one with nature when they are out in the country. I believe, as Natives, that is one of our greatest treasures— something we should continue to nurture in our children and grand-children. We must have a vision for our youth that they can share. What are we doing in this conference to expand this vision?

What is Community Empowerment and Academic Success?

Most of us would define academic success in terms of modern schooling, saying it is to be educated in school and home and go on to higher learning so that you can get a good job and have a successful and meaningful life. I'm sure you have your own definition.

How can we make bilingual education and cross-cultural educa-tion tools for community empowerment and academic success? When we talk about bilingual education, we are talking about speaking two languages. As an Iñupiaq, I will talk about the Native language ex-perience in Alaska. When the *Guidelines for Strengthening Indigenous Languages* were being developed, my concern was that someone needed to be responsible for providing a forum in which our people who had been punished for speaking Iñupiaq in school could come together and tell their story so that their experience could be validat-ed and they could hear an apology from the school system and some avenue for forgiveness and healing would begin.

The reason I brought this up is because it is a recurring story that I hear and in a way prevents grandparents and parents from partic-ipating effectively in the school system. When bilingual programs first began in the early 70s and as they continued in the 80s, some Elders expressed shock and surprise that the language was going to be taught in the school, because when they were young, they had been punished for speaking even one word in the school playground. As young children, they had a hard time seeing the difference be-tween stealing, lying and speaking Iñupiaq because they got pun-ished for doing any of those. Now years later, they were told it was okay and, today, there are people in their 70s who still feel hurt when they remember what happened and I think many people think no one wants to hear their story because it happened so long ago and we should forget it and go on with our lives.

We must realize that this action taken against our parents and grandparents had ramifications that occurred over the 20th century and an attitude of shame and humiliation toward the teaching of the Native language was passed from parent to child unintentionally, unknowingly and innocently, like Harold Napolean described in his book *Yuuyaraq: The Way of the Human Being*. He wrote that the symptoms experienced by the survivors of the influenza epidemic are the same symptoms of survivors of post-traumatic stress disorder and that the present disease of the soul and the psyche is passed from parent to child unintentionally, unknowingly and innocently.

Let us take time to reflect and understand what happened to bring us to where we are today:

William Hensley

In his 1981 speech at the BMEEC, Iñupiaq William Hensley said the following: "The policy of repressing the Native language in the school system has had the effect of repressing the ancient spirit of the people that enabled us to survive over many thousands of years. The values that have been beaten into our people were in direct contrast to the very values that enabled us to survive. In the place of common effort, individuality has been made sacred. In the place of cooperation, competition is fostered. In the place of sharing, acquisitiveness in our lives is pummeled into our minds through the media. It is no wonder that there are so-called Native problems."

Eben Hopson

Eben Hopson, at a bilingual conference, said the following which appeared in Cross Cultural Studies in Education: "Eighty-seven years ago, when we were persuaded to send our children to Western educational institutions, we began to lose control over the education of our youth. Many of our people believed that formal educational systems would help us acquire the scientific knowledge of the Western world. However, it was more than technological knowledge that the educators wished to impart. The educational policy was to attempt to assimilate us into the American mainstream at the expense of our culture. The schools were committed to teaching us to forget our language and Iñupiaq heritage. There are many of you parents who, like me, were physically punished if we spoke one Iñupiaq word. Many of us can still recall the sting of the wooden ruler across the palms of our hands and the shame of being forced to stand in the corner of the room, face to the wall, for half an hour if we were caught uttering one word of our Native language. This outrageous treatment and the exiling of our youth to school in foreign environments were to remain the common practices of the educational system. For eighty-seven years, the BIA tried to destroy our culture through the education of our children. Those who would destroy our culture did not succeed. However, it was not without cost. Many of our people have suffered. We all know the social ills we endure today. Recently, I heard a member of the school personnel say that many of our Iñupiaq children have poor self-concepts. Is it any wonder, when the school systems fail to provide the Iñupiaq student with experiences which would build positive self-concepts when the Iñupiaq language and culture are almost totally excluded?"

Changes in the 80s and 90s

Since these speeches were given in the 70s and 80s, much has changed. William Hensley was instrumental in developing the Iñupiaq Ilitqusiat Spirit Movement in Northwest Alaska, where the values were listed and parents were encouraged to speak Iñupiaq to their children. Immersion programs have been developed in Barrow, Bethel, Arctic Village, Kotzebue and other places around Alaska. We have powerful web sites such as the Alaska Native Curriculum and Teacher Development Project created by Paul Ongtooguk and his staff and the Alaska Native Knowledge Network, a by-product of the Alaska Rural Systemic Initiative, where we receive information from Sean Topkok under the direction of Ray Barnhardt, Oscar Kawagley and Frank Hill.

Although we have made some progress since then, the effects of the punishment inflicted on our parents or grandparents for speaking Iñupiaq lingers today. I was born in 1954 and when I went to school this did not happen to us. My mother lived in camp much of her childhood years so she didn't speak much English when I was young. My father, on the other hand, had attended school until he was in the eighth grade. He had heard stories of how people were punished for speaking Iñupiaq and knew the importance of speaking English. When I was very young, my mother's cousin and I were playing and speaking Iñupiaq with a high tone English accent saying something like this: *Uvuÿa aquvillagutin.* We thought we spoke English when we raised our voices and played "teacher." Well, my father pulled me over and said in Iñupiaq, "Daughter, you must try your best to learn to speak English." From that moment on, I did my best to speak English to him, but I spoke Iñupiatun to my mother and grandmother. Only recently have I started speaking in full Iñupiaq sentences to my father. I know he told me this because he wanted me to succeed in school. My father's generation did not have the luxury of welfare or government assistance, so their goal was for us to learn as much as we could so we could have good jobs that provided food and shelter for us. I dare say that at some point in the 60s, it seemed like the goal for many young women was to move to a city and work somewhere with a typewriter. Just come home once a year and see how everybody's doing. That happened with some people, but they found that they missed home, missed Iñupiaq food and all that goes on in a village.

Last year, we had invited an Elder from Kiana by the name of Tommy Sheldon to speak to the school staff about the history of Kiana. He spoke about how the schools were segregated when he was a child. Only the children of white people or half breeds attended school until they set up a school for Native children. He spoke about how he was punished for speaking Iñupiaq at school. The most common form of punishment for people who tell their story was to stand in the corner or next to the black board with your nose matched to a dot on the board. This was punishment for being Iñupiaq and speaking your own language. A beautiful language that had been used to communicate and verbalize concepts from a world view that existed for many years and helped the Iñupiat to survive in the Arctic.

Later he said that if they spoke Iñupiaq, then they were not allowed to attend the school party. If you didn't go to the school party, you didn't get to eat cookies and juice. That's when I thought, "We lost some of our language to cookies and juice." Today, the grandchildren do not speak the language because of this cookie and this juice.

When I spoke to my father, he recounted that boys who were older than him would refrain from speaking Iñupiaq just to attend a school party where beans were served. So we lost some of our language for a bowl of beans.

I also spoke to my friend Bertha Sheldon of Shungnak. She said that when they spoke Iñupiaq, they would stand in a corner.

They would also have to hold books from an outstretched hand and would be barred from attending the school party at the end of the month if they didn't.

If they couldn't go to the party, they would go to the window and watch the fun the students were having inside. She particularly remembers when apples were hung from the ceiling with string and the students raced to see who would finish eating an apple first without using their hands. It looked like so much fun and the apples looked so delicious. Mmm, they thought, this time I will not speak an Iñupiaq word. Later, they couldn't even look inside the window anymore because the curtains were drawn across the window.

Then I spoke to a former Iñupiaq teacher named Amelia Aaluk Gray of Kobuk. She said that if they spoke Iñupiaq in the school grounds, someone would tell on them and they would receive a black mark by their name on a piece of paper. If they got so many marks, then they could not go to the school to play games on Fridays (an equivalent to game night.) She said the teachers only wanted them to learn English so that they could learn what was taught in school. She was not bitter about what happened because by this time, she had learned to forgive them and tried to understand what had happened.

Okay, so we've heard those stories before. They happened many years ago. Right now is the time to move on.

Well, after Tommy spoke, a woman younger than me remembered how she had to hold books with an outstretched hand. She remembers the shame and humiliation and says that today, as a parent, it makes it difficult for her to speak Iñupiaq to her children although she speaks Iñupiaq to her spouse, siblings and parents.

Another woman shared with me that when she moved from the village to Kotzebue, where more people spoke English, whenever she started to speak Iñupiaq, her sister would whisper and scold her not to speak Iñupiaq. Especially since she spoke a slightly different dialect from the one spoken in Kotzebue.

That is when I realized that this problem has to be dealt with. I am not a therapist and I have no quick solutions. Because a public apology was not made soon enough, the attitude about the language silently crept from generation to generation during the 50s, 60s and 70s. Now there is a new young generation who wonder why their parents did not speak Iñupiaq to them.

Forgiveness and Healing

If we are to make parents and grandparents feel welcome in the school, we must invite them into the school and publicly apologize for what happened to them or their parents in the past. We must hear their story and validate it. We must not ignore it or it will continue to fester and more bitterness will grow until we have nothing left. We still have hope that more of the language can be shared and spoken in all its beauty for it is a language of the heart.

Language of the Heart

I read a wonderful article by Marilyn Wilhelm about heart language and how the ancient languages spoke from the heart as God created us. I began to think of our Iñupiaq language. I thought of the word meaning "to think": *Isuma-* or *isruma-*. *Isu-* or *isru-* is the end of something. *-ma* is "my" and I think then the literal meaning is "my end". This could mean that everything about us reaches our mind, which is like our end. It is our source of thought. Then I thought of the word for eye which is *iri*. To exist is *it-*. When you add *-ri*, it's a post-base that could mean something like "the means, the cause of", so everything we see, we behold and in our mind, it exists when we see it. *Nakuagi-* means "to like" or "to love". *Nakuu-* is "good" and when you *nakuagi-* something, you think that person or thing is good. It's like saying, "I think good of you." Isn't that wonderful? See what beautiful languages we are struggling to save?

Not only our we trying to save our languages, but also our history. I have been so fortunate to have translated many narrations from our Elders. There are so many wonderful concepts and world views that they knew and that are being lost as each precious one dies, slowly, one by one. I remember one particular story that I like to share about an Elder named Susie Stocking from Kobuk. She recounted how they used to gather willow bark to make into net twine and how they would walk barefoot among the thorns in the heat of early summer, among mosquitoes and gather the bark. They would pile it so high around their necks that you couldn't see the person anymore. Then when they brought it down to the birch canoe, they had to keep the bark covered and moist the whole way through. All through the process, they had to keep the bark moist or else it would become brittle, dry and break off into little pieces. The remarkable statement that I remember from her narration is that she said in all the hard work they did, they just simply viewed their lives as being normal—they didn't know that they were working so hard. Stories like these must be documented and handed down from generation to generation because that is our rightful heritage.

It is not too late. If we are to empower our communities, we must validate the pain that our Elders experienced and help them walk through that process into healing and forgiveness and a new resolve to speak the language and pass on the knowledge. God made us with forgiving hearts and we can help each other heal. So, that is one plan to get our parents to participate in the programs.

What about the schools and the education system? What can they do?

The AFN report on "The Status of Alaska Natives: A Call for Action" wrote on education: "In the words of the most thorough study to date of the federal and state school systems operated in Alaska from 1867 to 1970: policy makers over the years have vacillated between attempted assimilation of the Native population into white society and protection of their cultural identity.

Our history tells us this (from www.alaskool.org):

- In 1886 the policy was that in all schools conducted by missionary organizations, it is required that all instructions shall be given in the English language.
- In 1887, it said that the instruction of the Indians in the vernacular is not only of no use to them, but is detrimental to the cause of their education and civilization, and no school will be permitted on the reservation in which the English language is not exclusively taught. "It is also believed that teaching an Indian youth in his own barbarous dialect is a positive detriment to him."
- In 1990, an article appeared in Education Week, that stated that federal officials were assessing the potential impact of a new law that encouraged the use of Native American languages in schools run by the BIA and in public schools enrolling Indians or other Native groups. Spokesman for the Interior and Education departments had said that the statement of federal policy contained in a bill approved by the congress without public hearings and signed into law by President Bush might well result in an invigoration of Native language instruction. But they also said that the intent of the new Native American Languages Act could prove costly and difficult to realize because of the vast number of Native languages and the paucity of Native speakers who have been trained as teachers. The article quoted John W. Tippeconnic III, who headed the Education Department's office of Indian Education as saying, "On the one hand, it promotes the languages, which is positive, but it does create burdens for

the schools." The article further said that the law includes no penalties for noncompliance. But some officials had suggested then that it could provide legal ammunition for parents seeking Native language instruction, particularly in BIA schools and public schools with high concentrations of Native American students.

- The measure declares that the policy of the United States (this is in 1990!) is "to preserve, protect and promote the rights and freedom of Native Americans to use, practice and develop Native American languages." This act became public law 101-477 on October 30, 1990. The law states that the status of the cultures and languages of Native Americans is unique and the United States has the responsibility to act together with Native Americans to ensure the survival of these unique cultures and languages.

I remember being so excited when I read this bill. I thought there was going to be funding like Title VII that went with it. When I brought it to the attention of an administrator in Kotzebue, he looked at me and said, "Ruth, all this does is reverse the policy of 1887 which stated that Indian languages will not be taught." He thought it was long over due, or maybe too late. In addition, there was no extra funding attached. All it basically did was say, "Oh, by the way, it's okay to teach a Native language in the school now."

In any event, in 1991, Senator Frank Murkowski introduced the Alaska Native Languages Preservation and Enhancement Act. It was meant to preserve and enhance the ability of Alaska Natives to speak and understand their Native languages.

Today, under the Administration for Native Americans, there is limited funding for people to apply for grants to administer language programs, but they have to be applied for by the Native corporations or IRA offices, though they can do a joint project with the school. The problem is that there is very limited funding in this and it is competitive nationwide amongst Indian tribes. Several years ago, they started out with something like one to two millions dollars available on a competitive basis among all the Indian tribes in the nation. We applaud Senator Murkowski and his staff for this legislation.

In July 2000, Senator Lincoln worked with the Alaska legislators to pass SB 103 "Native Language Education Act." This requires Native language curriculum advisory boards for each school in the district in which a majority of the students are Alaska Natives. If the board recommends the establishment of a Native language education curriculum for a school, the regular school board will initiate and conduct a Native language education curriculum within grades K–12 in that school. We thank Senator Lincoln for her hard work to have this bill passed, but there is no additional funding attached.

In the meantime, What has happened with the state bilingual regulations? All this time, the whole intent of the bilingual education is to improve the English language of the student, always talking about exiting them out of the program as soon as possible.

Now the regulations say you can have a two-way immersion program but 50% of your students who come in have to speak the Native language. So only if the parents teach them and they enter the school that way can you get an immersion program funded. Otherwise, if they come to school speaking English, even if it is village English, then they just have the English programs available as an option.

So we need to get our programs identified as Native language programs by the village advisory board, but there is no special funding attached and if the school board decided not to have it, then that's it again.

As Native people who believe in bilingual education, we must work together for funds to be allocated for the "Native language education act" to be implemented.

So how does all this relate to our students who must live in this modern world and not lose their Native identity? If we believe our theme that bilingual education and cross-cultural education are tools for community empowerment and academic success let us remember the following recommendations.

The 1990 AFN report on the "Status of Alaska Natives: A Call for Action" wrote on education:

- Children are the most important segment of any community, for each community's future lies in its children. To assure that future, the children must be given, through education, the skills that will enable them to succeed in life and the understanding that will continue the community's values. For Alaska Native children, this means that they must receive an integrated education that encompasses two sets of skills and two sets of values.

- The first set of skills is that it is necessary for the children to succeed in traditional Native life ways. The second set of skills is that it is necessary for the children to succeed in Western society. The children's education must also integrate Native and Western values so that they are empowered in both cultures. The skills and values are inseparable, for mastery of one cannot be obtained without mastery of the other.
- This ideal of an integrated education has not been achieved, or even accepted, in the past. Alaska Native children enter an education system developed by Western culture. In past years the system had eradication of Native culture as one of its objectives. Even after this misguided goal was abandoned, the system still proved unable to meet its own fundamental objective: education of Native children in the skills and values necessary to succeed in Western society.

Those are the words conveyed by past Elder Chester Seveck, who advised us to take the good parts of the Iñupiaq culture and the good parts of the Western culture and blend them together for an integrated education. So how does bilingual education help us toward community empowerment? What is community empowerment? Let us take a moment now and visualize an empowered community with students learning to cope and succeed in the 21st century.

To me, an empowered community in the villages of Alaska means a community where children are well taken care of and they get enough sleep, enough food and their clothes are clean. They eat well and go to school on time and are hardly ever absent. Their parents take time to plan activities for them and train them to develop habits that result in good character traits. For example, they take them on long hikes on the tundra so that they can learn the value of hard work. They take them fishing so they can learn patience. They feed them wholesome foods, including Native foods so that they can be healthy and strong and realize what good health is. They speak their Native language to them and tell them stories and their people's history. If they don't know this, they take them to someone who can. They limit watching TV and playing electronic games. They monitor how the computer is used by the children. They provide time for them to do their homework and teach them to pray. They cook food and have the children bring some food to a needy person or an Elder. When they hunt and gather, they also have the children bring the food to share with others. They make sure that they know who their relatives are. Although they enjoy snow machining, skiing and other outdoor sports; they also make sure that their children can build an outdoor fire and survive if they had to live off the land in an emergency. In all of this, they speak respectfully to others, especially Elders. They show that helping Elders is necessary and important. If they have the opportunity, they allow their children to learn about the world outside and travel with them. They speak respectfully of teachers and other people in the community who work to help everyone else. An empowered community is where the children graduate from high school and go on for more training or school and still feel comfortable to come back to the village and work in jobs that pay well so that they can enjoy all the outdoor activities that our back doors in Alaska can provide. An empowered community has school systems that work to accommodate the needs of their students, including the provision of the child's language and culture being integrated into the curriculum.

That is my idea of how the lives of our children could be improved in an empowered community. Let us begin to visualize this empowered community and share the vision with our children. And in the words of John Pingayak of Chevak: "Our ancestral ways are always best for our future. Never forget them and learn them well . . . "

Thank you.

Inuit Studies: Some Reflections

Maricia Ahmasuk

Sharing Our Pathways, Vol. 7, Issue 5, Nov/Dec 2002

Inspired by the 13th Inuit Studies Conference held August 1–3, 2002, Anchorage, Alaska

The Inuit, "The People" of the world are one of the more studied people in recent history. This timeless research and documentation seeks to capture the essence of what it was like in a time when all one had was oneself and those immediately surrounding to sustain life itself. It is observed that since contact, Inuit have adapted to new ways brought on by outsiders, thereby changing the way Inuit operate in their daily activities and even in their mode of thought. Barrow's George Ahmaogak, Sr., mayor of North Slope Borough, put it interestingly in his keynote address at the 13th Inuit Studies Conference, titled, Science, Politics and the Bottom Line: the North Slope Experience: "

Your conversations can help to interpret what's happening in the cracks where Native culture and the mainstream culture rub against each other. It's a constant and silent and powerful movement, like the shifting of the earth's continental plates under our feet." Ahmaogak commented that these fault lines are not necessarily hostile or incompatible, but are simply hot spots that if taken so far as to interrupt the heritage of a people, such as banning the age-old practice of whaling, there are sure to be upheavals, or earthquakes. The whole subsistence issue is a prime example of how differing cultures tend to clash.

It is certain that we as Inuit have felt the ripple effect of two or more cultures coming together, as all cultures of the world continue to undergo, as we are drawn into this global village through modern technology. I view our current experience as a melding, an evolution. We are living in a time where the very existence of every single human being on earth depends to a certain extent on a network of governments and countries in globally negotiated positions. As Inuit, playing an active role in what is being documented even today is crucial in terms of preserving the accuracy of the image being portrayed. Faulty past records since outside contact have proven to haunt Natives with negative connotations and misinterpretations.

An important trend for Native peoples in the world of research is where the ownership of the surveys and their outcomes lie. Being involved from square one when the surveys are being developed is a must if they are to capture the essence of what Natives consider important information to relay to a public or agency reviewing the results. For example, the Survey of Living Conditions in the Arctic, headed out of the Institute of Social & Economic Research (ISER) at the University of Alaska Anchorage has organized a group of Alaska Natives to form the Alaska Native Management Board (ANMB), which basically steers the project. This board ensures that the information gathered for this project follows the concept of informed consent, as well as making sure that the survey is culturally sensitive. Respecting the whole process of including Native guidance on research projects brings useful information to light while at the same time defends a Native peoples' dignity and right to own what is really theirs.

Michelle Snyder shares a story using the storyknife on to our descendents?" while Nia White looks on.

After two-and-a-half days of listening to intelligent speakers such as Father Michael Oleksa and Angayuqaq Oscar Kawagley and visiting with Elder and author, Lela Oman of Nome, among other distinguished individuals, I was boiling with ideas, theories and a willingness to share my story with the group. I managed to offer my views with humor despite all seriousness of the issues at hand. I spoke of topics that ranged from language retention (or theory of retrieval through hypnosis in this case) to racism within our own Native society. The key point that I hoped to portray to the group was how important it is to find a balance between our modern lifestyle and the inner voice that constantly reminds us of where we came from.

Coming to terms with our identity as a Native person, or just as a human being in modern society, should be an area of concern and deserves some dedicated time and research on our behalf. Coming to terms with the small, still voice inside is key to our well being and long-range health. Perhaps some of the research that shows our people to be among the most devastated statistically is a result of over-looking our important role in a societal situation that is fairly new compared to where even our parents came from. Cultural adjustments do not happen over night, and we are not all naturally compatible with the modern Western values and mannerisms. Our whole life is a research project as we gather data and interpret its meaning as it applies to our selfhood. Finding meaning and truth is a universal, yet very individual concept and delves deep into the spiritual realm. If we think about it, just being outside doing activities such as berry picking, fishing or gathering wood for a fire grounds us, bringing us back to who we are as human beings, which is a spiritual experience—being one with the land and our natural surroundings. It is the simple things in life that make an individual or society feel grounded in a culture or heritage.

Finding meaning or purpose in life may mean putting the communal good over a personal pain, as it was traditionally. It is important to honor our heritage by practicing our values, so as to discover their true significance and intent. Discovering past morals and ways of living an honest life may lead us to a broader understanding of where we stand in today's world of individualism, even as we fight for a co-dependant relationship with the world-at-large. As we continue to adapt to the changing times, it is a comfort to know that there exists a wide collection of materials representing a time past when life appeared simpler. We have a big picture to work with in respect to the Native way of life as we move forward in progression toward an understanding of where we have been and where we are going. It is time to take authority over our own lives through our Native organizations.

Yaayuk Bernadette Alvanna-Stimpfle, Iñupiaq Lead Teacher

Integrating Culturally-Responsive School Standards in Education

Sharing Our Pathways, Vol. 8, Issue 1, Jan/Feb 2003

Last fall, the Bering Strait School District held their Third Annual Educational Conference from October 21–24. There were many workshops and meetings offered for all the participants from the fifteen sites within the region. It was exciting to see so many teachers coming together from the Bering Strait region.

On Tuesday, October 22 during the breakout sessions I facilitated two sessions on "Integrating Culturally-Responsive Standards." At both sessions I guided the participants in brainstorming on subsistence activities throughout each season.

In the first group, there were enough participants to break up into smaller groups to help each other in preparing lessons. In each of the groups, it was suggested that we create a circular calendar listing the seasonal activities. Teachers brainstormed with the students and they created a subsistence calendar. The following illustration shows activities both groups came up with.

Suggested Activities for Implementation of Subsistence-based Curriculum

- Have students brainstorm what activities are happening in the community.
- Create a circular seasonal calendar to record and display traditional activities with these labels:

Early spring	Summer	
Early fall	Late fall	Winter

- If possible, include the Native names of each season.

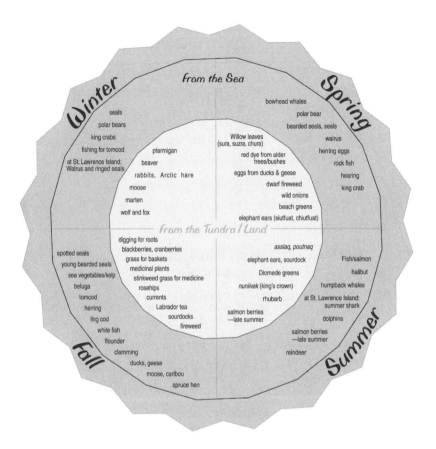

- Have students illustrate the calendar.
- Have students research and interview Elders or local experts.
- Compare and contrast traditional and modern subsistence activities.
- Create a website on the activities.
- Participate and get involved in the community activities.
- Invite guests for storytelling.
- Create and display student work.
- Hold a science fair on the research done by the students.

Assessment and Rubrics

- Teachers can create an assessment and a scoring guide for the projects.

Performance Assessment

- Hold a community night to display student work.

I know there are many activities I have left out from this list. Teachers can add them with their students. Both sessions I worked with were very good about sharing their activities and lessons.

Quyaana to all the participants who were part of the workshop during the BSSD Education Conference!

Sean Topkok | # Humility

Sharing Our Pathways, Vol. 9, Issue 3, Summer 2004

The warm Alaskan summer sun beats down on the students and counselors, including me. We've danced one song several times, learning and practicing it. When we finish, an Elder says, "Sean made a mistake. We're doing it all over again."

At this cultural camp, held years ago, the campers and staff had the good fortune to learn from Elders William and Marie Tyson from St. Mary's. Yup'ik dancing was part of the camp activities. Although I am Iñupiaq, I enjoyed actively learning along with the students. Not surprisingly, the Elders were aware of everyone, keeping a close eye on each person's progress.

Months later, I asked Mrs. Tyson if she would make me an *atikluk* (kuspuk) if I were to supply her with the fabric. Instead she thought I should make my own and she would teach me. As I was working on my *atikluk* there were times when she would undo the stitching and encourage me to do it correctly.

These are two examples of working with Elders and cultural-bearers, where I have gained significant experience. When Mr. Tyson said I made a mistake dancing and the whole group needed to start again, I did not feel humiliated, but honored. I realized he wanted to make sure I learned the dances correctly. Mrs. Tyson reinforced the same principle as I learned how to make my *atikluk* correctly.

Looking past my ethnicity, these two wonderful Elders focused on my learning process. Being Iñupiaq and not Yup'ik didn't matter to them. They saw something in me and, for me, that felt exceptional. Eventually I started to dance from within myself, knowing the motions have a meaning. I joined their dance group. On more than one occasion during a dance performance, Mr. Tyson felt it necessary to dance with us for a *pamyua* (encore).

I did not feel I had acted arrogant; however, through these learning experiences, the word "humility" has been further defined for me. These experiences have helped me realize it is okay to make mistakes. Originally I titled this article "Make Mistakes," but after reflecting on it, I felt it more appropriate to title it "Humility." Humility is part of my Iñupiaq values. Humility, like all our Alaska Native values, is something to teach our children. We need to let them know it is okay to make a mistake and encourage them to learn from their mistakes.

Humility vs. Humiliation

We have all been humiliated in our lifetime. It can negatively affect us and does not feel good. I could tell you a personal account of humiliation, but I would rather share how the Tysons and other Elders taught me humility. I am not, nor is anyone, a perfect person. I can learn from my mistakes, as long as I demonstrate I am trying to learn. Isn't that what we all want our children to learn—that it's okay to make mistakes and to learn from them? We, as parents and those guiding them, need to recognize and acknowledge they are trying.

I do not imagine Elders strive to become Elders, but rather to be the best they can be. Many people see me as just a computer person, however, I am actively involved in the Native community. I make mistakes on the computer, but I learn from them. I've also learned, that in order to learn from any mistakes in the Native community, I have to be active in the Native community. I must be involved, and I must try.

I have organized an Iñupiaq dance group in Fairbanks, the Pavva Iñupiaq Dancers. My whole family is involved with it. My wife, Amy, and I have never pressured our two sons to dance, but they look forward to practice and performances. Aaron, our five-year-old, is one of the strongest singers and drummers in our group. During the recent 2004 Festival of Native Arts, Christopher, our nine-year-old son, told a Native story passed down from one of Amy's relatives. It was his choice to tell the story in front of a large audience. I cannot tell you how proud we were of him. It was not how well he did it, which was awesome, but that he felt comfortable enough with his heritage to express himself in front of others.

We, as educators and parents, expect remarkable things from our students and children. Through our own actions and experiences we must share and reveal ourselves to them. We must act accordingly, whether we make mistakes or not. These are our Native, family and community values. As a parent, I feel that I want my sons to grow up culturally healthy. I also want them to grow up with a healthy self-esteem, regardless of their ethnic background. I want them to grow up to be the best people that they can be. I want them to grow knowing I love to be there with them to say, "I'm proud of you."

Author's note: This is dedicated to my mom, who allowed me to make my own mistakes and learn from them.

3

Tlingit/Haida Pathways
to Education

Andy Hope | # Reading Poles

Sharing Our Pathways, Vol. 3, Issue 5, Nov/Dec 1998

The following article originally appeared in Raven's Bones Journal, *Vol. 5, No. 1, Nov. 1996.*

The Tlingit occupy the northeastern Pacific coast of Alaska, the northern part of a region commonly referred to as the Northwest Coast (of the North American continent), which reaches from Yakutat, Alaska to the mouth of the Columbia River. Because many of the tribes that inhabit this culture area are related in one way or another, I refer to the Northwest Coast as the Raven Creator Bioregion. The Tlingit are one of many aboriginal groups in this bioregion that continue the tradition of pole carving.

To appreciate Tlingit pole art, one must understand Tlingit social organization: what Frederica de Laguna refers to as ". . . the fundamental principles of . . . clan organization, . . . the values on which Native societies are based," that is, the names and histories of the respective Tlingit tribes, clans, and clan houses.

The seventy-plus Tlingit clans are separated into moieties or two equal sides—the Wolf and the Raven. Tlingit custom provides for matrilineal descent (one follows the clan of the mother) and requires one to marry one of the opposite moiety. The clans are further subdivided into some 250 clan houses.

To underscore the duality of Tlingit law, Wolf moiety clans generally claim predator crests, whereas Raven moiety clans generally claim non-predator crests. For example, the Kaagwaantaan, a Wolf moiety clan, claim Brown Bear, the Killer Whale, the Shark and the Wolf as crests. The Kiks.áàdi, a Raven moiety clan, claim the Frog, the Sculpin, the Dog Salmon and the Raven as crests. Tlingit totem art is utilitarian as opposed to decorative art. Tlingit pole art depicts clan crests and histories.

> With the introduction of steel and iron implements among the tribes of the Northwest Coast, totem poles became numerous. Numbers of them could be seen in the more southern villages. But before modern tools, it is said, Totem poles were rare, not only on account of the difficulty in making—as stone and wood were used for tools—but the desire to keep them strictly distinctive as a reason for the scarcity. One often hears it said by the older people that originally totem poles were used inside of houses only, to support the huge roof beams. The carvings and painting on them were usually those of family crests. Those posts were regarded with respect very much as a flag is by a nation. Even when the Chilkats had acquired modern tools with which to make totem poles they did not fill their villages with tall poles like some other tribes, chiefly because they wanted to keep to the original idea.
>
> The figures seen on a totem pole are the principle subjects taken from traditional treating of the family's rise to prominence or of the heroic exploits of one of its members. From such subjects crests are derived. In some houses, in the rear between the two carved posts, a screen is fitted, forming a kind of partition which is always carved and painted. Behind this screen is the chief's sleeping place.
>
> —Louis Shotridge
> *The Museum Journal*, 1913

Archaeological field work has shown that the Northwest Coast decorative art form originated approximately 3,000 to 3,500 years before present, with appearance of decorated tools. In early seventies, a bentwood burial box was illegally taken from a cave at the west arm of Port Malmesbury on the west central part of Kuiu Island in central southeast Alaska. The US Forest Service eventually recovered the box and turned it over to the Alaska State Museum in the early 80s.

The box is of sacred significance, since it is associated with a burial. It is decorated on all four sides, with a killer whale form on one side and a half human, half bird (with a humanoid head) figure on two sides. The box was radio carbon dated in 1992 at 780 years before present, plus or minus 80 years, which makes it the oldest example of true northwest coast formline art.

The Port Malmesbury burial box discovery establishes that northwest coast formline existed well before contact with Europeans and was established well before metal tools were available. Some anthropologists had theorized that northwest coast formline was only established after exposure to metal tools brought by Europeans.

> What is significant in terms of art that the cultural pattern appears to be coalescing during this initial period. Symbolic modes of graphic expression have not emerged. Certainly to judge from available archaeological evidence, a distinctive coastal style did not begin to crystallize until about 1500 BC. We can only infer that the accumulation of historical and mythological traditions by the corporate lineages of northern coast villages was approaching the threshold where graphic symbols of corporate identity became meaningful. Implicit here is the assumption that graphic symbolism expressed in art works, requires a base of shared cognitive modes, belief systems, etc., which must develop to a certain point, perhaps over several millennia, before it can be meaningfully expressed in art works.
>
> —George MacDonald
> Indian Art Traditions of the Northwest Coast

Types of Poles

Mortuary

These poles usually depict one figure, the main clan crest of the deceased. The ashes of the deceased clan member being memorialized by the pole are traditionally placed at the base of the back of the pole.

The Raven Mortuary pole comes from the Prince of Wales Island in southern southeast Alaska. It was moved to the Sitka National Historical Park at the turn of the 19th and 20th centuries .

Crest or history of poles. These poles have multiple figures, representing clan crests and symbols depicting clan history. This type of pole is prevalent in southern southeast Alaska southward along the British Colombian coast to Puget Sound, where the Douglas Fir and Red Cedar trees necessary for carving large poles are more accessible.

Raven Memorial Pole

These poles are read from the top figure down. The Kiks.ádi clan of the Raven moiety. A replica of the pole stands in Totem Park in downtown Wrangell, Alaska.

House Poles

House poles are usually six to eight feet tall and usually have one clan crest figure, and are placed in the corners of the clan house.

Screens

House screens depict clan crest symbols. They are usually wall size and are placed at the back wall of clan houses, though in some cases a smaller screen is placed at the front entrance of the clan house.

The Kiks.ádi Naas Shagi Yéil (Raven Creator) pole from Wrangell, Alaska

The topmost figure is that of Naas Shagi Yéil and the highest of the Tlingit mythological beings that lives on a mountain about the headwaters of the Nass River. He is seated on the day box containing the sun, moon and stars in the front of which is carved and painted to represent the mythical sea spirit, Gunakadeit. Below this is Yéil, the Raven creator, who changed himself into a hemlock needle and was swallowed by the daughter of the guardian of light, which resulted in the rebirth of the raven child who stole the sun, moon and stars to prepare the earth for man, whom he later created. The female figure, indicated by the labret in the lower lip, is the mother who was carried up to the sky to escape the flood caused by the jealous uncle, to be pierced with his bill to sustain him until

Illustration by Joanne George

This pole is on display at the Sitka National Historical Park. Raven is portrayed on this memorial column, distinguished by his rather large, slightly hooked beak. The carving is in the style and is believed to have come from the village of the Takjikaan on Prince of Wales Island. In Sitka, the Tlingit placed their memorial poles on the ridge behind their village (along present-day Katlian Street) overlooking the channel. Memorial poles, along with house posts, are among the oldest forms of totem poles.

Illustration by Mike Jackson

Kiks.ádi Naas Shagi Yéil (Raven Creator) pole from Wrangell, Alaska

Illustration by Joanne George

The house poles illustrated at left come from the SheeAtiká Kwáan Tlingit Tribe. They are owned by the Kaagwaantann clan of the Wolf moiety. They come from Gooch Hít. The poles are housed at the Sitka National Park in Sitka, Alaska.

Illustration drawn by Harold Jacobs

The screen at left is from the Huna Kaawu Kwáan Tlingit tribe. It is owned by T'akdeintaan, clan of the Raven moiety. It comes from Yéil Koot Hít (Raven's Nest House). It is said to represent the man who guided boats into the entrance of Lituya Bay. The screen is housed at Sheldon Jackson Museum in Sitka, Alaska.

the waters subsided. The next figure below, which in the form of a raven, was named by informer as Ch'eet (murrelet) on the back of which the Raven tell, when dropping from the sky, and which carried him and the mother safely ashore. The female figure with the large labret through the lower lip at the base is "Old woman underneath," who, seated on a post, supports the earth. In her hands she carries a club for protection against the enemies of mankind who would drag her away, thus destroying the world. In the dualistic creed of the Tlingit, all nature has two existing and opposing forces which beset one on every hand.

—George Emmons
*The History of Tlingit
Tribes and Clans*, n.d.

Roby Littlefield | # Elders in the Classroom

Sharing Our Pathways, Vol. 4, Issue 2, Mar/Apr 1999

Elders do not Preserve Culture, They Live It

All students can benefit from inter-generational contacts. In Alaska Native cultures, grandparents were held in high regard as they contributed to the community by passing on knowledge and skills. Children learned by listening to and watching Elders and often didn't realize they were in training. Bringing grandparents in to share personal knowledge when studying subjects like nutrition, customs, plants, biology and history can benefit the entire class.

To begin, first look to your class members. Send home a note or survey expressing your desire to include parents, grandparents and Elders in your lessons. Get referrals for possible speakers from organizations that work with Natives and/or the elderly.

The way to ask Native American Elders for help is different from Western customs. Initial and subsequent contact should be subtle. Visit with them, allowing time for the conversation to wander. Allow for extended pauses, giving them time to think and decide. If their hearing is poor, sit on the side of their better ear and make sure your lips can be seen. Direct eye contact should be limited. Standing or sitting at an angle can increase an Elders comfort level. Keep your questions basic and specific.

Begin the request by telling a little about your class and how the Elder could help. If you are not sure if the Elder is interested, hint strongly that you would like to have their help and ask if she/he knows of someone who might be willing to participate. Custom teaches that it is rude to give someone a frank "no" to a request for help, so you need to recognize that a noncommittal response might mean "no", or it might mean that the request is being considered. If at some point the Elder changes the subject more than once while you are explaining your request, you should be aware that she/he might be trying to say "no". Don't force a response; if it is clearly not a "yes" let it go, or suggest they can contact you after they've thought about it.

It is important to ask before a meeting for permission to make audio or video recordings. Don't show up with the equipment because you may force consent and cause bad feelings. Permission to listen to or tape a story or lecture does not give you any right to re-broadcast or write the story with you as author.

Elders Concerns & Expectations

- How can I find the room? (transportation, personal guide)
- Will I be respected and appreciated by the students?
- Will I be able to hear the students questions? (background and noise level)
- Can I speak within the attention span and understanding of the age I am speaking to?

If an Elder has agreed to participate in a classroom activity, provide them with optional dates and the logistics. It would be helpful to explain the routine, consequences for students misbehavior, and possible options if problems come up during the lesson. It is your responsibility to ensure discipline is maintained. Be aware, however, that Elders generally do not support strict discipline in a public setting. Discuss how to make a smooth transition to help the Elder leave the class. Agree on some visual signals and ground rules.

When the Elder arrives introduce her/him so the Elder sees your respect for them. The teacher should be alert for visual cues from the Elder during the visit as well as be prepared to give unspoken signals back. The teacher should stay in the room.

Give the Elder a chance to use traditional discipline. Be prepared to move a child to sit by an adult who can role model how to listen respectfully. If you have problems with students degrading or ignoring an Elder, have a teacher's aide or adult Native quietly intervene.

Most traditional stories are like a round, crocheted pot holder. The storyteller goes round and round the subject until it all comes together and finally comes to the lesson or point. Be patient, allow the Elders to share their culture in their own way. Your students are learning how to listen. Students should refrain from interrupting to ask questions. There will be a proper time to ask questions.

As a thank you, Elders usually appreciate student and teacher letters, pictures and story booklets which are treasured and shown to friends and relatives. This may also encourage other Elders to participate in classroom projects.

Sometimes you will find a resource person who will be available for a wide variety of subjects and projects. If you use an Elder more than once, the school should provide some type of stipend in appreciation of the energy and knowledge the Elder is contributing. Be careful not to burn out your Elders. Whenever you make a request be sure the Elder understands she is not obligated.

Keep your lessons flexible in case the Elder can't come at the last minute. Once an Elder has agreed on a time to come into your classroom, avoid changing or postponing the visit.

From *The Tlingit Moon and Tide Resource Book* (K–4), editor Dolly Garza. Published by Alaska Sea Grant, 1999.

In the Presence of Stories

Vivian Martindale

Sharing Our Pathways, Vol. 8, Issue 5, Nov/Dec 2003

"The storyteller is one whose spirit is indispensable to the people."
—N. Scott Momaday

According to Kiowa author and poet, N. Scott Momaday, the Native person lives "in the presence of stories." He claims the storyteller is many things: magician, artist and creator as well as a holy man. "He is sacred business" (Circle of Stories). Stories are meant to be told. They enrich our lives and for educators they can enrich our classrooms as well.

We are humbled and gracious in the presence of storytellers, yet how do we incorporate that knowledge into education, especially higher education? Most students come to the college classroom expecting the standard lecture and the required readings. Long forgotten is the Socratic method, which promotes listening by the students and gentle facilitating by the instructor. This method is similar to many Native American methods of teaching by example. Elders often engage the observer or learner in what they are doing. For example, if a carver is teaching an apprentice, the Elder often sits and carves while telling a story. To the untrained listener the story may not relate to what the apprentice should be learning, but usually the storyteller/carver gets around to bringing the meaning into what they are doing. Eventually the apprentice, when he is ready, picks up the piece of wood provided for him and begins to carve. Also, in Native cultures it is common to give the child or student the tools to learn and let them experiment with their learning. One example is when a child is learning to fillet fish. He may be given a small fish and a small knife and allowed to slice the fish without instruction because the child has observed the women slicing fish at the fish camp. As well, the child learning to carve will be given a piece of wood and the tools to carve without being instructed by reading a book, or a "lecture." Children are allowed to experience life, they are allowed to just "be."

These methods, translated to learning in the classroom, allow the student to listen to the stories, read the poems or other literature, and then interpret that knowledge without being "wrong" or told how to think. Interpretation and the variations of interpretation of knowledge are viewed according to one's culture, therefore the cultures of individual students must be appreciated.

There are similarities between the Socratic method and the methods of teaching in Native American traditions. The Socratic method of teaching, according to the *Catholic Encyclopedia*, is divided into two stages: negative and positive:

> In the negative stage Socrates, approaching his intended pupil in an attitude of assumed ignorance, would begin to ask a question, apparently for his own information. He would follow this by other questions, until his interlocutor would at last be obliged to confess ignorance of the subject discussed. Because of the pretended deference, which Socrates played to the superior intelligence of his pupil, this stage of the method was called "Socratic Irony". In the positive stage of the method, once the pupil had acknowledged his ignorance, Socrates would proceed to another series of questions, each of which would bring out some phase or aspect of the subject, so that at the end, when all the answers were summed up in a general statement, that statement expressed the concept of the subject, or the definition. Therefore, knowledge through concepts, or knowledge by definition, is the aim of the Socratic method. (*Catholic Encyclopedia*, 2003)

I would not categorize the two steps into the terms "negative" and "positive" because all learning can be applied to our lives in a positive way. I would re-word the term "negative" to "exploring". In the exploring stage we examine new concepts and learn new things. Often we make mistakes and are very aware of our ignorance. But this is not "negative" so-to-speak, but learning by doing. The Socratic method can bring out concepts and ideas by the questioning of the instructor and allow for the students to explore what they have learned and what that knowledge means to them. It is not enough just to lecture on how the facts are interpreted in the mainstream society, which is usually with a Euro-American twist, but learning in a multi-cultural environment must allow for the students to see through another's worldview, whether they are Native or from another ethnic background.

However, in Native American cultures many concepts within those cultures can only be taught through the original native languages, which is why it is important to bring those languages into the classroom through stories, songs, dances and other customs. The instructor and students can view videos, such as the ones on the "Circle of Stories" website produced by the Public Broadcasting System, and use the Socratic method to bring out any ideas or questions that the students may have. "Circle of Stories" is just one such site among many available on the internet that promotes listening and interaction by the educator and or student. According to the PBS site, they use documentary film, photography, artwork and music to honor and explore Native American storytelling.

The website is divided into five parts: Storytellers, Many Voices, We Are Here, Community and For Educators. As a learning tool, this site can broaden instructional techniques and allow for an increase in listening skills as well as bringing Native culture into the classroom.

Because literature is not limited to the written form, in many Native American communities such as those in Alaska, oral traditions are considered literature. This makes sense because poetry is considered literature; short stories are considered literature, yet both are best enjoyed when read aloud. Stories and poetry are meant to be read aloud, therefore incorporating the storytelling process into the classroom can be a rewarding experience for both students and teachers. Even if a student doesn't particularly enjoy nor want to tell a story, he or she can participate by listening. Because listening is a valuable part of Native American society it should be honored. Part of the benefit of incorporating storytelling into the curriculum is that some students haven't been taught to listen properly or respect the listener as many people in Native American communities have been. Television, internet, video games and many technologies are geared for the "viewer" and not the "listener." A good website such as "Circle of Stories" can be enjoyed by a listener as well as be used as an interactive visual aid.

According to the website:

> In the basket of Native stories, we find legends and history, maps and poems, the teachings of spirit mentors, instructions for ceremony and ritual, observations of worlds and storehouses of ethno-ecological knowledge. Stories often live in many dimensions, with meanings that reach from the everyday to the divine. Stories imbue places with the power to teach, heal and reflect. Stories are possessed with such power that they have survived for generations despite attempts at repression and assimilation. (Circle of Stories)

In Native American communities songs, dances and music are all considered stories. They tell something. There are consistent themes in the stories. Stories tell us about the culture in which they were created and are an excellent way to learn about a particular culture. Students can listen to a story from a specific period in time, comparing an old story to a modern one, or a hero story to one that is intended to teach a lesson. One can also compare stories that are similar or different from region to region.

Understanding rituals and ceremonies within the context of a culture is another way of learning about a Native community. The Mojave Creation song is just one example, "Some Native songs are sung in great cycles, containing over 100 songs for a specific ritual. *The Mojave Creation* songs, which describe cremation rituals in detail, are a collection of 525 songs and must be performed for the deceased to journey to the next world." Stories can be symbolic, teach a lesson, teach how to conduct ceremonies, promote understanding of the natural world, how to survive in the environment, oral maps for travel, transformation stories and stories about love and romance. (*Circle of Stories*)

In *Circle of Stories*, the section for educators consists of lessons designed to enable students to examine Native American storytelling, as well as create their own stories. The lessons are also intended to explore indigenous and Native American cultures and the issues within those cultures. Students are encouraged to research and explore their own cultural heritage by recording family stories and heritage.

Although these lesson plans are designed for grades 6–12, one could incorporate them into the college curriculum.

The section for educators is divided into three lessons. The first, entitled "It's All Part of the Story," is about instructing students on the rich cultural and religious heritage of the generations before us, and it leads us to understand how our past has influenced our present. Use this plan to help students learn to share their story while learning to appreciate stories from others. The second section titled, "Our Small World" examines the contributions of Native cultures to our modern society as well as how to keep the cultures alive and the role of storytelling in that process. The third lesson, "Record and Preserve Your Family Heritage," is about learning how to record stories and the proper protocols involved with gathering stories. (Circle of Stories)

Featured under the heading "Storytellers" in the main menu, are three or four storytellers and their stories. Included is a biography of the storyteller, something about their culture and then a story told by that person (Real Player is the software used to listen to the downloaded audio.) Also some of the stories are told in the original language of the storyteller. One featured storyteller is Hoskie Benally, a Diné (Navajo) spiritual leader, from Shiprock, New Mexico. He tells the story of the Five Sacred Medicines, which is the story of how the Navajo acquired their medicines: sage, tobacco, cedar, yucca and eagle feathers.

Another storyteller featured on this site is Tchin from the Narragansett people, who inhabited the area now known as Rhode Island for millenia. Tchin is also part Siksika, more commonly known as the Blackfeet people. Like many Native American cultures, the Narragansett were nearly wiped out by settlers who brought disease and violence. According to Tchin, "In 1880, the state of Rhode Island illegally detribalized the Narragansett, terminating the tribe on paper. The Narragansett lost their remaining 3200 acres of land, leaving them with only a church on a scarce two acres" (Circle of Stories). Eventually with the introduction of the Indian Reorganization Act in 1934, the government recognized the Narragansett as a distinct people, but fell short of federal recognition and unfortunately they were unable to acquire back their land. But in 1978, tribal members filed a lawsuit, which resulted in the government returning 2000 acres to their possession. Federal recognition eventually came about in 1983.

Tchin uses these facts and his knowledge of storytelling to bring the listener into his story of why rabbit looks like he does today.

The stories and information on this site are excellent tools for instruction. Adapting the site to individual instructors need only take a bit of imagination. Whether we are in a grade school, high school or the college classroom, our educational experiences are enhanced by stories. In the presence of stories our knowledge can increase, especially our knowledge of the cultures around us. Many Euro-Americans grow up in regions without knowing the richness of their Native neighbors. Stories are just one way to incorporate knowledge, language and culture within the classroom. In our classrooms as well as our lives, we are enriched by the presence of stories.

References

Rogerson, Hand and Jilian Spitzmiller Producers. Electric Shadows Project. *Circle of Stories*. Public Broadcasting Service, 2002. Philomath Films. http://www.pbs.org/circleofstories. 16 June 2003. Knight, Kevin. Editor. Socrates.

Catholic Encyclopedia. Updated April 20, 2003. http://www.newadvent.org. 17 June, 2003.

Native American Perspective and the Classroom Experience

Ted A. Wright,
Southeast Alaska
Tribal College

Sharing Our Pathways, Vol. 8, Issue 5, Nov/Dec 2003

When I am asked to represent the Native view on one or another issue, I usually say something like, "It really isn't fair for me to try and speak for Indians, indigenous or Native peoples. Just like it wouldn't be fair for me to ask you to speak for all Caucasian, Euro-American, middle-class men from the Northwest." I typically add that I can speak about Native peoples, insofar as I have studied my own and others. But even then, the information I provide is generalized from a variety of sources and interpretation of information, especially when it has to do with Native tribes, is a risky business. So, the question becomes, to what extent can I represent Indian peoples and how do I approach the issue in practice, as a teacher?

Well, for one thing, I have studied Native groups other than my own. It would be impossible to teach and learn in a Native American Studies program or a tribal college if we were confined only to talking about our own tribe, clan or community. But the issue here is one of perspective, not knowledge. It is possible to have access to and familiarity with a vast store of information about Native peoples and indigenous life ways, but to speak from a group's perspective a person pretty much has to be a part of that group. And even then, each group has different and competing voices. For example, among my people I am considered mixed-blood and somewhat non-traditional, depending on whom you ask. I might also be labeled as over-educated, elite, middle-class—one who has been away to school and come back home. Also, I am a northern Kogwaantan (wolf clan), transplanted by virtue of my grandmother's journey to the middle of Tlingit country—Sitka. Well, you get the picture. Now we are talking issues of identity and group affiliation. And in the era of self-determination and casino gaming, these are muddy waters in which to wade.

So let's simplify what is decidedly a complex issue. There is tremendous diversity among Native American peoples, certainly more so than within the general American population. The reason for this is that American Indian and Alaska Native peoples, through their cultural, political and social institutions, tend to reject the notion that we should melt into the all-consuming culture that is America in the 20th and 21st centuries. Does that mean we don't wear Levi's or drive sport utility vehicles? Or that pizza doesn't taste good and we don't watch baseball? Hardly. It just means that we try harder than most to maintain an intact culture, one that is distinct from the American way. We sing our songs, dance our dances and eat our foods. We want to remember our own histories, practice our own brand of spirituality. We want to be Native in a society that tries to dominate and assimilate. But it isn't necessarily true that Indian people understand how different we all are, one tribe to the next, even considering our similarities.

I was reminded of this again a while back when I read an article about a presentation on tribal sovereignty by a Lac Courte d'Oreilles tribal councilmen published on the American Indian Policy Center website. The Councilmen said:

> We are seen as different and we are different. American Indians have a special legal relationship with the United States government . . . The way of life for Native Americans is different. Tribes have worked to maintain their sovereignty because American Indians want to maintain their traditional ways . . . We're not a part of the melting pot. We are a proud people. Many people do not understand this, creating conflict and misunderstanding. There is a lack of accurate information about American Indians in mainstream educational institutions. Schools generally do not teach about traditional American Indian values and beliefs, or about the legal and historical basis of tribal sovereignty. Often times, questions that non-Indians ask about American Indians reflect cultural, legal and historical misunderstanding . . . We're continually asked by non-Native people "why don't you want to

bring wealth and possession to your people?" and "Why do you continuously pursue and promote the treaties from so many years ago?" Questions of this sort reveal ignorance about the relationship between Indian tribes and the U.S. government, and differences in values. This ignorance could be reduced if more schools taught accurate information about American Indians.

One of the reasons I read the article is because I noticed in the beginning that the speaker is from the Wolf clan of the Ojibwe people. I thought, hey, I'm from the Wolf clan of the Tlingit people. I also served on the tribal council for my people in the mid-80s. And I have had an abiding interest in the issue of sovereignty. So I felt like I had a lot in common with the Ojibwe councilmen, like he was my counterpart from a different tribe. Well, his statements are reasonable and he has obviously thought deeply about sovereignty and why he fights the battles he does. But after I read it a second time, I began to think about how much the speaker generalized and the wheels started to turn. On a napkin (I was at a restaurant) I began to list his statements that reflected a Native American perspective:

We, American Indians, Native Americans, Tribes:
- are seen as different and we are different,
- have a special legal relationship with the United States government,
- want to maintain . . . traditional ways,
- are not part of the melting pot,
- are a proud people.

As you have noticed, the speaker also discusses the fact that many of the misconceptions about Indians could be remedied if schools would provide students with accurate information. But this begs the question, "What is accurate information and who decides?" I agree with the Ojibwe speaker that we are seen as different—our tribes have a special relationship with the U.S. government; we want to maintain our traditional ways; we are not part of the melting pot in the sense that we are in the pot and striving not to melt; and, of course, we are proud to be who we are. But from my point of view, the truth about perspective lies in the details. Getting and using accurate information about tribal, Indian people is not simply a matter of sharing the most common set of facts, or providing a superficial description.

To illustrate this point consider my own people, the Tlingit. How would I help apathetic, less eager students learn about my people's politics, history, language, culture and more to the point, their perspective? After all, there are about twenty sub-regional and community groupings within our extant panhandle territory and dozens of related and unrelated clan and clan house affiliations within each of those sub-regions. Even to begin to talk about larger issues of Tlingit tribal history, politics, law, spirituality and language, the basic cultural family and clan connections must be covered. And yet, when Tlingit people themselves get up in front of a group and say the Tlingit this and the Tlingit that, they sometimes forget they are only talking for the Wolf people of the Salmon Stream Tribe of the farthest north Tlingit people, for example. There are a few Elders that do not forget this, but they are seldom invited to speak at the kinds of gatherings where people talk about Tlingit people as a generic subset of Alaska Natives inhabiting the Southeast panhandle.

So, what's a teacher to do? When I first started in education, nobody had a clue. Nowadays we understand that sticky issues of Native or indigenous perspective are actually opportunities for students to take on a subject in-depth. So don't be afraid to bring people like me into your classrooms. But do make certain your students aren't afraid to ask direct questions about comments that over-generalize and categorize issues and people. Your students will be better for it and it is possible that the speakers will be better for it as well. I am inviting teachers I work with to use materials developed through the Alaska Rural Systemic Initiative—in cooperation with the Southeast Alaska Tribal College and a number of school districts—to open an ongoing dialogue about Southeast. Native peoples through an in-depth analysis of the places they live and the cultures they still maintain today.

Native American Songs as Literature

Vivian Martindale

Sharing Our Pathways, Vol. 9, Issue 1, Jan/Feb 2004

U tilizing the richness and variety of Native American songs is one way to open up the world of Native American literature in the classroom. After all, Native American cultures have a rich oral tradition and many stories are told through the medium of songs. Rhyme, rhythm, drums and dancing have the ability to enhance the memory while simultaneously healing the spirit, mind and body, providing for an enriching classroom experience.

Classrooms don't have to be boring. Literature classes especially can be enhanced through the medium of song. In David Leedom Shaul's article "A Hopi Song—Poem in Context", he claims that the listener is similar to an audience during storytelling, in that the listener is also interacting with the music. The listener, as a participant, is not passive; the listener is hearing rhythms, words, patterns and much more. The listener does not have to understand the Native language in order to appreciate the song. Shaul calls attention to the genre called "song poems." These songs are in a category by themselves, separate from poetry and prose. "The text of song-poems in Hopi culture, like much poetry, seemingly create their own context by virtue of minimalist language" (Shaul 1992:230–31). Therefore it would be interesting to include the concept of song poems or poetry as music into a curriculum.

Poet, songwriter and saxophonist, Joy Harjo, is one such example of an artist/poet whose work could be shared in a class on Native American literature. Other than being a poet, Harjo is in her own band called Poetic Justice. Harjo is from Oklahoma and is an enrolled member of the Creek Tribe. Her work combines music with poetry. According to Harjo, "The term poetic justice is a term of grace, expressing how justice can appear in the world despite forces of confusion and destruction. The band takes its name from this term because all of us have worked for justice in our lives, through any means possible and through music." Harjo's lyrics to her songs are a reflection of her poetry, "a blending of rock, blues and prophecy" (Princeton 2003).

I include here an excerpt from Poetic Justices' song "My House is the Red Earth," words and music by Joy Harjo and John L. Williams:

> My house is the red earth. It could be the center of the world. I've heard New York, Tokyo or Paris called the center of the world, but I say it is magnificently humble. You could drive by and miss it. Radio waves can obscure it. Words cannot construct it for there are some sounds left to sacred wordless form. For instance, that fool crow picking through trash near the corral, understands the center of the world as greasy scraps of fat. Just ask him. He doesn't have to say that the earth has turned scarlet through fierce belief, after centuries of heartbreak and laughter (Poetic Justice 2003).

Poetic Justice is just one example of how contemporary musicians use poetry to express issues facing Native Americans today. Song poems, in themselves, hold a unique element of language and culture.

In a more traditional manner, songs from around Native America could be included, not just for listening enjoyment, but also could include students' input on the lyrics afterward asking how the students thought the poet/artist expressed themselves and how they felt when listening to the songs. Traditional singers could be invited into the classroom to perform. But of course permission to perform the songs and dances must be given by the owners of the song so educators need to be aware that there is an aspect of ownership as well as some songs and dances are only to be performed at certain times of the year and by specific persons. Usually dancing and other forms of expression accompany songs. Students could be encouraged to close their eyes briefly and afterward record what they heard as a participant compared to what they saw as a participant. Also ask the students if they felt as if they were participants on some other level or were simply an observer or listener. In many of the contexts, songs may not have to be translated if they are performed in their Native languages. One can simply enjoy the language, how it sounds, how it feels to the soul.

For further studies on Native American song poems a good source is by author and editor Brian Swann called *Song of the Sky: Native American Songpoems* (1992). Although adding music and song in a literary context may seem like a revolutionary idea, Native Americans have been using songs to educate since time immemorial. According to an article on the Alaska Native Knowledge Network, "Singing and dancing were very important to the Athabascan people. People often made up songs about events, love songs, war songs or about relatives who had died for the death potlatch. The children at potlatches and community events observed the adults as a means to learn how to dance and sing. Children learned to sing very early as it was very important to the Athabascan way to carry on their teachings through oral languages" (ANKN 2003). And yes, even college students enjoy learning through the medium of music and song, especially when it opens up the world of literature from other cultures.

Another resource for educators comes from Canyon Records called *Traditional Voices*, which includes recordings made in the 1950s and 60s. These rare songs were recorded by "historically important singers from all over United States and Canada." This collection offers a glimpse into the rich and varied tribal cultures of twenty different Native American tribes. Samples from the works include songs such as the Navajo " Yei-Be-Chai Chant," Northern Cheyenne "Sun Dance Song," and the Tohono O'odham, "Song Of The Green Rainbow." Through traditional songs and dances this recording would be an excellent tool to introduce students to Native American literary forms.

Songs or song poems, whether traditional or contemporary, can be one instrument for educators to utilize in order to explore various Native cultures. Involving local singers and dancers is also important as well as any students who are willing to share their songs and dances with their classmates. Dance and songs are a means to understanding Native American cultures. To appreciate other cultures, it is good to immerse ourselves in each other's songs.

References

Alaska Native Knowledge Network. 2003. *Athabascan Winter Studies: The Dene' Indigenous Peoples of Interior Alaska*. Electronic document, http://ankn.uaf.edu/ANEunit/aneindex.html, accessed July 14, 2003.

Harjo, Joy. 2003. *Joy Harjo*. Electronic document http://www.princeton. edu/~naap/harjo.html, accessed July 14, 2003.

Harjo, Joy. 2003. KACTV Publishing/Muskogee. Mekko Productions, Electronic document, http://www.joyharjo.com/index.html, accessed July 14.

Shaul, David Leedom. 1992. "A Hopi Song Poem in Context" In *On the Translation of Native American Literatures*. Brian Swann ed. Washington: Smithsonian Institution.

Swann, Brian. 1992. *On the Translation of Native American Literatures*. Washington: Smithsonian Institution.

Traditional Voices. Electronic document, http://www.canyonrecords.com/ cr7053.htm, accessed July 14, 2003. Phoenix: Canyon Records.

The School of Custom and Tradition

Andy Hope

Sharing Our Pathways, Vol. 5, Issue 5, Nov/Dec 2000

Where do traditions come from?
Where do customs originate?
How are customs and traditions learned?
Carried forward?
What are the sources of inspiration?
Look to ones that know
Look to creative ones
Look to ones with ideas
Look to the artistic
Look to Elders
Look to the young
Look to the energetic
I attended the school of custom and tradition
A school of vitality and richness
A school of ideas
A school where one will always learn
Something new
Where people meet
Where people teach
Where people learn
From each other
Support each other
And move on to become
The school of custom and tradition
Reflected
In their lives
In their minds
In their eyes

S'áxt': Incorporating Native Values in a Place—Based Lesson Plan

Vivian Martindale

Sharing Our Pathways, Vol. 9, Issue 2, Mar/Apr 2004

In many Native American communities, plants have medicinal, spiritual and cultural value. They aren't just some green things that grow in the woods or in your front yard. According to Tlingit oral traditions, Raven created man from a leaf. At first Raven was going to create man from a rock, but then man would have lived forever and that wouldn't have been right, so by using a leaf man could move faster and also man would die. This story illustrates the importance that plants have in the lives of the Tlingit people.

One such plant, which is highly valued among the Tlingit people, is found predominantly in the temperate rain forests of Southeast Alaska. This plant is sacred to the Tlingit people. The Tlingits call it *s'áxt'*; science calls it Oplopanax horridum (Araliacea) and local residents call it devil's club. The *s'áxt'* is also related to the oriental ginseng and is sometimes called Alaska ginseng. According to *Alaska's Wilderness Medicines* many different Native peoples in Alaska use this plant for a variety of reason: cold, flu, fever, stomach ailments, tuberculosis and poultices for wounds such as black eyes and burns. Modern pharmaceutical, naturopathic companies and other researchers are studying the plant for its commercial medicinal values. Their studies reveal that *s'áxt'* may possibly have hypoglycemic capabilities because the plant contains a substance similar to insulin (Viereck 1987). Many Elders believe that the plant will also prevent cancer or help in healing many types of cancers.

In Southeast Alaska, among the Tlingit people, the *s'áxt'* plant was used by shamans and contains very powerful medicine and when placed above doorways and on fishing boats it is said to ward off evil. In the past, devil's club was associated with shamanism. "Shamans may carry a power charm made with spruce twigs, devil's club roots and their animal tongue, acquired during their quests. During the quest (a novice who feels called to shamanism quests for his power) a novice goes into the woods for one or several weeks, eating nothing but devil's club" (Alaska Herbal Tea 2002).

Devils' club can be found in small or very large patches throughout the woods or beach areas. The plant likes wet, but filtered soil. *S'áxt'* grows up to eight feet tall and the large maple—like leaves and stalks of the plant are stems covered with stickers, similar to slivers of glass or wood that can easily get under the skin or through light clothing. Stickers from the plant can cause infection and pain if not removed immediately. The plant also contains blooms of berries in the summer. These berries are not edible by humans but bears do eat them. According to local harvestersT, the roots and shoots of devil's club are edible, however, the stage for harvesting the plant is in the spring when the stalks first sprout new green growth. This is the best time to harvest the roots and new shoots, which can be ground into a powder and made into tea. Some Elder sources say that in late summer or fall you can harvest the bark from the stalks and the rootstalks. It is best to consult the local Elders rather than rely on conventional scientific documents or public agencies. Despite this, the U.S. Forest Service advises, "The leaf spines, though visible, are soft and pliable at this stage. Once they stiffen, however, the shoots should NOT be eaten." The leaf clusters may be nibbled raw, or added to omelets, casseroles and soups like a spice. One or two is enough to add a unique tang to a common meal.

Hence the reason I have chosen the subject of *s'áxt'* is so I may illustrate how educators can create a lesson plan that will enable the introduction of one or more of the Tlingit values, as outlined by Elder Dr. Walter Soboleff, into the curriculum. The Native values, by region, can be found on the University of Alaska Fairbanks' Alaska Native Knowledge Network website located at www.ankn.uaf.edu. Dr. Soboleff lists these values:

- Respect for self, others including Elders
- Remember our Native traditions, families, sharing, loyalty, pride and loving children
- Responsibility
- Truth and wise use of words
- Care of subsistence areas, care of property

- Reverence: *Haa Shageinyaa*
- Sense of Humility
- Care of the Human Body
- Dignity: *Yan gaa duuneek*
- Peace with family, neighbors, others and nature

As well, this lesson explores the concept of "naturalist intelligence" as outlined by Howard Gardner (19). By enhancing the student's naturalist intelligence a curriculum such as this guides the students to the understanding of how their Native values work in everyday life. The naturalist intelligence refers to the ability to recognize and classify plants, minerals and animals including rocks and grass and all variety of flora and fauna. Author and educator Karen Roth examines this intelligence in her booklet *The Naturalist Intelligence: An Introduction to Gardner's Eighth Intelligence.* Implementing naturalist intelligence into the classroom setting is accomplished by introducing students to the practicality of the natural world—one that they can relate to their own lives in their own regions. Many local Elders are rich with this intelligence, able to identify, classify and relate the plants to the spiritual and cultural workings of the Native communities. By utilizing this naturalist intelligence, Elders and educators can introduce the Native values into the classroom and community.

Roth introduces educators to the various ways with which a classroom could implement this intelligence. In one method, Roth outlines a model based on four stages. This model, designed by David Lazear, is used to awaken the naturalists' intelligence. ". . . he suggests the naturalist intelligence be triggered by immersing the student in the natural world of plants, animals, water, forests, etc., using the five senses" (Roth 1998). First, there is the "Awakening" stage, which is accomplished through immersion. The second stage is called "Amplify" and in this stage the intelligence is strengthened through practice, such as learning about where the plant grows and why. The third stage, "Teach," is "using specific tools of this intelligence and applying them to help learn"; it is the stage when your objectives are achieved. "Transfer" is the fourth stage. This is when students apply the naturalist intelligence beyond the classroom. In other words, students will be thinking about how to view their Native values beyond what they have learned about the *s'áxt'*.

Through the study of the abundant and highly recognizable local plant, students will be able to recognize how the Tlingit values play out in their everyday lives. In *A Yupiaq Worldview: A Pathway to Ecology and Spirit*, Dr. Angayuqaq Oscar Kawagley points out how important it is for students to acquire knowledge from the experiences in the world around them. Kawagley contrasts this relation to the whole with the Western classroom that may pose an "impediment to learning, to the extent that it focuses on compartments of knowledge without regard to how the compartments relate to one another or to the surrounding universe" (1996:87–88). It is knowing about the plants in our environment, such as *s'áxt'*, and how to use that knowledge in our environment that makes the knowledge we seek worthwhile. Therefore students, searching for knowledge in their natural environment will flourish and be able to apply new concepts to their familiar place.

The introduction of Native values need not be difficult. I suggest a dialogue to open up the discussion about the values and how they are transmitted from one generation to another. Students will be able to see the difference between rigid book learning and field-based or place-based learning models. Then introducing a teaching unit that will tie in one or more of those values will get the students to thinking about how those values are transmitted through daily life. In the article *The Domestication of the Ivory Tower: Institution Adaptation to Cultural Distance*, Barnhardt illustrates how the field-base environment is prime for learning. The field-based program outlined by Barnhardt is "a reality-based, collective learning process." In a field-based program Barnhardt points out the benefit to both teachers and students when the students are required to participate in experiences. The experiential learning environment is not detached, but thrives in the interactions between people and their experiences. This place-based or field-based environment is key to relating the Native values to the curriculum and to the outside world.

S'áxt': Incorporating Native Values in a Place-based Lesson Plan

Grade Level

Middle school, high school and possibly college level

Course Objectives

Utilizing placed-based education to introduce the Tlingit values (see list of values above)

Curriculum Area

Math, science, art, writing, language and cross cultural studies

Objectives:

1. Working with Elders:
   a. Elders explain the cultural significance of *s'áxt'*: spiritually, medicinally, etc. (value: reverence, care of human body, responsibility, dignity).
   b. Elders can show students the best places, times and type of plants to harvest (value: care of subsistence areas, peace with the world of nature).
   c. Elders can talk about the methods of harvesting and assist with this in the classroom and outside the classroom (value: remember Native traditions, responsibility).
2. Proper identification of *s'áxt'*, its habitat, uses and preparations.
3. Introduction to Tlingit terms for the parts of the plant and words and phrases associated with the activities.
4. The role of *s'áxt'* in art: beads and/or rattle and then translate to ceremony (value: dignity, remember traditions).

Activities and Methods: Harvesting & Preparation

A. Harvesting the *s'áxt'*
1. Have Elders or other local plant experts assist with appropriate harvesting tools, what types of plants to look for, appropriate clothing such as gloves for protection, thick pants and coats (value: care for human body).
2. Roots: Dig up long, straight pieces that are 1/2" thick or larger.
3. Make sure there is a time for thanking the plant for its gift (value: care, respect, reverence, truth).
B. Explore methods of preparation:
1. Salve or ointments: One method is to shave the bark off the stalks and boil with canola oil, strain it, mix^{oo} it with beeswax. Afterwards this mixture is poured into empty medicine containers for use as a salve (value: care of human body, sharing).
2. *S'áxt'* tea: The roots and greenish inner bark can be shredded and dried or fresh steeped into tea (value: humility, peace).

3. Roots:
   a. Students can peel, roast and then mash the roots.
   b. Wash the roots as soon as possible with a plastic bristle vegetable scrubber. Then peel off the root bark with a knife and place on screens to dry (value: sharing, respect, peace).
4. Making Beads, Jewelry or Deer Hoof Rattles:
   a. Pauline Duncan's instructions for Deer Hoof Rattles can be found on the ANKN website (value: remember, reverence).
   b. Beads: Beads are made from dry stalks of s'axt'. They are cut from the stalk, hollowed out and then dried. They can be painted or left natural. The twine for stringing the beads is usually made from mountain goat (value: sharing, humility).

Resources

- Local Elders
- Local plant experts: Elders, U.S. Forest Service, local medicinal healers, herbalists
- Pauline Duncan's Tlingit Curriculum Resources: Picking Berries can be located at http://www.ankn.uaf.edu/curriculum/Tlingit/PaulineDuncan/index.html
- Alaska's Wilderness Medicines: Healthy Plants from the Far North by Eleanor Viereck
- A good kitchen and work space for making salves, beads, etc.
- Harvesting tools: knives, small shovel, cooking implements, beeswax, oils
- Other books illustrating what the plant looks like, paper and pencils for on-site illustrations

Evaluation

Evaluation methods should be culturally and community relevant. Students can keep a journal or write about what values they observed in action. As well, students should be able to produce salve, brew tea, know the basics of harvesting and prep procedures and also to be able to make a piece of jewelry or art from the plant. Afterwards students should be able to relate what they have done, at every step of the way, to one or more of the Tlingit values.

In conclusion, educators and Elders should be constantly considering where and how values can be incorporated into learning activities. At first it might be necessary to point out where the values might fit in, however, as the lesson and the relationships with the Elders progress that will no longer be necessary. Prior to undertaking the lessons, have the students be aware that they are looking for those values. At the end of each day, excursion or lesson, students can be asked what values they observed at work and how they might pass on those values to others or apply them in their daily lives, stressing that almost all the Tlingit values can be applied in one way or another to any daily living situation.

Raven knew what he was doing, creating man from a leaf. By using the simplicity of a leaf, Raven connected us to our environment forever weaving Native values into our creation thus into our lives.

References

Barnhardt, R.
Gardner, H.
Kawagley, A.O.
Roth, K.

Vivian Martindale
and Vivian Mork

Perspectives from a Lingit Language Instructor

Sharing Our Pathways, Vol. 10, Issue 2, Mar/Apr 2005

The following narrative with Yéilk' Vivian Mork was conducted and transcribed by Vivian Martindale in 2004 and edited for Sharing Our Pathways. Yéilk'is a twenty-seven-year-old Tlingit woman from the Raven moiety and the T'akdeintaan clan and is a full-time student at the University of Alaska Southeast majoring in Alaska Native Studies. She is an instructor in the Lingít language in the Dzantiki Heeni Middle School in Juneau, Alaska, and has taught at the 2003 and 2004 Kusteeyí Lingít Immersion Camps sponsored by Sealaska Heritage Foundation.

Yéilk' Vivian Mork Narrative

I decided to learn the Lingít language when I was living in Washington State. My mother called and asked me when I was going to return to Alaska to go to college. My mother was living in Hoonah and learning the Tlingit language with local high school teacher Duffy Wright. She was excited about it. My mother would call me and tell me something in Lingít. She was persuasive, so I decide to come back home. I realized I wanted to be a part of the revitalization effort. Growing up, I was told that the language is dead. When I found out the language wasn't dead and that you could learn it, I was amazed because I come from a family of non-speakers.

In the beginning [learning the language] was important because I knew that people weren't learning [it]. No one in my family spoke Lingít fluently despite the fact my grandfather heard Lingít when he was younger. When you come from a family with no fluent speakers, you really don't have too many choices about where to go in order to learn. I soon found out that they were teaching the Lingít language at the University of Alaska in Juneau. I decided to incorporate learning the Lingít language into my studies. And after a couple of years of learning the language, it has taken on a whole new life. A lot of us new speakers feel that when we speak, we are waking up the ancestors by using the language, giving them respect and calling on them. When we introduce ourselves, we are telling someone in the room who we are and calling our ancestors to stand with us.

It wasn't an easy transition to go from a learner to an instructor of the Lingít language. As college students, several students and I got better at speaking the language, and suddenly we started to get job offers. We learned that the school system has a difficult time hiring Elders because often an Elder doesn't have a degree or the skills to teach in a public school. As students we had the credentials to work at the school, so we paired ourselves with Elders and entered the system in that way. I've taught 6th, 7th and 8th grades, 4- and

The Tlingit class was held during the Sealaska Heritage Institute's Tlingit Immersion Retreat in Hoonah last August. Yeilk was one of the teaching interns during this program. The group ranged from pre-school to middle school. Yéilk' Vivian Mork holds the ball. Students are left to right: Sophia Henry, Karoline Henry, Harlena Sanders, Rachel White, Donnita White, Chauncey White and Louie White.

5-year-olds, and college students as well as at the community level, including Elders. It's scary to teach. As a learner-teacher you are aware that you don't know everything. You know you make mistakes, you pronounce things wrong, and that sometimes you are going to be judged and criticized for it. But it is important so you do it anyway. You take the criticism and the judgment; you take it with a grain of salt and keep going. Fortunately, when pairing a student-teacher with an Elder to teach the language to others, we find that we learn along with the children. In fact, we learn a lot quicker. We learn to have conversations and we understand learning is more than memorization and commands; communication flows in that environment and spills into other areas of life. Everything becomes a teaching environment: the home, the street and grocery store—it isn't limited to the school system.

For example, at the grocery store when the cashier hands you your change, you say *"Gunalcheésh."* If they want to know what you said, you tell them that means "thank you" in Lingít. In fact, I was once at the Fred Meyer in Juneau when I said *"Gunalcheésh"* to a cashier and she said, *"Yaa xaay yatee,"* which translates loosely to mean, "You're welcome." She was blond-haired, blue-eyed and white-skinned. I never would have guessed she was Tlingit, but it made me smile all day long. This illustrates that you can make any experience a learning one. Most of my teaching and learning experiences, although they have been challenging, have been rewarding.

When I taught at the middle school I had 33 kids and 90 percent of them were boys. In the beginning, they were rambunctious and disrespectful. But the one thing that comes with teaching the language is the culture; you can't teach the language without teaching the culture, if you want it to stick. In teaching the Tlingit language you teach people about respect. It wasn't long before my class became well-behaved and even some of the most difficult kids started being respectful. We taught the children introductions, about their clans and the clan system, how all the Ravens and Eagles are brothers and sisters, and the proper way to interact with one another. I had a student who is a Teikwiedí, a brown bear. Because the Teikwiedí is my grandmother's people I had to address her as my grandmother, which would make her giggle and, more importantly, it made her interested. She listened and a level of respect emerged between us. This young girl was 13-years-old. Later in the summer, at [Juneau's] Celebration, a teacher asked this young girl what her best experience in school was.

All she talked about was the language program. She said that learning the language is important because she felt keeping the language alive depended on her and her fellow students. At a young age, this girl knows the value of learning the language. She knows who she is and her place in the web of life. I'm proud she is one of my students.

The pride in learning your Native language is a big change from past generations. We've come a long way from the boarding-school generation who were forbidden to speak their languages. American boarding schools were a main contributor to the loss of language, not just in Alaska, but also for Native cultures throughout the United States. When you look through old government documents regarding the boarding schools' progress, you find references that the government knew that in order to get rid of the "Nativeness" in Native people, they had to remove children from their homes, out of the culture, out of the influences, and take away their customs and their language. Because language and culture are intertwined, the government schools had to take it away to assimilate them. It was almost successful.

Unfortunately, because of past policies, there is a huge loss of the language and the knowledge that comes with the language. It wasn't just the boarding-school experiences that created the loss; it began with epidemics such as small pox and tuberculosis. These diseases wiped out entire villages including their traditional knowledge and language. In no time at all, whole dialects disappeared with no possible way of getting them back. Each Elder, being a life-long library, was gone in an instant.

There is another reason for language loss. There were entire generations of people who decided that the language was dead and let it go. This came after the push to assimilate Natives into mainstream American society. There were reasons why people went to the schools and reasons why people sent their family members to get educated. Native peoples knew there was a lot of change coming. They needed to be ready and one way was to educate leaders within the Western system. But it didn't have to be done in such a traumatic way. If only the American government would have known how much better off they would have been if they allowed Native people to keep their culture. You have groups of people living around each other whose entire life is about taking care of each other and they use a language system that had been indigenous to the land for thousands of years. There is so much knowledge within the system, and it is ridiculous to just throw it away. Intruding cultures could have learned so much about this land, about the people. It could have made Alaska a better place.

But we still have hope. Now though, when we look at old videos and recordings, we hear the Elders speak and note the differences in the language. We realize that people who learn languages today in a university setting differ in dialect and pronunciation from the language learned in the villages, which is the difference between a natural acquisition and a rather "fake" acquisition. Despite those differences, however, it is all right to pronounce words incorrectly when you are first learning. You have to think of each language learner as a "child of the language." When they are six months into learning the language, they are six months old.

Although the process of re-learning the language is difficult, you notice that through learning, the students, both young and old, have been changed. There are people who have decided to dedicate their lives to learning the Lingít language and have devoted themselves to making sure it will never die. It has changed how we language-learners relate with one another. Knowing we are going to interact with each other for the rest of our lives, we treat each other with respect.

When you learn the language, you begin with a basic introduction. You learn what moiety and clan you are, what house you are from, and who your grandparents are. When you give that introduction in a room full of speakers, every Elder in that room knows who you are without having met you. This introduction can be basic and take a few minutes to recite, but a real Tlingit introduction can be from 10 to 20 minutes long. This is an important aspect of the Tlingit culture. When we teach children the basic introduction, we are teaching them who they are, who their ancestors are and how their names and clans connect them to this land and to each other. We teach children that they have a bigger family than the typical nuclear American family and that we have a larger family and a responsibility to the people around us.

Despite the lack of natural settings to teach the Lingít language, teaching in the school system is important. It instills a sense of pride for Native students, especially in Juneau, since we experience cases of racism. When children start to learn the language, they realize where their pride can come from. We tell them daily that they've been here since time immemorial and this land is theirs—they belong to it. Another thing occurs. People in the classroom who are not Tlingit start to ask questions about their own ethnicity. We've had Yup'ik and Aleut students in the classroom. Even a kid with Norwegian heritage was excited about looking into his history.

We teach them they are genetically half of their parents, and part of their grand parents and great-grandparents. This way, children learn that inside of them, they are literally their ancestors. By speaking the language and by introducing themselves in Lingít, they are respecting their ancestors by respecting themselves. The idea of respect is something a lot of Native children don't have today. Gangs, media, television and music have a profound influence on them. They are reaching out and searching for something; they are lost. When you can teach children in their language, however, they start to find out who they are. When they really know who they are in the language, no one can take that away from them. This is amazing to hold on to. It lifts their spirit and it makes them happy and excited to come to class. They usually like the language classes more than their mainstream classes. It makes their spirits stronger.

4

Unangan/Alutiiq Pathways to Education

Cultural Innovation at Netsvetov

Ethan Petticrew

Sharing Our Pathways, Vol. 2, Issue 1, Jan/Feb 1997

A *ang-aang*! Exciting and new things are happening at Atka's Netsvetov School. The staff, community and school board are busy creating a curriculum that is radically different from the traditional American approach to education. Through this revision of curriculum, we thoroughly believe that we are creating an atmosphere in which our students can excel at their own pace in both western and Unangan education. Although this is an arduous task, the size of the school makes it somewhat simpler than if it were a large school setting. There are twenty-two students from K–12. The staff consists of three certified teachers (two are Aleut), one bilingual teacher and a

Atxam Taligisniikangis members back row: Jimmy Prokopeuff, Crystal Swetzof, Ethan Petticrew and Debbie Prokopeuff. Front row: Tina Golodoff, Larisa Prokopeuff, Louise Nevzoroff, Lucinda Nevzoroff, Mary Swetzof and Nancy Zaochney. Not shown are Sally Swetzof, Jason Dirks and Annlillian Nevzoroff.

secretary who is adept at handling bilingual classes and also teaches a reading group everyday. Through the cooperation of these individuals we are able to give the students a strong background in education, combined with traditional Unangan practices and values.

The highlight of our school is the dance group which was started several years ago. This group, Atxam Taligisniikangis, has made great leaps in the last year. It has built pride in our cultural self-esteem, created a greater awareness of what it is to be Unangan, revived ancient rituals and dances, and has spawned a hunger to learn as much about our ancestors as possible in this day and age by our students. The group has performed in many places around the state, and is constantly getting requests and invitations to perform all over the country. In the past, we have performed for Alaska Federation of Natives, the Metropolitan of the Russian Orthodox Church and last year we were selected to represent all of Alaska at the Arctic Winter Games. Each student at the school is required to take this class daily. It has replaced "traditional" physical education (P.E.) classes at the school. Students who want to do other P.E. activities are encouraged to attend open gym night. This is radically different than other schools who make Native dancing an extra curricular activity. Students attend dance class daily with enthusiasm. In fact, if the class is canceled for reasons related to scheduling, then our students are disappointed and on the verge of revolution. The group not only uses ancient dances, but also creates dances from traditional stories and from every day life in our islands. The use of the old stories in our dances has created a greater understanding of the natural and supernatural world as seen by our ancestors—something that was overlooked and scorned as useless by the Western educators of the past. Needless to say, dancing is back and very strong in the Aleutians. Now we are committed to revising our entire curriculum to reflect the practices and philosophy of our ancestors. The revival of dancing at Netsvetov School has overflowed into all other subject areas.

The Unangan language class is currently engaged in building an *ulasux*. This is a traditional Aleut sod house. The applications for applying knowledge learned in the construction of this house are vast and not only do the students learn the Aleut terms for every part of the house, but it can also be tied into Aleut and Western math. It is wonderful to see the students so excited about learning language and, finally, math. This house will serve a number of purposes when it is finished, some of which are the launching and training area for the *iqyax* (kayak) project. This project will be completed within the next two years. Students are also looking forward to the day when we can hold a traditional dance in the house.

In the past few years the school has also had a number of important cultural projects which took place. These include Aleut bentwood hunting hats, beaded headdresses and drum-making. All of these activities have incorporated traditional patterns and measurements with Western-style math. The primary grades spent a good part of last year studying the old patterns in both the traditional regalia and beadwork. We believe that this activity truly helped our students in understanding the concept of patterns, which made the transfer to Westernized math patterns much easier. Last year's high school history class spent a majority of their time studying traditional Aleut society. Topics included: Aleut tribes, social structure, kinship, laws and consequences, environmental factors, life cycles, gender roles and traditional religious beliefs. In the future we will be having school-wide classes in gut skin-sewing, sealskin pants sewing and construction of an *iqyax*.

As a result of immersing our students in a strong cultural program and seeing the educational benefits and positive results, we are moving forward and committed to improving instruction in all areas of our curriculum. This has brought us to our present position in revising curriculum.

Currently, we have begun work on our science curriculum. We have just finished aligning our benchmarks and standards with state and federal standards. The next step for us will be to define materials and activities in which to attain these goals with our students. It is our desire to incorporate the knowledge of elders in designing these activities and materials, so that we have a balance of Western and traditional Aleut influences. We hope to implement our science curriculum in the fall. This spring we will begin to revise our math curriculum in the same manner. Over the next three years we are hoping to have our entire curriculum revised and fully implemented in the daily learning of our students. This is a slow process, but then again, Western education has taken years to undo the educational practices developed by our ancestors over thousands of years. In the future, we hope our students will be better able to understand our unique cultural values and to make wise decisions in a modern world with all of its challenges. After all, when we look through the eyes of our ancestors perhaps our vision will be clearer.

Interview and
transcription by
Moses L. Dirks,
Unalaska,
November 28, 1999

Elder Interview: Nick Galaktionoff

Sharing Our Pathways, Vol. 5, Issue 1, Jan/Feb 2000

I was born in Makushin, Magusim kugan aganaqing 1925. This month or next month. And after I was born, kids they didn't know how they were born anyway. My dad and my mom they were going to move into their own house. My dad built a house and finished it. So then my mom and dad was ready to go. I had an older sister named Malaanyaa. They went out and pack things over. And me, I was left with my grandmother. So my grandmother grew me up all the way.

When I was five years old I started helping my dad. I didn't know what I was doing. He always told me that I was doing good. I suppose I was making a mess, but he always said I did good. I ran into the house and tell my grandmother. My grandmother was a very important person to me that time. She would always teach me; I didn't really know my real mom and my dad. She told me that was my dad. But I never called him my dad. I always call him Ludang, "my oldest." So I don't know my real mom because my dad call her Ayagang, "my wife." So I start calling her my Ayagang. We grew up that way.

Before he (dad) go to St. Paul, he would take the *baidarki* skin off 'cause you save the ribs anyway. You don't want them rot away. After he come back from

St. Paul, them guys were working for forty dollars a month. People make more than that in one day now days. Then after he come home from St. Paul, take a rest for one week and start work on his *baidarki*, changing the string ropes on there and soak the skin in the creek. After it got dried up it don't get stretch or shrink anyway (the sealskin). After two days you put them on. People come in and help him sew it up and everything and no time he finished it. No party, but they always had tea parties after that. So my dad told me I was five or six years old. I know I was small. I don't know how old I was. My dad said that he was going to take me out in a *baidarki*. But, my grandmother told him, don't take him too far out. I know I can't see nothing. I have nothing but a smile on my face. Finally, he got me in a *baidarki* hole (in the front). Boy my eyes were barely sticking out. Then he launched his *baidarki* giving me a ride around from that house all the way far as the creek and from there turned back, all the way as far as that point. And we finally landed. My grandmother lift me up from the *baidarki* take me out, take me home. I thought that it was a lot of fun I ever had.

Because we didn't have our own toys, we all made toys. That's all we had. Pretty tough them days. But everything I do this better and what anybody do it looks better. But when I was eight years old I started fishing. I am not alone but always go with them fishing, seining right in the front. Those were the days when it was a lot of fun. It was a lot of fun for every kid. Them days the people work on fish and after that my dad is gone. Go out and get some wood and fish. My dad and my dad's brother and his friend and guy named Matfii Burenin, John Burenin, Akiinfer Galaktionoff—he was my dad. John—that was his brother but he got different dad. He never come home. There was not even a storm, not even windy. People there looking for them. They didn't find them. Finally, Iliya Burenin find the boat in another bay all chopped up. Japanese got them. Japanese started to move into Unalaska in the mountains, hide away spying Dutch Harbor.

So that was 1939. The marshall got there on the mail boat. Not the mail boat, but Coast Guard boat. He found out my grandmother and mother did not have no help. And back to Unalaska again. Finally try and find a place for us to stay. Finally Coast Guard got there and pick us up and we come in 1939. I don't like it but as kids we can't do nothing by himself. I was 13 years old.

And after that I am doing something like everybody else, helping my mom.

In 1939, just about 1940, my grandmother died. She was seventy-nine years old. I didn't know she was seventy-nine but after she died, after I grew up until fifteen-sixteen, I found out she was seventy-nine years old. So I've got nothing to do so I had to move in with my real mom. I didn't like them kids in there, but they were my brothers and sisters. Always doing something. For ten cents you tell them to do something. I am getting ten cents from somebody else. Ten cents was a lot of money. I would buy two big bar candies. Now days them forty, fifty cent bar candies are twice as small as the big candies before.

And from there I work most of the time. When I was fourteen years old, school started. And they wanted me to go to school. I was happy for a while. I might learn something. I was in school but I didn't like my teacher. If I don't say "Good morning Miss Jorgensen," she would always hit my head with a little ruler. Boy, I didn't like that. I have been up at the school. I know how to sign my name. So one morning I got sandwich and I got a big coat. I make a big sandwich and put it in coat pocket and I left. People go up to school but me, I kept going all the way to the trail, Biorka Trail. I walk all the way over to that Beaver Inlet. I am not even scared but I will be scared later. I did not have a place to stay. I take walk on the beach for a while. Dark comes I start eating my sandwich. I stay by the small creek, put my head down and drink water. I did not have a cup. I eat half of my sandwich. Later I went into the grass and went to bed. I sleep good for a while and I wake up, pitch dark. Boy, I am kind of nervous. Early winter started, right after school started, oh, about a month and a half after school started. I got into Beaver Inlet over night. Next morning, I got up and finished my sandwich. No I don't want to stay there again. So I come home before I lose my trail. No truck road up on top side, just a trail. I could have come in to town earlier but I don't want to come to town when it is daylight. And I am scared of the goats up there. We got to go through this pass, about twenty goats up there. Belongs to Mr. King. Boy, pretty soon they would be teasing me all the way. I got chased from them animals; run before they hit me and I went over the fence. When I come on this side I feel safer. I come all the way to my house and my mom said, "We have been worried about you, where have you been?"

"I've been camping." Well I didn't see no camp in Beaver Inlet.

Next two days the marshall, Mr. Bill, I forgot his last name, he wanted me back to school. I told him if you put me back to school I am going to run away for good. I was scared but I said that anyway.

So later he said okay stay home if you want to. He left me. That was Bill Brown. He was a marshall before Vern Robinson. Somebody else was the marshall before Bill Brown too. He died in Seattle. He was an Aleut. His Mother was Aleut I guess. He talked Aleut because everybody talked Aleut around here anyway. Not any more.

Nick "Nicholai"Galaktionoff was born in the village of Makushin on the island of Unalaska in 1939. Nick comes from a large family; he and his sister Marina are the only survivors. Both of his sons reside in Unalaska.

Nick's hobbies include halibut and salmon fishing. He used to go out seal hunting and fishing whenever he got a chance. He now has poor eyesight and does not go many places anymore. Nick likes living in Unalaska and enjoys fishing and walking around town.

Sally and
Sperry Ash

Leave No Language Behind

Sharing Our Pathways, Vol. 8, Issue 3, Summer 2003

Presented by Sally and Sperry Ash at the 29th Annual Bilingual Multicultural Education/Equity Conference, Anchorage, Alaska, February 5, 2003

*C*amai, gui ataqa Kuku, nupugpakarpilama Quyana—kcagyumiam-
ci nupugt'sllunuk mugtamllu unuarpak. Sugpia'ukuk Nanwalegmek
nupugcilluki Sugpiat taumi Aluttit. Guangkuta uturpet Sugt'stun.
Sungq'rtukut Nanwalegmek ernerpak ililillemta aualarnirt'slluku lit-
naurwik Sugt'stun. Katia Brewster, Ataka Moonin taumi Guitka
Guangkuta Dynamic-kegkut, guangkunuk allu kimnuk, nanluta. Cali
tainenguk Nanwalegmek Acuuk Kvasnikoff taumi Qelni Swenning.

Camai! My name is Sally Ash. Before I go on I would like to thank you very much for letting us speak here this morning. We are from Nanwalek and we are representing the Sugpiaq people from the Alutiiq-Sugpiaq region. Our Native language is Sugt'stun. There are some people from Nanwalek today that helped us get the immersion program started: Kathy Brewster, Rhoda Moonin and Sperry Ash. We are a dynamic team, not just the two of us, but all of us. Also a couple of people who didn't make it are Natalie Kvasnikoff and Emlie Swenning.

I am Sugpiaq-Russian born to Sarjus and Juanita Kvasnikoff. I was born and raised in Nanwalek, which used to be known as English Bay. I didn't realize it but as I was growing up, my village was slowly changing from Sugpiaq to a more Western lifestyle. Forty-five years ago big changes came to Nanwalek—a big BIA school was built. Speaking only Sugt'stun, to me it was exciting, new and bright but the teachers who came were different—frightening, authoritative and appearing superior to my grandparents, aunties and uncles or even my own parents. Our Elders encouraged us to learn as much as we could and to speak English. I was a good learner, always interested about the outside world, as much as any of my peers. The teachers were always promising us great things if we finished school. The Elders wanted us to get an education and get back something that was taken away from us, not to mention the pain and shame they went through for speaking a Native language. They were only trying to protect us from what they went through. It wasn't until I had to go out of the village for high school that I realized what my Elders were talking about. How different the outside world became.

I was happy to finally finish school, and then I got married and had kids. I was proudest when our kids were born because I was back in the village and learning once again from my Elders and women in the village about the rules on being a mother and raising a child in the Sugpiaq ways. It was through my children's eyes when I realized the important ingredients needed for life that I had left off in my rush to fit into this world. We moved to Anchorage for a few years when the kids were small. As I attended their parent/teacher conferences, the teachers would always end the meetings telling me how much the kids talked and wrote about the village. That sounded to me like their hearts belonged in the village, so we moved back. When I got the school bilingual instructor job I felt so lucky! What an important job. I didn't know what I was doing but I really took my job seriously. It was only then that I really realized how much of the language was dead and dying in my home and in the Alutiiq-Sugpiaq region. I had always thought our language would be alive and well in Nanwalek, but it seemed in a blink of an eye that only the Elders and a few young adults were speaking the language. This void, this emptiness had come silently, subtly. How did I, a speaker of the language, let this happen?

Where did the Elders and I fit in our community and school to pass on our God-given knowledge of culture and language? I tried my best to teach with no real support from anywhere until I finally met Sandra Holmes, to whom I am forever grateful. She literally opened my eyes and ears. She critiqued my classes and helped me understand how I need to teach in order to be effective. She moved and after that I had no real support from the school district. Over the years I came to realize that forty-five minutes a day, five days a week was hardly making a dent in saving our language. At the bilingual conferences

I'd hear the bilingual representative from our district talk with the Russians about their school and they sounded like they were really doing good and moving along. Our program was so sad that I started dreaming of an immersion school. With the help and inspiration of individuals from other Native language immersion schools—Dr. Jeff Leer, our main linguist from UAF Alaska Native Language Center; Dr. Roy Itzu-Mitchel; Loddie Jones from Ayaprun Immersion School in Bethel; my husband Marlon and so many others (some of you may be even here today)—we were finally able to see our dream come true.

We started our immersion school for our pre-school kids three years ago. Our Nanwalek Village Council sponsored us. With the support of parents and grandparents who could see the erosion of our language and culture and the rate we were losing our Elders, and with financial support from various agencies, we got started. Getting started was both an exciting and frustrating time for us. We just converted everything in the head start preschool curriculum into Sugt'stun. We used traditional songs and made up songs and borrowed from our Yup'ik friends. We wanted to work with our district school but they wouldn't even acknowledge us as a school. I remember when I used to teach as a bilingual teacher my credentials were never questioned—supposedly I knew enough to run the program and have complete responsibility. But when I suggested an immersion program, all of a sudden I knew nothing! They tried to discourage us saying that our kids would get confused in school if we did not teach in English. I did some worrying because my own daughter, Ivana, was one of our first students but the thing that kept me going was "Hey, English is all around us through TV and music and even our own people so it will always be there." I can tell you, Ivana is in the first grade and she is doing just fine and so are the rest of our first immersion graduates. We have the happiest times in our little school when our kids are responding to us or to each other in our language or when parents proudly let us know what they hear or what their kids are bringing home. Nothing in the world can beat that!

In the mornings we do regular school work, songs and arts and crafts. Then we have lunch followed by some physical education and some total physical response (TPR) and everything is done in Sugt'stun all day. Our cook, Angun Seville, prepares as much fresh and healthy Native foods as he can. We have a long way to go, but as I look back, I am proud and grateful for our little school, for our Elders who share their knowledge so freely, for the parents who give us their little ones to pass on our language, and as our Yup'ik sister Loddie says, to pass on our inherited gift from our ancestors.

When I hear of other villages struggling to keep their language alive, I say, "work harder; this is our opportunity and maybe our only chance." Our wildest dream is to teach a Sugt'stun immersion program from preschool to high school in the school that BIA gave us. We want to be a part of the healing that needs to take place for our lost culture and language. Are we, the Elders in our village, really the people our young kids look up to? We want to be. We should be.

We, like any other village or community, want our children to be successful students and young adults. As our Elders say, "*Agun'lu kinautacin*—don't forget who you are." We are doing it the best way we know works. I know that when my grandfather said about our language, culture and traditions, "I hope this will go on forever," he meant well. On behalf of all Alaska Native languages that are struggling to survive I urge, "Please don't leave our language behind."

Continued by Sperry Ash

Mom just told you her experiences. I would like to discuss some other aspects of our language situation so I want to begin by saying we Sugpiaq/Alutiiq people, especially in the Kenai Peninsula, are minorities in our Native land. I think that is also the case for other Sugpiaqs in their regions—Prince William Sound, Kodiak and the Alaska Peninsula. Because of our minority status the use of our language suffers, especially within our educational systems:

- We receive no meaningful Native language support from our school districts.
- We are not allowed to have an immersion program for K–12 students, even though immersion programs do exist in our very own district for the Russian language.
- Our immersion school is not recognized by our school district.
- Not once has there been a Sugpiaq representative on any of the various school boards formed to determine education policies for our village.

All of these decisions are made for us Sugpiaqs by others. Someone somewhere tells us what's good for us. As many of you are familiar, the history of American education with regard to cultural and language learning, especially in Alaska, is not one to be proud of. The educational flavor of the month is "Leave no child behind." Forgive my negative view, but as far as we can tell this is a new name for doing the same thing they were doing before. All it amounts to is teaching kids to pass some tests. Personally, I think a more appropriate name would be "One size fits all." Whether you agree or not, I can tell you it has not worked well in our village.

The truth is we have only two graduates from Nanwalek. That's a pretty bad record. Even though we, in our village, pay the price for this miserable record, we lack the control to try things our way. Everything about the borough school in our village permeates with the attitude "we know what's best for your kids." Immersion is the unmentionable "I" word. This situation makes it very hard to make any progress when it comes to revitalizing our language.

Besides our language we want to teach our kids to be proud of their culture, who they are, to be risk-takers and to have that can-do attitude they will need to solve the problems that they will face later on in life. The reality though is us kids will be just like our parents. We need to see our parents in charge instead of being helpers, having fun speaking their language instead of ashamed to say it in front of the principal, doing something proactive instead of crying or being consumed by anger about the situation and sharing our culture instead of being only observers and consumers of another culture. The struggle we continue to fight against alcoholism and other social diseases is in part a result of not being in control of our lives. These are the things we aim to promote in our school and none of them are on a test.

I have heard it said "Your culture is so important . . . don't lose it," but when you try to actually do something then they say "first get your college degree and then we'll talk about it." For example, I took a lot of math in college. I was able to solve quadratic equations long enough to solve a few on a test. But you didn't invite me here to do that. Nobody does and probably never will. All you want to know and many like you is about our language and culture—all of which I could have learned from people who never went to college, maybe not high school or even grade school.

My mom never went to college. It is an honor to sit beside her and talk to you about our situation. She, like so many of the parents and elderly in the Sugpiaq region, went through the period as a child when speaking Sugt'stun/Alutiit'stun was shunned, shameful or even forbidden. As children they swallowed this guilt. They held on to it.

They also raised their children with it. I see it in the common mannerisms and attitudes towards our Sugpiaq language by this generation. Some still hold on to this. But my mom and a few others finally came to realize that it's okay to be Sugpiaq, Aleut, Alutiiq. It's okay to talk Sugt'stun, Alutiit'stun. Speaking Sugt'stun is not equated with being dumb or slow. Heck, they have two languages in their brains and we only have one. Who's using their brain more?

I don't want to leave you with the impression that it has been a one- or two-person show. Many, many people have contributed to the effort of passing on the Sugt'stun language. There are many proactive community members in the village that share the high hopes for Sugt'stun. Just as we have support in the village, we also have support outside of the village. These connections have been equally as vital to the continuation of our efforts. Mom has mentioned a few so I will not run through the names again but I just want to reemphasize that the support we get is truly helpful. *Cali, Quyana*! Unfortunately, we also have people in our small village of 250 and some outside the village who do not see value in teaching our language to future generations and that has been an additional burden to our efforts. Maybe I shouldn't have talked like this; those that are in disagreement with us might not understand what they are doing. Maybe we ourselves don't know what we are doing either. As my departed grandmother taught us many things about prayer, I ask you, the audience, to please pray for all of us. Pray for us and our efforts, that they are pleasing and acceptable to God.

There are many more issues that need to be addressed related to language and its continuation, but of course we could not discuss them all in this time. I look forward to hearing from the rest of you and especially what you have to teach and share with us. *Quyana*.

From Sally & Sperry Ash

We really want to thank the organizers of this bilingual conference for inviting us to speak. We enjoyed the experience and the warm support we received. One of the things we do regret is that we did not adequately thank the many people and organizations that have helped us get to this point. Some of you that we would like to thank are:

- Guilia Oliverio, UAF Alaska Native Language Center
- Dr. Jeff Leer, UAF Alaska Native Language Center

- Jennifer Harris, Chugachmuit
- Sherrie Buretta, Chairman, Chugach Alaska Corporation
- Teri Schneider, Alaska Rural Systemic Initiative
- Staff of Ayaprun Elitnaurvik Immersion School in Bethel
- All the parents who sent their kids to our school and Nanwalek IRA Tribal members who supported us
- Our corporate donors: Chugach Alaska Corporation, CIRI, English Bay Corp, Rasmusen, DCRA, North Pacific Rim Housing Authority
- Many of the staff and management from Chugach Alaska Corporation, Chugachmuit and the Nanwalek IRA Council.

We also know that there are probably a few people and organizations who we forgot to mention. Please forgive our omission. There are also many of you out there who may not have time or money but support us in spirit. We thank you all for your support.

The Education of a Seal Hunter

Moses Dirks

Sharing Our Pathways, Vol. 9, Issue 2, Mar/Apr 2004

A prime example of the way learning occurs in an out-of-school setting is when Native people go about their subsistence activities. The topic I will use to illustrate traditional learning is sea lion hunting.

Long ago, Unangax̂ men were the main hunters of sea mammals. The men would prepare to go hunting by cleansing themselves before a hunt by sleeping separately from their wives, because they did not want the sea lion to get jealous of the hunter if s/he found out that he had slept with his wife the night before. This also had to do with the woman's scent. If the animal smelled a woman it would scare the animal away and the man would not experience a successful hunt. The scent of a woman was considered bad luck for hunters. When I was growing up my sister or mother were not allowed to touch the firearms used in hunting. The men believed that it caused the hunter to come home empty-handed.

Long ago Unangax̂ men hunted from an *iqyax̂* (one-man) skin-boat with only a harpoon. He would harpoon the animal and the tip of the harpoon would enter the animal and detach inside the animal without killing it. On the other end was an inflated seal stomach, which served as a buoy. The hunter pursued the animal until it got tired and then he would pull up alongside and club it to death. Once the animal was dead, he and his partner would tow it ashore and the butchering took place on the beach. All parts of the animal were used. The seal-skin was used for clothing and covering the *iqyax̂*, and the stomach was used for packing dried fish and meat. The intestines were used in making gut skin raincoats, called *chigdax̂*, which were durable and light enough so they did not hamper the paddler from maneuvering his *iqyax̂* in tricky waters. The whiskers of the sea lion were used in decorating the hunter's hat, called *chaxudax̂*, The length and stoutness of the whiskers determined the status of the hunter. All the meat was preserved by drying until the Russians introduced rock salt, which was then used in storing the meat for the long winter months.

All of the traditional form of education occurred in the natural world. The young hunters responsibility was to observe and learn by watching and imitating the moves that were produced in making the event happen. The young hunter was most likely the nephew trained by the mother's brother. He would be the apprentice hunter learning under the tutelage of his uncle. Training at times was really harsh. Cold water bathing was one of the tactics used, where the young man was told to take a bath in the cold saltwater early in the mornings. They called it "toughening the hunter up" so that he could endure the cold frigid waters when hunting on the sea.

The training started at a very early age when the young boys arm was stretched back while sitting down on the ground as if sitting in the *iqyax̂*, so that he would grow up naturally to throw the harpoon with velocity and distance. Other kinds of training included hanging from the *barabara* roof rafters to strengthen their arms in case they had to climb cliffs for bird hunting or egg gathering. The exercises continued until he could prove to his uncle that he was capable of being a successful hunter. He would prove that by getting his first seal or sea lion. Only then would he be considered a man in the Unangan hunting and gathering society. Before the coming of the Russians, the Unangan were a very self-sufficient and healthy people. Even with their crude weapons they were excellent hunters.

Today hunting technology has changed so much that by the time I was old enough to go hunting, all traditional technology was gone. The wooden dory or homemade plywood skiffs replaced the *iqyax̂*. Later came the fiberglass skiffs and aluminum boats. High-powered rifles, more powerful and accurate, replaced the harpoon. Bolas were replaced by shotguns for hunting birds. Now we have to learn how all these machines work, because the repair shop can be a thousand miles away.

There is usually someone in each village that knows about fixing motors. My cousin, for instance, has never completed high school but he is a master mechanic. He can fix outboards, cars and trucks. How does he do this with no formal training? His aptitude for fixing engines is very high, so he is depended on to fix the machines.

Now-a-days, owning and running a skiff is expensive and if you don't have a job it is hard to get out there for hunting, etc. You have to buy gas and oil for the motor, paint and a trailer for your boat as well as a truck or an ATV to haul it back and forth. Rifles and shotguns need to be kept clean and oiled otherwise they don't function right. Rust is the major culprit on guns. Along with the gun you need to buy shells that are expensive from the local store. These days, hunting is an expensive proposition.

I have taught Unangan culture for the last 15 years and I still can't believe how different it is to teach in a classroom setting. Whenever you want to bring a seal or sea lion into a classroom you have to get permission from your principal, then get approval from DEC to make sure it will be safe to handle the blood pathogens and raw meat. In the past this was never a problem, because most of the butchering was done out in the field before the animal was brought into the village. As a result, if you are trying to teach a unit on traditional activities in a classroom, you often have to resort to textbooks and there are very few texts that deal with the inner organs of a sea lion. What little are available often do not clearly explain where the organs of the animals are located and most of the texts come in black and white so you can't even positively identify the organs.

Elders don't like coming into the classrooms; they were never allowed in the past, so they feel uncomfortable in schools. It is so unnatural to be sitting in a classroom hour after hour learning from a book. I once knew an Elder from one of the villages who told me that he was getting sick because he was not getting any exercise since he moved in from the village. He sat around too much and he said that it was not healthy. He would rather do hands-on type of work, so he always found things to do around town. The Elder lived to be in his nineties.

Classroom settings are good for the Unangax̂ for the first hour. Listening to a person talk for more than an hour is unheard of in my culture—the only time you would hear talking amongst the Unangax̂ would be when they were telling stories at night. Unangax̂ people are used to hands-on, kinesthetic type of learning; learn by watching how it is done, trying it out and if you don't master it the first time you do it again and again until you know how to do it.

I would sometimes be awestruck by what some of my relatives could do—machinist, electrician, carpentry—you name it, and they never went to school for these trades. If you ask them, "How did you learn how to do that?" they would credit God for giving them the skill so that they can do what they need to do. As I venture down the road and think about those intelligent people that I knew, I sometimes shudder to think, what would have happened to them if they had gone to school?

5

Yup'ik/Cup'ik
Pathways to Education

Earth, Air, Fire, Water and Spirit as a Foundation for Education

Angayuqaq Oscar Kawagley

Sharing Our Pathways, Vol. 1, Issue 4, Sept/Oct 1996

Modern science studies that which is visible using many techno-logical devises to refine their observations. Theories are con-structed, used, modified or discarded as new information and findings warrant. The task of modern science has been to simplify Nature, learn of its underlying logic and then use that logic to control Nature (Briggs, 1992:14). Indigenous societies study that which is invisible to temper the development of technology and guide its association with Nature. The Yupiaq society deals with trying to understand the irreg-ularities of Nature which is underlain with patterns of order. Many unseen forces are in action in the elements of the universe.

To begin to understand these phenomena, Yupiaq science education must begin with the five elements—earth, air, fire, water and spirit. The sacred gifts of each must be understood, as well as the human activities which contribute to the despiritualization and reduction of these life-giving gifts. In order to be holistic, the activities must include Yupiaq language and culture, language arts, mathematics, social studies, arts and crafts and sciences. All must be interrelated as all of earth is interrelated. For example, in dealing with the element air, the teacher could select the sacred gift of weather. And what an unpredictable choice! Like many Yupiaq myths, weather is so very dynamic, ever changing, and, like the myth, very mystical.

The wind has irregularities of constantly varying velocity, humidity, temperature and direction due to topography and other factors. There are nonlinear dimensions to clouds, irregularities of cloud formations, anomalous cloud luminosity and different forms of precipitation at different levels. There are patterns, however tenuous, such as the path of a jet stream or fronts to be studied. The Native students' visual acuity and memory for detail could be used to advantage. There is very little in this universe which is linear, in a grid or in a two-dimensional square or three dimensional cube. The weather's dynamic is that the part of its part is part of a part which is a part of another part and so on. The local Native elders could explain how they were able to predict weather based upon subtle messages given to them by the sun twenty-four hours before it happened. This involves the language of feelings of the inner world coupled with the language of reason. Being inclined to the spiritual, the Native was able to understand and accept the unpredictable permutations of weather. The Native people had learned certain general predictable patterns of weather connected to the seasons and moons. Yet, the Native student could get acquainted with some more predominate tools of the meteorologist such as the thermometer, barometer, anemometer, hydrometer, satellite pictures and other tools to give the elders' knowledge depth, detail and a broader view. Introducing students to the notion of irregularities and anomalies of form and force (chaos and fractals) necessarily introduces them to holism. The key idea is for the students to understand the interconnectedness of all things in the universe.

Of utmost importance in using the five elements of life to teach science is assuring that the students understand that the sacred gifts of each is a gift to the life-giving forces of the living earth (or Mother

Earth). The teacher must be careful to explain what those gifts are absolutely necessary for life on earth to continue. All these five elements' gifts make possible for creation on earth to continue. The Yupiaq honored and respected these gifts in the rituals and ceremonies. Take for example, the Nakaciuq or the "Blessing of the Bladders." The Yupiaq people believed that when the seal or some other sea mammal gave itself to the hunter, that the spirit of the seal entered its bladder upon giving up its life. This required that the people take care to remove the bladder, inflate it to dry and save it for the winter Bladder Festival to honor the sacred gift of the element, spirit. In this way the Yupiaq people honored and showed respect for the gift of the element earth for giving birth to animals upon which they depended for survival as a people.

During the festival, the bladders were reinflated with life-giving air and hung on poles for the duration of the activities. In the *qasgiq* were placed two three-to-four foot stout poles in front of the place of honor for the elders. The honors seating was located at the rear of the community house. On the flattened upper end were placed two earthen lamps with wicks which were *then filled with seal oil. The wicks were lighted and the lamps kept burning during the entire festival. One or two people were given the responsibility of keeping the lamps going. The gift of the element fire was used to light and give some warmth to the community house. To purify the air and the participants in the house, wild parsnips were burned. Another gift of the element earth, the parsnip plant was used to create purifying smoke with the transforming gift of the element fire. Fire, with the gift of air, transformed the seal oil to heat and light.

At the conclusion of the Bladder Festival, the bladders were taken down, deflated, and carried to the ocean or river where an opening in the ice had been made. With collective mindfulness of all the Yupiaq participants that the spirits of the animals were happy and satisfied with the care and careful execution of the required rituals and ceremonies, and that they would return and give themselves to the hunters, the bladders were returned to the sacred gift of the element water, the womb of creation.

A multi-disciplinary and -sensory study of the elements can be undertaken for the entire school year. The students would begin to understand that the experience of knowing and making the place a friend takes time. The students can be helped to fine tune their endosmotic sense-makers through carefully planned and executed lessons of observation that incorporate their Yupiaq language of feeling with the language of reason. The ultimate gift is that of the element spirit. Through the Yupiaq language, mythology, rituals and ceremonies, the students are taught the "correct lifeway, a lifeway appropriate to place" (Mills, 1990:159).

The modern schools are not teaching students how to live a life that feels right. Rather, the schools are giving a lot of information to the students without also showing them how they can transfer the information into useful knowledge for making a living. Another step is to individually and collectively as a people see how the usable knowledge could be transformed into wisdom to make a life. The students now look at an innovative teacher who refuses to use existing curricula, syllabi, lessons plans, media presentations, photocopied materials and so on, as not really teaching. They expect to be given a lot of information and to be entertained. The many machines, modern tools and the vaunted computers are not enough to teach a lifeway that feels right. It is more important that we use the Yupiaq values and culture well interspersed with imagination or intuition from within and the element spirit to make the new lifeway that feels right.

During the years which this activity is being done, the participants will explore, plan and implement ways to make the Alaska Native mythology as a teaching tool for the sciences as well as the humanities. Within the humanities (mythology) are the sciences and within the sciences are the humanities.

Kindergarten through third grade could possibly talk about the five elements generally. This is what earth does: it provides homes for people, animals and plants. Air is what you breathe. Fourth through the sixth grades can begin to talk about certain gifts that each element gives to earth to make it good and beautiful. They can begin to talk about the water cycle and begin to see how it is affected by the sun, water, land, air, plants and people. The junior high grades can begin to talk not only of the gifts, but how the activities of the human being affects the life supporting gifts of the five elements. The high school students can begin to discuss and research the five elements' gifts and how people and pollution reduce the life supporting role of the gifts. They can expand their knowledge of the Yupiaq peoples' perceptions and behaviors to the natural and spiritual worlds to keep them sustainable.

The teachers and teachers-to-be must be taught that the world is nonlinear and that, as a result, science will never understand everything about the universe. They must also realize and appreciate that in modern scientific and technological endeavors, mathematics, science and technology are interrelated as are all other disciplines. It behooves that science education and teaching in general become aligned to the common philosophical thread, or the "distant memory," as it is called by N. Scott Momaday, of the ecological perspective. All peoples of the earth began from this vista, and therefore such a perspective makes it more probable and possible for attaining a new consciousness for a sustainable life.

References

Briggs, J. (1992). *Fractals the patterns of chaos*. New York: Simon & Schuster.
Mills, S. (1990). *In praise of nature*. Washington, D. C. and Covelo, CA.: Island Press.

Yupiaq Mathematics: Pattern and Form in Space and Place

Angayuqaq Oscar Kawagley

Sharing Our Pathways, Vol. 2, Issue 2, Mar/Apr 1997

The Alaska Native people have always had a way of seeing and understanding patterns in the land (*nuna*) around them. They identified patterns in plants, rivers, weather, landforms, animals and the heavens. Upon the careful observation of patterns, they were able to make predictions for the future. This critical analysis involved the past histories, the present conditions and thus presented sensemakers for the future. This is the practice of ecopsychology at its finest. Everything that one needs to know about life and to seek freedom and happiness are found in Nature. As stated by Barry Lopez, the landscape becomes the mindscape and the mindscape becomes the landscape (1986).

For Yup'ik people, according to elders Joshua Phillip and Fred George, the various parts of the body were their measuring instruments. The outstretched arms became the measure for the length of a fishing net. The closed fist defined the opening of the blackfish trap. Other units of measure, such as one arm's length, the distance from the elbow to the tip of the index finger, the span between the thumb and index finger extended, stepping off to mark the diameter of the *qasgiq* and various combinations of these became the units of measure for tasks such as making clothing, tools and shelter. Consequently, the clothing people wore and the tools needed for hunting and trapping were made precisely to fit the dimensions of the user.

The women used precise patterns for making parkas and mukluks. The parka required the maker to look at the body of the person for whom it was to be made and to visualize proportions in body form (including bone structure and musculature) and size in order, for instance, to determine the number of ground squirrel skins needed. In sewing together the skins, the sewer is reminded of the family history of the patterns, tassels, decorative designs, and the use of various furs, taking advantage of their beneficial qualities.

The Alaska Native people also had a numbering system (Lipka, 1994). For the Yupiat people, their numbering system used a base of twenty. Ten fingers and ten toes are needed to make a complete person. The digits are attached to appendages which are in turn attached to the body. The counting system was necessary for determining the number of furs needed to make an article of clothing. For example, it takes 45 squirrel skins or six otter skins for a man's parka. For net-making, special wooden measuring tools were constructed, again using body parts to determine the width for different species of fish. However, there was no need to count the precise number of dry fish to last the whole winter. This was done by estimating how much storage area needed to be filled with fish to feed the family and dogs, provide for ceremonies and share with others. Always, they had to have food supplies beyond the immediate needs of the family. Sharing and reciprocity were key to their preparations. Thus, for the Yupiat people it was not necessary to quantify in precise numerical terms, but rather in proportional terms relative to size of family, time until next food supply would be available, weather conditions and nutritional uses of various foods.

The Alaska Native people had many geometric designs in the things they made such as utensils, fishtraps, weirs, clothing designs and ceremonial paraphernalia. Again, it was not necessary to quantify in terms such as surface area, degree, angle, volume and other numerical dimensions. Such information alone would be considered insufficient knowledge for you were also required to know the history of the design, its replication of a natural or spiritual form, the meaning of the color and the story behind the artifact.

The Alaska Native people also had no precise measurements for distance such as feet, meters and miles. Rather, distance was calculated qualitatively-measured more in terms of time and terrain than distance. The Yupiaq person would consider the mode of transportation, weather conditions, topography over which he would have to traverse, history of various sites that one would encounter along the way where food is available and, if traveling a great distance, where logical and safe rest areas were located. In considering the above, one can see that units of measure for distance alone would have rendered their knowledge incomplete and unreliable as a basis for moving from one place to another. The all-important knowledge of place would be lacking in the details that are necessary for the landscape to merge with the mindscape.

Space and time were thought of differently too. Space was a multi-dimensional place that the human, spirit and nature occupied at the same time. The self or consciousness was considered to be time and timelessness at the same time. One accomplished what needed to be done at the right time. There was a place and time for everything. Timing in drumming and singing was important, however there was no need for a metronome because it was implicit in the act itself. To pay attention to such a device would detract from the sacredness of song, beat, motion and story. The circadian rhythm of the universe was the sacred timepiece of the Native people.

Western mathematics and sciences, because of their emphasis on objectivity and detachment, introduce us to an abstract and lifeless world that has a tendency to set us apart from the rest of our relationships in the universe. However, with fractal geometry and the new sciences of chaos and complexity, the Western thought-world seems to be shifting from the quantitative and impersonal study of tangible "things" and is becoming more attuned to the qualitative dimensions as more and more of its members recognize the importance of inter-relationships (Capra, 1996). Western scientists constructed the holographic image which lends itself to the Native concept of everything being connected. Just as the whole contains each part of the image, so too does each part contain the makeup of the whole. The relationship of each part to everything else must be understood to get the whole picture (Wilber 1985). We are finally getting there.

There are many bright Native people who would make excellent elementary or high school teachers. Many of these students have problems understanding mathematics, in part because teachers don't themselves recognize it as another way of knowing with a language and logic of its own. We present mathematical abstractions as though the purpose was to practice the virtuosity of the human mind and its creativity and we lose sight of its practical applications. Native students often have trouble visualizing abstract mathematical constructs and their application to real life. Perhaps, we can overcome this problematic academic gatekeeper by introducing Native students to recognizing and understanding the patterns and forms in their own world through which they can visualize the problems and then move from qualitative to quantitative explanations. From the tangible we can go slowly into the intangible. The interest that such an approach can spark is evident in the work of the Iñupiaq students from Kaktovik, who have created their own system for representing Iñupiaq numerals (Bartley, 1997).

We are in a modern world which was described ably by Lewis Carroll in Alice in Wonderland: "Now, here, you see, it takes all the running you can do to keep in the same place. If you want to get somewhere else, you must run at least twice as fast as that!" New information is bombarding us from all quarters with entropy setting in and the decay of knowledge brings about confusion. It behooves us then to slow down and see what knowledge and information will help us to build the kind of world that we would like. What aspects of mathematics and the sciences will help free us from the obsession with self and materialism? We can learn from the way our ancestors made sense of the world and used keen observation of patterns and form in relation to space and place to maintain balance between the human, natural and spiritual worlds. You see, our problem is a crisis of consciousness. Ralph Waldo Emerson once wrote, "Society is in conspiracy against the manhood of every one of its members. Society is a joint-stock company in which the members agree, for the better securing of his bread to each shareholder, to surrender the liberty of the eater." We experience resistance to making change in the world, but our efforts must continue with spirit and determination.

References

Bartley, W.C. (1997). Making the Old Way Count. *Sharing Our Pathways, 2*(1), 12. (Available from the Alaska Native Knowledge Network)

Capra, F. (1996). *The Web of Life: A New Scientific Understanding of Living Systems*. New York: Doubleday.

Lipka, J. (1994). Culturally Negotiated Schooling: Toward a Yup'ik Mathematics. *Journal of American Indian Education, 33*(3), 14–30.

Lopez, B. (1986). *Arctic Dreams: Imagination and Desire in a Northern Landscape*. New York: Charles Scribner's Sons.

Wilber, K. (1985). *The Holographic Paradigm and Other Paradoxes: Exploring the Leading Edge of Science*. Boston: New Science Library.

William Beans

Learning Put Into Cultural Perspective

Sharing Our Pathways, Vol. 2, Issue 2, Mar/Apr 1997

I have observed interaction in a number of situations where I have watched students learning in an out-of-school situation. The adults who taught them were always willing, when given an opportunity, to teach skills they used in their everyday lives. They were the "elders", or professionals by right, in their daily life activities. I will give two examples—one of a male and the other of a female—teaching skills they have mastered in their respective roles.

The first one I would like to describe is the making of a *taluyaq*, or trap, used for catching black fish, mink, otter or muskrats in the traditional way. The instructor already had straight grain driftwood split into strips for the students. He explained that this wood can be found during the summer when at camp, etc. He explained that not just any wood can be used for this purpose. Students were able to look at and touch the wood as he explained. He described the grain of the wood and how it could bend easily without breaking. The straight grain wood was three and a half to four feet long. The drift-wood had to be carved down to approximately one-half inch wide by three-eighths of an inch thick. The instructor then had the students get a feel for the *canasuun*, or carving tool, by giving them one. He demonstrated how to use it. Then he gave the students scrap wood so they could practice using the tool before they began carving the material for the traps. He explained that it was important for all the strips to be carved down and he told them how many they needed to complete the trap. Once done with the strips, he went on to make the neck of the trap, estimating how big he wanted the trap to be. He made his estimation based on materials at hand. The students carefully observed as he worked on the neck of the trap. He showed them each step of the way how it was to be done. The instructor also had roots of alder trees that he had gathered for tie downs. The roots had been gathered during the summer months from along the river bank.

The elder showed in detail the process of putting the trap together, giving the students examples and having them work through the process firsthand step-by-step. With every success he gave them praise, letting them know that they have the ability and skill to make anything that they set out to. The students experienced success with each step they completed and were excited about what they were doing. The trap is considered completed when the apprentices, or students, set the trap and provide a meal for the elder and his family. The apprentice type teaching by the elder works with great success.

The next teaching situation I would like to describe is the making of a parka. An elder, in the process of making her own parka, had two young ladies working with her while cutting, measuring and sewing materials. She did not use measuring tape, but rather used herself as a mannequin. She talked her students through the steps, describing how and which cuts and measurements went where. The elder had the students do the actual hands-on as she went about making measurements and cuts. She laid out the materials and explained why certain pieces went where. That is, there are certain patterns on the skins that the maker wants to match up. It is like working a puzzle, by piecing the skins together to get the visual just right. The cutting of the materials has to be just right, so that when the sewing begins the skins will not be lopsided or uneven. The elder got the visual of the pieces together then began the process of cutting. Under her close supervision the students were tasked with helping her cut the materials. As they completed a task, the elder explained the steps to the next one. Parka making involves a number of tasks. The ruff and trimming are added to make the parka complete. Each step involves sewing. The elder continually demonstrated how to do this while explaining the importance of the stitching. With each phase of work, the elder praised each lady's work. The students gained self-confidence as their efforts were acknowledged. The end result was a nice, completed parka for the elder. For the ladies, there was a feeling of accomplishment and a good feeling inside, knowing that the elder would have a parka to keep warm in the cold. The ladies also sensed that they would receive praise from other women about what great skills they possessed for being able to do a good job.

In both of the tasks I have described, the teacher/elders showed much patience in working with the students. The frequent encouragement, praise and help they gave along the way kept the students from becoming frustrated, giving up and quitting. Learning the skills became a meaningful, unforgettable and enjoyable experience.

In comparing and contrasting these examples to how learning occurs in school, it is to be noted that in the classroom setting this type of teaching and learning very rarely occurs. Why? In the classroom setting, teachers are textbook driven. Lessons are designed in such a way that teachers stick to teaching in a chronological order. Teachers are locked into a method of teaching that goes from addition to calculus, from Columbus to World War II. This method of teaching is very contradictory to the learning and teaching that occurs in our daily lives.

The educational system we impose on students is contrary to the methods used by our elders. This puts into perspective why it seems our educational system is not working. In the classroom, our students are not interacting with someone, but rather are taking symbols and numbers and trying to make something of them. In many situations, students get frustrated and angry and as a result, do just enough to get by. In an interactive teaching situation, such as with the elders, students learn what is being taught and they grow through experiencing. The elders gain as they share with and learn from the students with whom they are interacting.

In summing up, I would like to say, from the observations made, that we need to step back and look again at the population with whom we are working. We need to reassess how we can become better educators, using the rich resources available to us, and capitalizing on the elders and what they have to offer.

Angayuqaq Oscar
Kawagley

Active Reality Research

Sharing Our Pathways, Vol. 2, Issues 3–5, Summer, Sept/Oct, Nov/Dec 1997

During recent times many articles have been produced that address ethical values of doing research in the North. I will not address them except to say that confidentiality is important, that villagers know what they are participating in and that research results be provided to the villagers. It has been too long that Native people have been subjects of research without the honor, respect, reciprocity and cooperation due them. It is now time that we recognize that they are human beings with particular ways of knowing, being, thinking, behaving and doing. They have successfully survived for many thousands of years.

For the Yupiaq people, culture, knowing and living are intricately interrelated. Living in a harsh environment requires a vast array of precise empirical knowledge to survive the many risks due to conditions such as unpredictable weather and marginal food availability. To avoid starvation they must employ a variety of survival strategies, including appropriate storage of foodstuffs that they can fall back on during the time of need. Their food gathering and storage must be efficient as well as effective. If this were not so, how could they possibly hope to survive? To help them achieve this balance, they have developed an outlook of nature as metaphysic.

The Alaska Native world views and technologies are conducive to living in harmony with the universe. Their lives, subsistence methods and technology were devised to edify their world view. After all, the Alaska Native creator is the raven. So, how could the human being be superior to the creatures of Mother Earth? How could their hunting and trapping implements be made of offensive materials to animals that they have to kill in order to live? Thus, their tools were fashioned from resources which were formed and shaped using the natural materials. Their tools, housing and household utensils had to be with and of nature. Harmony was the key idea behind this practice. They believed all plants, creatures, winds, mountains, rivers, lakes and all things of the earth possessed a spirit, therefore had consciousness and life. Everything was alive and aware, requiring relationships in a respectful way so as not to upset the balance.

The four values of honor, respect, reciprocity and cooperation are conducive to adaptation, survival and harmony. The Native people honored the integrity of the universe. It is a whole living being. As it is living, all things of the earth must be respected because they also have life. The Native people had the ability to communicate with all things of the universe. This is called reciprocity. From observing nature, the Alaska Native people learned that the earth and the universe are built upon the premise of cooperation. Researchers must implement these tour values to advance knowledge and expand consciousness. The constructs and understandings of the Alaska Native people must be honored for their integrity on the level of the modern scientific holographic image.

The holographic image does not lend itself to reductionism nor fragmentation. Reductionism tries to break reality into parts in order to understand the whole without realizing that the parts are merely patterns extant in a total web of relationships. The Native world views do not allow separation of its parts as each part must be understood in its relationships to all other parts of the whole. Respect for the Native people who formalized this view must be practiced. The Native people have transcended the three-dimensional, quantifying and sensory constricted studies of nature practiced by the modern world. It behooves that there be cooperation between the researcher and Native people. The researchers must forget about human superiority to things of the universe and to people considered primitive and backward. The Native people must be treated as equal human beings with powers of observation, critical analysis and a gift of intuition and the magical.

Following are some examples that make the practice of the four values difficult or impossible from the perspective of the modern world for doing research in a Native world.

The tools of mathematics have given us some ideas about patterns and forms as well as abstract and esoteric formulae that sometimes leave us confused and questioning the use to which they will be put. For example, when will the hunter need to know the exact distance across a river using trigonometric functions? However we agree with a lot of mathematical and scientific theories and concepts, such as the shortest distance between two points is a straight line; that a circle is a line that keeps falling in toward the center; that the radii in a circle are equal length; that the circle has no beginning and no end; and so forth. These are common sense ideas that indigenous people can readily subscribe to.

To the Native people there are many things in this universe that are cyclical and describe a spiral or a circle. Examples of these include the seasons, the solar system, the Native timepiece of the Big Dipper going around the North Star, the atom, the raven's path across the sky visible at certain times (part of the Milky Way spiral), an eddy in the river, a whirlwind and many other examples. In each instance there is a drawing force in the center. In the Native world view, we can think of this as the circle of life. In each Native person's life the central drawing force is the self (Fig. 1) . Down through many thousands

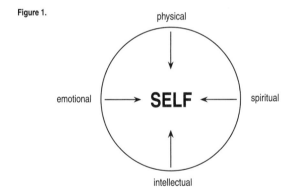

Figure 1.

of years, this is what kept the individual in balance. The energy (self) kept the values, attitudes, and traditions from being flung out. It allowed the Native individual to be constantly in communications with self, others, nature and the spirits to check on the propriety of existing characteristics of life. They knew that life is dynamic. In the process of change in the world views, many of the values have remained the same and are very applicable today.

With infringements of new people from other parts of the world, came a weakening of the self with all its strengths of what to be and how to live. At first the circle remained strong. However, with the encroachment of missionaries from various Christian religions, traders, trappers, miners and explorers came diseases unknown to the Native people. Following this came a calamity surmounting any experience that the Native people have ever had. Many elders, shamans, parents, community members and children died as a result of these unknown diseases. With the loss of so many people, especially the shamans who until this time were the healers, left the Native people questioning their own spirituality. Was it really the work of the devil and his evil allies that the Native people subscribed to and believed in as the missionaries pointed out? This dealt a crushing blow to a people who had direct access and communications with the natural and spiritual worlds through their shamans. The first rent to the circle of life was

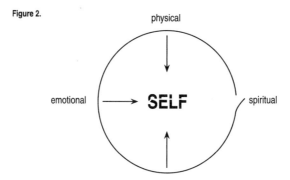

Figure 2.

in the spiritual realm (Fig. 2), and we have been suffering from a spiritual depression ever since. Alaska Native spirituality can in no way be wholly replaced by orthodox Christian religions, Eastern belief systems or other ways of knowing about a spiritual life.

Where the break occurs, one side of the curved line becomes more linear to reflect confusion. Through this break occur leaks for new ideas, values and ways of life that cause much doubt about their own world and beliefs. A maelstrom of values, beliefs and traditions result causing a confusion of what to be and what to do. The sense of self becomes weakened, thus its drawing force is weakened causing some original and traditional ideas of life to be lost. The turmoil, like that of a tornado, continues. The amalgamation of Western and other cultures from throughout the world are mixed with Native traditions. Although the Alaska Native people did not readily accept modern education and religions and gave initial resistance, breaks eventually occurred. If conditions had been different, the Alaska Native people could have controlled what was allowed into their world view. But such was not the case. The encroachment of various peoples and their cultures overwhelmed the Native people. Not only did these new people come with new ideas, but with new species of dogs, plants, domesticated animals, bacteria and viruses. This not only caused turmoil for the human beings but also caused ecological havoc. Armed with their new technological tools—hunting, trapping and fishing devices—along with the need to make money to buy these "needed" items, the newcomers battered down sacred ideas of harmony in many Native people.

The next onslaught was in the emotional realm (Fig. 3). Not feeling good about themselves because of the message being told them by the missionaries, teachers, miners, trappers, traders, federal agents and so forth, they became emotionally depressed. They had been told that their languages and cultures were primitive and had no place in the Western or modern world. The educational system was established to dissipate and destroy their languages, spirituality and cultures. The

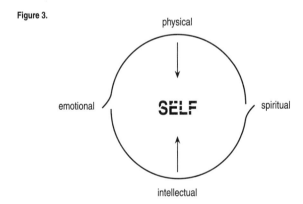

Figure 3.

physical

emotional   **SELF**   spiritual

intellectual

barrage came in many forms from institutions of the colonial hegemonic force. The once proud hunter/provider and successful homemaker now felt little worth living for in their ravaged world. There was nothing promising left to allow them to feel good about themselves, have confidence for self-governance or self-reliance. Only despair was left.

The intellectual arena was the next rupture to occur in this circle of life (Fig. 4). Rationality and empiricism coupled with intuition had been the Native peoples' forte´. Nature was their metaphysic and thus they lived in reality. They had successfully devised their world view to allow them to live life with all its difficulties but developed coping

Figure 4.

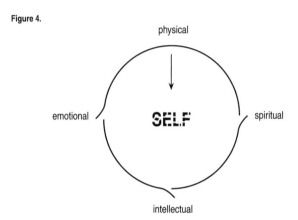

tools and skills to deal with the hard times. Now with their spirituality and emotions on a downward spiral, the people became intellectually dysfunctional. They became docile and robot-like, expecting everything to be done for them. Their original clear consciousness or awareness was now unclear, as if being viewed through a stigmatized and scarred corneal lens. Things were dim, shaded, with some channels opaque and confusion followed. A framework for assimilating new experiences no longer existed.

The last fissure occurred in the physical well-being whereby the Native people in their demoralized state became susceptible to diseases such as tuberculosis, influenza, cancer and many nutritional deficiencies and psychosocial maladies (Fig. 5). The foundations upon which a whole person was produced by the culture was now broken asunder with a new fragmented culture, a mix of many cultures represented by newcomers, producing fragmented Native youngsters susceptible to new ideas, diseases and yearnings.

The ruptures allowed some aspects of Native characteristics to flow out or become modified by allowing new fragmented ideas, ways of being, thinking, behaving and doing to seep in. This has caused much confusion among the Native people.

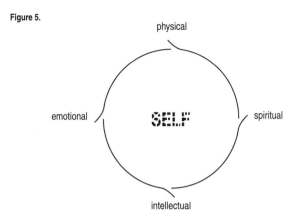

Figure 5.

The Native ways of science have always been multi-dimensional to include the human, natural and spiritual worlds. This was a conscious effort to keep in balance. Everything on earth, including earth and self, was endowed with a spirit, therefore life. And because of this spirit or energy from the Spirit of the Universe (Ellam Yua), the Native people must do things in ways that no harm nor disrespect happen to life on earth. It then required that the Native people come up with elaborate rituals and ceremonies to pay homage to all, to maintain or at times to regain balance in one's life or that of the community. They had transcended the need for quantifying and establishing laws of nature.

Much of the subject matter in the schools' curricula is one-dimensional because it is linear. The vaunted mathematical and scientific disciplines and their offspring, the technologies, are often one-dimensional. These tools have the wonderful capacity for new discoveries in other worlds but because of the Western society's need to learn to control nature they lead to confusion and a feeling of being weaned from the life force and its inherit relationships. They are bereft of the values extant in the indigenous societies which open doors for new world discoveries. Western mathematics, sciences and technologies have values, however, they are proscribed to ambition to learn in depth and greed to use this knowledge for gain. This is arrogance, a senseless and meaningless ambition, leading to the disintegration of the human experience. Through them, the more we know, the less we know about life. This says to me that Western mathematics, sciences and technologies have been superficial, never getting to the meat of things. What has been missing from the great potential of these and the other disciplines?

From all indications, nature thrives on diversity. Look at the permutations of weather during a day, month or year. Climates differ from one part of the earth to another. Flora and fauna differ from one region to another. Continents and their geography differ. No two snowflakes are exactly alike. The stars, constellations and other heavenly bodies seem to be unchanging, yet our learned astronomers tell us that many changes are taking place. According to them, novae, supernovae, black holes, stars dying and being born and so forth are happening in the universe. The science of chaos and complexity shows us a diversity of patterns we never thought existed in nature. These all point to diversity—the balance that makes nature thrive. The Alaska Native people knew this and strove for harmony with all of life.

Alaska Native people have come full circle and are seeking to heal the breeches that have put life asunder. *Seggangukut*, we are awakening, we are being energized, is what the Yupiaq say. They have nature as their metaphysic and have drawn energy from earth whereby things in times past were often quite clear and thus could be attended to or a resolution reached. One aspect of energy exchange that has often been spoken of by Native people who are ill is that of being visited by various people from the community to show care and love for the ill person. They have expressed the feeling that some people will cause the person to feel worse while another person will make the person stronger and clearer of mind. It is said that in the former case, a person who does not have the right mind or balance in life will draw energy from the ill person thereby making the ill person worse than before the visit. On the other, there will come a person who is kind, upright and is with a mind of making you better. Instead of drawing energy from the ill person, this person shares some of his/her energy with the sick person. The ailing one feels better.

Another example of energy exchange is the story of a man out on the ocean. He gets caught on an iceberg that gets cut off from shore and drifts out. He has no choice but to try to keep warm and survive the night. The next day, he finds that the iceberg is stationary but is not attached to the shore ice. New ice has formed overnight in the water between. He remembers the advice of his elders that to test the newly formed ice and its ability to hold up a person, he must raise his ice pick about two feet above the ice and let it drop. If the weight of the ice pick allows the point to penetrate but stops where it is attached to the wooden handle, he can try crossing on the ice. If, on the other hand, it does not stop at the point of intersection, then it will not hold up the man. In this case, the former happened. The man looked around him at the beauty, the might of nature, and realizing the energies that abound, he gets onto the ice. He must maintain a steady pace for if he stops or begins to run he will fall through because he has broken the rhythm and concentration. The story goes that when he began his journey across, there was a lightness and buoyancy in his mind. This feeling was conveyed to his physical being. Although the ice crackled and waved, he made it to the other side. He drew energy from nature and was in rhythm with the sea and ice and, coupled with lightness and buoyancy, made it safely to the other side.

In the another story, two youngsters come into being and they find themselves in an abandoned village. It has been some time since the people disappeared by indications from the decay of semi-subterranean houses and artifacts in the village. One possible explanation of why the people were gone might be that these Yupiaq people may have reached the apex of spirituality which is pure consciousness. Their bodies became the universe and their pair of eyes became part of Ellam iinga, the eye of the universe, the eye of awareness. This could explain how some communities became mysteriously deserted.

Western physics with its quantum and relativity theories say that we are mostly energy. Why then should not our spirit or soul be energy? Scientific technology has given proof of energy fields, personal aura, findings from near death experiences and many other human experiences. Theory of relativity tells us that matter is condensed energy and also conveys that the world is made up of relationships. Can we not then say that our spirit is made up of energy? If this is true, the Alaska Native must be able to draw energy from earth because we are a part of it. All life comes from earth. Alaska Native peoples' metaphysic as nature becomes corroborated by the Western theories. This also strengthens the argument that the laboratory for teaching and learning should be placed where one lives. Being outdoors in nature enjoying its beauty and energy, and becoming a part of it, energizes the youngsters. This could bring back the respect of personal self, and if one respects oneself then certainly one would be able to respect others, nature and the spirits that dwell in and amongst all things of nature. The students will be able to whet their observational skills while learning from nature and drawing energy to themselves. They can again attain love and care with all its concomitant values and attitudes that give life. It is imperative that the students from all walks of life begin to experience and get close to nature. There is a vast difference in learning about the tundra in the classroom and being out in it. Being in and with it the whole year round, they can experience the vicissitudes of seasons, flora, fauna, sunlight, freezing, thawing, wind, weather permutations, gaining intimate knowing about place and using their five senses and intuitions to learn about themselves and the world around them.

It is this drawing of energy from nature that will allow the self to again become strong so that the breaks in the circle of life become closed. Then the individual and community can allow chosen outside values and traditions to filter in which they think will strengthen their minds, bodies and spirits. The Alaska Native people will again become whole people and know what to be and what to do to make a life and a living. They will have reached into the profound silence of self to attain happiness and harmony in a world of their own making. *Quyana!*

A "New" Old Way of Understanding

Joe Slats

Sharing Our Pathways, Vol. 2, Issue 4, Sept/Oct 1997

During the summer of 1997, Kuskokwim Community College in Bethel offered a class entitled Education 693: Native Ecological Education. This class was taught by Yup'ik Native elder professors. The elders told the class stories illustrating old traditions, old ideas and old ways of looking at things. As Yup'ik/Cup'ik people of the 1990s, students found some of the old ways difficult to comprehend.

The here and now Y/Cup'ik people were brought up in Western schools with Western thought. When we listen to our elders speak, we listen with our Western ears and use our Western analogies to attempt to comprehend what our forefathers did. Stories told to the class by our elder professor Louise Tall, and our responses to them, are an example of how we as Y/Cup'ik people attempt to translate and comprehend these old Native thoughts and customs.

In order to understand some of the concepts and ideas behind our ancient traditions and customs, we had to try to set aside Western thought processes. We found this to be difficult. One of the ideas was that of rewards from the gratitude of orphans and elders. This gratitude is said to be strong or to have power. There is a relationship between the decisions one makes when young to help those in need and the rewards one may reap as an older person. This is the power of the gratitude of the orphans and elders one has helped in the past. The linear thinking of the Western world makes this a difficult concept to comprehend.

Another story Louise Tall told was about the idea of "pretend husband and wife." She told how some young Yup'ik males and females created a "pretend husband or wife." These young individuals would see a person entering through a window to be with them. They would begin to keep themselves clean and to look forward to the evenings with their pretend spouse. They would carry ond conversations with this "imaginary" person and not pay attention to other human beings around them. It is said that one female took off to the tundra with her non-being male mate. She was not seen or heard from again until a young bow-and-arrow hunter found her next to a lake. She had a drying rack with *telleqcaraqs* (small swimming birds) and *augtuaraqs* (red water birds) carefully skinned and drying. These birds had been caught by her pretend husband and in her mind they were loons. Therefore she had skinned them and hung them to dry.

At one time an individual used *ayuq* (Labrador tea) to *tepkegcaq* (smoke herself as perfume) prior to the evening visit of her pretend husband. The male non-being arrived and *"Ayurutaanga"* (to block the way or entrance). It was learned that smoke was to be used to block the way of non-beings. Other human beings heard the non-being say *"Ayurutaanga."*

After hearing this story, the class attempted to analyze and comprehend it. With our Western ways of thinking we concluded that perhaps the young adults in the story were suffering from some form of mental illness.

Louise also discussed shamanism through a number of stories. It became apparent that the shaman played a very important role in the lives of the Yup'ik people long ago. After the arrival of the missionaries, shamanism came to be referred to as "Satan's agent." Western thought has turned what used to be a very important tradition and religion into an unaccepted and evil practice. Here and now Y/Cup'ik people, raised with Western thought, must struggle to make sense of ancient practices and customs. In a short discussion regarding whether shamanism would ever return to the delta, it was felt that perhaps it is too big of a leap for the church community to accept. The elders within the church community are still struggling with the concept of allowing Eskimo dancing to enter their villages. The group felt that a return to some of the shamanistic ways is an important idea and that it will be too late if it must wait for the elder community to accept its reintroduction. The knowledge will be lost or kept from being handed down.

As modern day Y/Cup'ik people living in the 1990s, we have been taught Western ways of thinking and looking at things. If we are to truly understand the lives, stories, thoughts and wisdom of our elders, we must relearn the skills of hearing with Y/Cup'ik ears and seeing with Y/Cup'ik eyes.

An Alliance Between Humans and Creatures

Angayuqaq Oscar Kawagley

Sharing Our Pathways, Vol. 3, Issue 5, Nov/Dec 1998 and Vol. 4, Issue 1, Jan/Feb 1999

Paper presented to the International Circumpolar Arctic Social Science conference in Copenhagen, Denmark, June 1998

Basic philosophical questions are raised in the course of observing and questioning people with respect to notions of inquiry, explanation, technology, science and religion as they relate to particular lifeways. Accordingly, world view as discussed here will attempt to answer the questions deftly set out by Barry Lopez. Lopez refers to "metaphysics, epistemology, ethics, aesthetics and logic—which pose, in order, the following questions. What is real? What can we understand? How should we behave? What is beautiful? What are the patterns we can rely upon?" (1986:202). Added to the above list will be "ontology:" Why are we? Is there something greater than the human? Lopez goes on to point out, "The risk we take is of finding our final authority in the metaphors rather than in the land. To inquire into the intricacies of a distant landscape, then, provokes thoughts about one's own interior landscape, and the familiar landscapes of memory. The land urges us to come around to an understanding of ourselves" (247).

The concept of "worldview" is very closely related to the definitions of culture and cognitive map. A worldview consists of the principles we acquire to make sense of the world around us. These principles, including values, traditions and customs are learned by youngsters from myths, legends, stories, family, community and examples set by community leaders. The worldview, or cognitive map, is a summation of coping devices which have worked in the past, and may or may not be as effective in the present. Once a worldview has been formed, the people are then able to identify themselves as a unique people. Thus, the worldview enables its possessors to make sense of the world around them, make artifacts to fit their world, generate behavior and interpret their experiences. As with many other indigenous groups, the worldviews of the traditional Alaska Native peoples have worked well for their practitioners for thousands of years.

Native ways of knowing imply action, states of knowing that entail constant flux of doing. The universe and Mother Earth are constantly changing. If we are looking at and trying to make sense of the world in which we live, we must speak of it as an active process. So our Alaska Native words describe pieces of activity. The Native words are sound symbols garnered from nature which then lend themselves to reality defining itself. The English words used to describe nature merely define nature and supplant reality. The scientific objectivity allows looking at "things" in nature and then as commodities to be used and exploited without regard to its habitat and niche in the ecological system. The institutions of higher learning teach us to look at "things" for in-depth detailed knowledge in a fragmentary approach. It allows us to develop technology to hasten our extraction of minerals, deforestation and agriculture. We are not mindful of the carrying capacity of the land and its ability to regenerate. Our affluence as industrial nations is merely a borrowed affluence. Borrowed from countries like Ghana, Philippines, Columbia, China, and India to name a few. Our technological prowess and its concomitant concepts of growth and development and that the "whole is the sum of its parts" has brought us to the brink of disaster. I quote the following poem from Elisabeth Hermodsson:

once upon a time

we were to be pitied
we were in mortal fear
we believed in spirits, gnomes
god and other kinds of superstition
now we feel safe for we know everything
control everything
we have rational explanations
for everything
we make use of matter's minutest particle
for our purposes

and we are much to be pitied
more than ever before
never has space been closer
never has responsibility been greater
never have we known more fear
and we do not believe in good or evil powers
nor in gods and other superstitions
we believe in ourselves
and never has space been wider
and never have we had greater power
and never have we been more powerless
we believe in progress
and never has catastrophe been so close

We certainly have a totalitarian and dehumanizing technological system. And most certainly, as a Native people, we have been unable to evaluate our satisfaction with the technological gadgets and tools that have been given or forced upon us by this all consuming giant. Its technocratic society questions the maintenance of our Native languages, subsistence, ways of knowing and Native rights to an education befitting our worldviews. But it espouses, through lip service and pronouncements, multiculturalism that many of its members deem evil. I don't remember the source of the following quote but: "Too much think about white man, no more can find dream." We have become aware of the materialistic and scientific sophistry with its inherent ability to obfuscate who we are, what we are and where we are going. After this vitriolic attack, I now get to the subject of my talk.

I have enclosed a diagram which I call the tetrahedral metaphor of the Native worldview. I have drawn a circle representing the universe or circle of life. The circle represents togetherness which has no beginning and no end. On this circle are represented the human, natural and spiritual worlds. There are two-way arrows between them as well as to the worldview at the apex of the tetrahedral. These two-way arrows depict communications between all these functions to maintain balance. The Yupiat say *"Yuluni pitalkertugluni,"* "Living a life that feels just right." One has to be in constant communication with each of the processes to know that one is in balance. If the feeling is that something is wrong then one must be able to check to see what might be the cause for unease or disease. If the feeling of being just right comes instinctively and this feeling permeates your whole being,

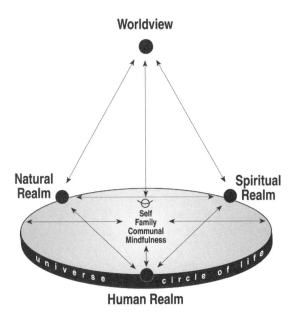

then you have attained balance. This means that one does not question the other functions intellectually, but that one merges spiritually and emotionally with the others. The circle brings all into one mind. In the Yupiat thought world, everything of Mother Earth possesses a spirit. This spirit is consciousness, an awareness. So the wind, river, rabbit, amoeba, star, lily, and so forth possess a spirit.

Thus, if all possess a spirit or soul, then all possess consciousness and the power that it gives to its physical counterpart. It allows the Native person the ability to have the aid of the spirit to do extraordinary feats of righting unbalanced individual psyche, community disease or loss of communication with the spiritual and natural world through irreverence toward beings of Nature. Grof refers to this as "power animals" (Grof, 1993) which gives its possessor the power to "communicate with them, adopting aspects of their wisdom or power and re-establishing links with them when the connection has been lost through negligence or lack of reverence, or by offending either the animal spirits or one of the greater spirits of the natural world." These are not available through Western scientific research methods but through the ancient art of shamanism. From this you can see that when we rely on Western means of research only, it is a limiting factor, and this is what our institutions of higher learning teach. All areas of social and scientific research teach only one way of trying to learn and understand phenomena. Our technological and scientific training imprison the students' minds only to its understandings, much to the detriment of the learners who enter the mainstream Western world to become its unerring members of progress and development.

The Alaska Native needed to take lives of animals to live. To give honor, respect, dignity and reciprocation to the animals whose lives were taken, the Native people conceived and put into practice many rituals and ceremonies to communicate with the animal and spiritual beings. These are corroborated through the Alaska Native mythology which are "manifestations of fundamental organizing principles that exist within the cosmos, affecting all our lives" (Grof, 1993).

It behooves the Alaska Native person to leave something behind, such as a piece of dry fish when getting mouse food from the tundra. The mouse food is gathered in the early fall so that the mouse and its family will have an opportunity to collect more food for the winter. The seal when caught is given a drink of water so that its spirit will not be thirsty when it travels to the animal spiritual kingdom. This is done to show respect to the animal for having shared and given its life to the hunter.

Medicinal plants are gathered respectfully knowing full well their power to heal and recognizing that they were given freely by Nature, thus requiring that we share these freely. The Alaska Native person is aware that if we do not use these gifts of Nature regularly, mindfully and respectfully, they will begin to diminish through disuse or misuse. The essential elements of earth, air, water, fire and spirit must always be in balance, as each has an important niche to play in the ecological system.

With this concept in mind, we must carefully examine the lifestyles and technology that is extant in this world. Our lifestyles have become materialistic and we are given to technological devices and gadgets galore that are not always geared to sustainability. Our modern cities with their complex network of buildings, transportation structures, communications systems, and commodity distribution centers are often disjointed and given to fragmentation.

Likewise, the studies of natural resources are often approached in a fragmentary way, where an expert in harbor seals may not know what the expert in herring fish has discovered in the same ecosystem. Such research has the effect of objectifying the species studied, often for commercial purposes, and contributes little to sustaining Mother Earth. However, in the Western world of science and technology there also exists many alternative approaches that are nature-friendly and sustainable. They await the time when the global societies evolve from consumerism and materialism to an orientation toward conservation and regeneration.

Perhaps, now might be a proper time to begin to use the traditional ecological knowledge of indigenous people as a "strange attractor" that can serve as a catalyst to bring meaning and understanding to the mountains of data on phenomena across a vast spectrum of possible knowledge. We need to pay heed to the warnings and recognize the consequences of the over-manipulation of Nature: wonder drugs of a generation ago are producing new resistant forms of bacteria; our aseptic hospitals are generating iatrogenic diseases; we are losing agricultural lands at a terrific pace; deforestation is accelerating; and global warming is a fact of life today.

I, as a Yupiaq, taught in a traditional and Western way, worry about my seven, grandchildren and the legacy that I will leave behind for them. Will they be able to enjoy the biological diversity and freedom that I had growing up in a traditional Yupiaq household and village? Will they experience starvation and want because the carrying capacity of the lands has been atrociously outpaced? This behooves all of us to rethink whether our objectification and commodification of natural resources has led us to the verge of catastrophe. We must strive to have the various ways of teaching and learning converge to give new direction for living, regeneration, cooperation and sharing, and thus forging a new pathway to a vision of life, liberty and the pursuit of happiness. Thank you.

References

Grof, S. (1993). *The Holotropic Mind: The three levels of human consciousness and how they shape our lives.* New York: HarperCollins Publishers.

Lopez, B. (1986). *Arctic Dreams Imagination and Desire in a Northern Landscape.* New York: Bantam Books.

Ayaprun Loddie Jones, Ayaprun Immersion School, LKSD

Collaboration in Education

Sharing Our Pathways, Vol. 4, Issue 1, Jan/Feb 1999

The following was a keynote speech given to the Alaska Native Education Council Conference, October 9, 1998.

My parents were my first teachers who taught and made me very knowledgeable of my Yup'ik culture. They collaborated in my educational upbringing, each one knowing their specific roles. My father was the head of the household—sheltering, feeding and loving all the thirteen children in the family. My mother's role was to raise the family, take care of my dad's catch and model what a mother should be. They taught me in my first language: Yup'ik. They taught me using the traditional methods where my mother was the only one who talked to us every morning about what to do and what not to do. She used the traditional discipline method but never raised her voice and my father never intruded but gave his support.

What are the discipline policies in the schools doing to our children? Those of us who were raised by our Elderly parents know that the Western schools are doing the opposite. Our children don't show a lot of respect. One reason is because we, the working mothers, had them raised by a line-up of babysitters.

To follow up on the roles my parents had, I have a story about the time that my family and I came back from a long, tiring day of berrypicking. Just before we had dinner, my mother said, *"Kitak tauna neqliurru,"* meaning get your husband's plate ready. Without thinking I responded, *"Atam ellminek piyumauq,"* "Oh, he gets his own food!" My mother got up and said, *"Takumni pingaituq,"* "Not while I'm around," and she gave a plate of food to my husband. My husband said, "See!" and he looked like he had just made the winning touchdown of a super bowl game!

In this day and age now, most women have jobs and the roles seem to be reversed.

For my teacher preparation I was trained in a field-based teacher preparation program called the Alaska Rural Teacher Training Corp. There are a lot of professionals, principals, etc. from the other culture who gave me the confidence and belief that I can be a good teacher and who believed in me. They also helped raise my self-esteem and helped me seek to improve myself.

We, the Native speakers, were trained in the Western school system. Why can't there be collaboration and have the teachers be trained in our culture and language? When the missionaries had to reach and convert their Native followers, a lot of them learned our languages.

We have to have pride in what was given to us by our parents. I once wrote that every year we are losing our most precious and important resources—our Elders. What a fine gift it would be to give the gift of our Native tongue back through our Yup'ik-speaking young people. I feel proud to be involved in the Yup'ik Immersion Program. At least this community knows the importance of retaining our language and culture.

In this day and age there are too many controversial issues facing our lives, both in our communities and schools. We must get self-esteem and pride back into our children or else we'll keep losing them to drugs, alcohol and finally suicide. Let's work together and aim for one goal—the happiness of our young people.

Traditional Yup'ik Knowledge—Lessons for All of Us

Esther Ilutsik

Sharing Our Pathways, Vol. 4, Issue 4, Sept/Oct 1999

What kinds of "experiences" and "practices" do we provide within the school setting that transfers to the real world? Are "experience" and "practice" an important element of life? Can we teach something that we have not experienced or practiced ourselves? If so, how effectively?

A Yup'ik Elder, John Pauk, a well-known *nukalpiaq* (a great hunter), shared the following information during a discussion with other Yup'ik members at a conference in Aleknagik, Alaska in January, 1999. He said, "Experiences and practices are very important parts of the learning process. Without experience and practice you will not learn how to do something better or understand it very well. You will not be able to teach and share your information with someone unless you yourself experience and practice it." He shared that observation after many years of hunting while he was looking back at some of the hunting implements he had made in his earlier years. At the time, he thought they were good. But examining them now, he found them inferior and imperfect. His many years of experience and practice were not reflected in this earlier work. He emphasized that experience and practice bring about an understanding—an educated understanding—that brings other experiences and practices together.

Why is it that when we, the Native people, bring up the idea of teaching the local indigenous culture in the school, we still hear comments like, "They should just teach it at home if they think it is so important." Many of the things we want our children to learn we, as Native parents, haven't learned. So how can we teach the cultural knowledge that we feel is important to our children when we have not been taught these things ourselves?

Many educators or even community members do not realize that, as a result of boarding schools, we have a generation of parents who have not had the opportunity to engage in activities that would make their culture more meaningful to them. They sense that it is important and know that it is something that will help their own children gain a better understanding of who they are. They see it and hear about it, but since they have not experienced and practiced it themselves, they are not able to pass it on.

Therefore we, as educators at the university and public school levels, have an added responsibility—the responsibility of educating those who missed out on these traditional learning opportunities. Those of us who have had the opportunities to be educated by our Yup'ik Elders need to pass the information on. We need to explore ways we can share this information with those who want it, but do not have the financial capacity to pay for workshops or university-sponsored classes. Many people do not have the financial capacity to pay the tuition costs or participate in a program that will once again educate them in their own cultural practices, so we need to seek other avenues.

"Here is the mouse cache . . ." L to R, Elder Henry Alakayak, Sr. of Manokotak, teacher Ina Bouher of Dillingham City Schools, Elder Helen Toyukak of Manokotak

"This is how to pull back the earth (ground)." L to R Elder Henry Alakayuk, Sr. of Manokotak, Elder Helen Toyukuk of Manokotak, and UAF student assistant Virginia Andrew of Aleknajik.

Traditional Yup'ik Learning

Let's take a look at a traditional Yup'ik learning situation. In the past, the Yup'ik people learned a lot by participating and observing. This does not imply passive observing as defined in *Webster's Dictionary* (to watch attentively), but rather immersing yourself in the activity. This could be with immediate family or extended family members or at the community level. Consider the following scenarios:

Scene 1

A young girl plays near her mother as her mother is making a squirrel parka. She is playing with her dolls. Her mother gives her some scraps of fur to make a simple piece of clothing for her doll. She tries her hand at sewing with her mother showing her how to thread, to make a knot and doing the first few stitches for her as she observes (this time the Webster definition is valid.) Then she finishes what her mother started and has her help with tying the knot.

Scene 2

The young girl is outside playing with a few older girls as well as girls her own age. They are all seated in a circle each with a *yaruin* (a story knife) and are taking turns telling a story. She watches as the other girls draw a squirrel parka detailing all the parts of the parka, sharing the stories and meaning behind each design and pattern. She also draws as she watches and listens. When it is her turn, she is helped by the other girls.

Scene 3

The young girl is with her mother and father at a gathering and observes and listens. She notices that her mother and father greet certain people as relatives. She notices that the parkas that they wear are all similar. One part of the parka stands out as the important symbol that signifies relationships. She also notices that those with the most similar designs are invited to the home as overnight guests.

Scene 4

The young girl is a little older and again sits with her mother as she sews a parka. The girl indicates to her mother that she would like to make a small parka for her doll detailing some of the family

"Here is the mouse trail."

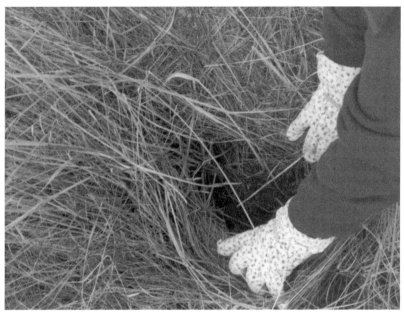

"Pull back the grass to get to the mouse cache."

patterns. The mother shares with her the most significant part of the parka design, then shows her how to make it and has her make one for her doll.

These scenes are played out over-and-over again until the young girl has reached marriageable age. She has all this knowledge, experience and practice which she brings to her early years of marriage and now, with her own family, continues the cycle.

Education and Western Influence

To what degree has traditional Yup'ik education been influenced by the Western world? Let's take a look at the following scenarios:

Scene 1

A child is playing at home near her mother. Her mother is working on a parka. But the child and mother are both distracted by the television. The child is playing with a Barbie doll or other manufactured doll. This doll doesn't need homemade clothes. All the clothes are pre-made.

Scene 2

The child is playing with other children at a preschool. They have puzzles and other toys they are playing with. They are acting out roles they see within the community: going to church, going to a birthday party or even going shopping at the local store. A teacher is sharing stories, showing the children different social skills. She has the children participate in art activities and reinforces certain types of behaviors. The teacher models the behaviors that she expects of the children.

Scene 3

The child is with her mother and father at a gathering. She observes and listens. She notices that her mother and father greet certain people as relatives. But all the people at this gathering are dressed in Western clothing. She makes an assumption that certain people are related to her based only on how her parents greet these people.

Scene 4

As the child gets older, she enrolls in the local school. Her whole day and many evenings are spent at the school. She rarely spends time at home and when she is at home, she's doing homework or watching television.

Western education and influence have taken over the responsibility for raising these children. It is no longer the mothers, parents and even peers sharing and teaching each other. It has been replaced by another method of learning. No wonder there is a "gap" between the parents and the children. Neither of the participants knows what the other is doing. The parents want their children to learn and understand certain things from their own culture, but the school is not teaching these skills.

Let's take my own personal experiences as an example. I grew up and was educated within the school setting. My parents knew that education was important for survival, but they had little idea what was being taught in school—only a vague understanding. They knew that reading, writing and mathematics were all very important. They assumed that some of the things they were doing at home were being taught at school, such as the art of cooking and preparing food. But little did they know that the food preparation that was taught had very little to do with how food was prepared in the home.

My father first came to that realization when my mother was not home to prepare food he caught. I was home when he came back from hunting with a couple of ducks in hand and asked me to prepare them for the next meal. I had, as a young girl before I started school, observed my mother and tried my hand at plucking birds, so that part was easy. But when it came to cutting up the bird, I had no prior knowledge. I may have observed, but did not have the opportunity to experience or practice it. So there I was, afraid to admit my ignorance to my father, I cut up this poor duck. I literally chopped it up to make some soup and threw the rest away. When the soup was done, my father came in to dish himself up, while I quickly made myself scarce, but within earshot. I heard him mutter under his breath, "Oh my God! What do they teach in school? This poor daughter of mine does not even know how to properly cut up a simple little bird. How will this poor creature live. She has no respect for this poor bird."

Documenting Traditional Yup'ik Knowledge

Interviewing is the most popular way of collecting and documenting traditional Yup'ik knowledge. The interview process has many different variations. For example, public school teachers have students interview Elders on subject areas that they are interested in. This process is usually teacher-directed and, most often, the information gathered is limited due to barriers in communication. University students also collect information by interviews and these again are usually teacher-directed. Depending on the interest and background of the students participating in these sessions, they usually contain more or less detailed information. There are also research groups that are comprised of Elders, professional educators and paraprofessionals who meet and gather together to document traditional knowledge. They use a form of interviewing where Elders and educators bounce information off one another. This method of interviewing brings about more detailed information which is further discussed in depth by the participants. But even this process does not take into consideration the type of information that would be collected and documented if the participants were able to actually experience it.

For example, there is an art to gathering the edible roots from bush mice. You hear about how mouse food is gathered. You learn that it is gathered during a certain part of a season. You may even have the opportunity to see it, but you have not had the opportunity to engage in this activity to see how it is done. It is like looking into another world, because when questions are asked of the Elders, they share what they know, but in many cases they forget to share significant details because they assume everyone already knows those things.

On one such occasion, we interviewed and recorded as much information as we could about edible mouse food from our Elders: what the names of the edible roots were, what they might taste like, the process used in preparing them for meals and even having the Elders attempt to draw what the roots and tubers look like. It was then decided that we should go out and gather these edible roots.

During the field trip we, the students, observed the Elders in action. They knew exactly where to go and we followed. We observed as they looked for a certain area with the types of plants that they knew the mice would cache. Then they would look into the grass. When questioned, they said, "Oh, we're looking for telltale signs of mice. You see they have little roads in the grass." So we, the learners, looked and to our amazement saw all these little highways. Then they started taking little steps and moving up and down. When questioned, they said, "Oh, we are feeling for a spongy area. If it feels spongy it might be the mouse nest or it might be the food cache." Then, when a mouse cache was found, the tools were taken out: an *uluaq*, a bag and even some bits of dried fish and crackers. The nest had to be cut in a special way so that the Elders would be able leave it as naturally as they had found it. After the edible roots were taken they were replaced with dried fish and cracker crumbs and thanks was given. In this way they shared more detailed information that was not initially evident during the interviews.

In experiencing and practicing the gathering of edible mouse food, we were able to document a great deal more information then we would have if we had just relied on the interviews. We, as educators, had acquired information that was validated by our own experience and practice. When learning passively from our Elders, we are able to bring only limited information and insights back into the classroom, but through participation in the actual field activity, the information takes on much greater validity and meaning.

Sharing Yup'ik Knowledge

As teachers and educators, we are responsible for sharing the information we gather with students who want to learn more about their culture, as well as with other individuals who are within the present school system and community. What avenues are available to share such information so that others may also benefit from this knowledge?

There are many new materials being developed for integration into the school environment that address the approaches to the teaching described above. Specific ideas and suggestions are outlined in the Alaska Standards for Culturally Responsive Schools, available through the Alaska Native Knowledge Network. One of the initiatives involves implementing "Native Ways of Knowing" into school teaching practices, including documenting traditional cultural knowledge and incorporating it into the curriculum using experiential methods. As a result of this initiative, many new materials are now being developed and integrated into the regular classroom. Schools are beginning the process of becoming grounded within the local culture.

We, as Elders, educators and teachers, are very optimistic that the educational environment within the Western schools will change so that learning will fit the needs of the students; so that the teachers coming into the area will have an understanding of and sensitivity to the local culture, so that we will begin to see some positive changes for our people and communities. One area that has been overlooked, however, is the education of the generation who are presently the parents—about their own culture and traditional roles and responsibilities in child-rearing. This is especially critical for those who had to leave home to attend a boarding school—how do we begin to bring their heritage back to them?

Collecting Knowledge Into Action

The Ciulistet Research Association, working through the Bristol Bay Campus in Dillingham, has begun to address these issues and concerns. The Native educators who make up the Ciulistet Research Association come from the two main districts within the Bristol Bay area: Dillingham City Schools and Southwest Region Schools. It was decided that one of the ways to begin to address these concerns and issues was to present public workshops. This would serve as a means of educating the public without cost to the participants. We would not only serve the needs of our people, but also people from other cultural groups. It was also decided that we would seek funding from the Alaska State Council on the Arts, which funds artist and educational workshops. Money was obtained to pay honorariums for two Elders to assist us with the workshop.

The community workshop is designed to model, as close as possible, the Ciulistet method of collecting information—that is bringing together Elders with professional educators and inviting the children and people from the general public to participate. To attract educators, the workshop is offered as a university-level course through the Bristol Bay Campus. By involving the educators, we are able to narrow the communication gap between the school and community. All of this is to be reinforced through opportunities for firsthand experience and practice in the knowledge and skills that are being shared— out where the mice make the highways in tundra.

Our vision is that the information presented at the workshop will generate interest among the parents, community members and teachers, thus creating a domino effect in education—teachers teaching the ideas and themes in the classroom, while the parents and community members share the information with their own children as well as others in the community.

It truly is an exciting time in education!

Cecilia Tacuk Martz

Never, Never, No Matter What!

Sharing Our Pathways, Vol. 4, Issue 4, Sept/Oct 1999

Kuskokwim Campus 1999 Graduation Address

Teggnerulriani—Quyana tailuci maavet ukut ilagaryarturluki gradu-ate—alriit. Quyanaqtuuci tangernaugaqavci waten quyurtaqamta.

Graduates, Regent Croft, Dean Gabrielli, faculty, staff, students, parents, friends—especially those of you who traveled to Bethel to be part of our graduation ceremony—welcome and *Quyana cakneq* for coming.

For you, the graduates, this is a special day. You will remember this day, April 30, 1999, as a significant experience in your lives. It marks what you have accomplished and completed up to this time in your life, but it does not mean that you quit accomplishing and completing other objectives you have for tomorrow, the next day, next year and five years from now. Days such as this one elicit recollections of other significant experiences from our past.

Our past experiences have made us who we are today, shaping how we think, what values we have, how we treat other people and how we view the world around us.

Certain people figure prominently in our lives—people who have had a tremendous influence on our lives—and we give those people a very special place in our hearts. One person who helped shape my perspective of other people, religions, races, regions and anything different, was a religion teacher I had when I was going to school at St. Mary's High School. We had nuns (sisters), priests, brothers and later, lay volunteers as faculty and support people. I was in junior high and we had been studying about heaven and hell—places where we go after we die. I had been told that only Catholics would go to heaven. That really bothered me for years because it went against what my dad and other relatives had taught me about judging other people. Anyway, I raised my hand (we had to raise our hands to be recognized and once recognized, we had to stand up to ask our question or say what we had to say). The nun (her name was Mother John), looked at me with a martyr's look on her face. She was probably thinking, "Oh, dear, not her again!" but she called my name. So I stood up and quickly said, "Mother, if only Catholics go to heaven, I don't want to go there." I could hear the other students' loud intake of breath and I could also imagine them thinking, "Surely, she is going to be excommunicated and she certainly is going to hell." Well, Mother John looked at me and the other students very thoughtfully and said, "Cecilia, no, that is not true." The other students again did their audible intake of breath . . . surely Mother John was also going to hell. She continued: "There are many religions in the world. All people, whether they are Baptists, Methodists, Zen Buddhists or whatever, will go to heaven if they live good lives according to how their religion and their cultures dictate." I said, "Good, then I'll go to heaven." I will never forget the lesson in tolerance she taught me. She also taught me to do my best in everything that I do—washing dishes, writing a course outline, cutting fish, making a presentation or giving a speech.

One other very influential person in my life and one who has the most space in my heart, next to my husband and children, is my father, who passed away 23 years ago. He always knew the appropriate times to say to me what he felt I needed to know. He showed me and other young people proper conduct by his actions and by pointing out the actions of others.

One morning at camp, when I woke up, he said to me, "*Tacung*, (a special name just for me from him) *anqaa* (go outside)." So I went outside and stayed out there for a while and then went back in the tent. I had no idea why he wanted me to go out. When I went back in, I had my tea with milk and fry bread. After a while, my dad asked, "Which direction is the wind blowing from?" Had I checked where the wind was blowing from? Of course not. I had just gone out like he told me to and came back in. Some time later, he again asked me to go out after I woke up in the morning. So, again I went out, and what did I make sure I did? I checked where the wind was blowing from. I went back in and had my tea and fry bread. A while later, my dad asked, "What do the clouds look like?" Oh dear, did I look at the clouds? No, I had not looked at the clouds.

Still later, he again asked me to go out in the morning before breakfast. This time what did I make sure I did? I made sure of the wind direction, made sure I could describe what the clouds looked like and I went further. I looked to see if the river tide was up or down, if the mountains looked high or low, if there was a blue reflection where the sea was, what birds were flying, what animal sounds I heard. I made sure I could answer any question my dad asked. After a while, I went in and had my tea and bread, at the same time waiting for "the question." While I was eating, my dad said, "When the clouds are stretched, the wind will pick up that day. If you see shimmering on the horizon, the ground is pushing the heat from the sun upwards. When you see what looks like fog rising from the lakes and ponds, their heat temperature is balancing with the air's."

From that day on he started teaching me about the weather in different seasons because he knew I had learned to observe my environment. To this day, I still take careful note of my surroundings and can tell, generally, what the weather is going to be like each day.

My dad was giving me scientific knowledge about our environment. In the same way, he taught me social studies by alerting me to different people's behavior. He taught me to read and write my own language. He taught me environmental biology and he kept teaching me until the time came for him to leave us. He also approved of Mike, who later became my husband.

He also gave to me what has become one of the cornerstones of my personal values, a solid foundation for who I am. When I started leaving for school at St. Mary's, one of those times, he said to me, *"Tacung,* learn as much as you can about the *Kass'aqa,* they are here to stay. Their numbers will increase over time. *Taugaam angurrluqapiareq qaneryaraput, cayararput-llu nalluyaguteryaqnaki."*

Angurrluk is a very strong word which translates roughly to "Never, never, no matter what!" or as Nita Rearden said, "Ever, ever, ever, not, not, not!" It's that strong of a word. My father said, "Never, never, no matter what, are you to forget our language, traditions, ways of doing things." (The English language sometimes is very inadequate to convey equivalent meanings.) So I follow that strong directive to this day to the best of my ability.

Many of us who are following that directive in our lives and our work, especially people of my age, are starting to retire. Those of you who follow us must take up the responsibility to ensure that our language and culture continues to thrive. Our Elders have repeatedly begged us to do so. The Yukon/Kuskokwim Delta is the heart and soul of the Yup'ik language and culture. It is imperative that you remain vigilant and outspoken so that agencies, especially the educational institutions, will continue to show us, the people they are here to serve, that the continuation of our language and culture remains one of their highest priorities. This is a heavy responsibility that should never be ignored.

There are many more people who have taught me and shaped me to what I am and affected how I think, and I thank those people from the bottom of my heart and soul. As you reflect on your own lives, think of those people who have influenced you and thank the Creator for them, and if you have the opportunity, thank them in person.

So our lives go on. We keep on accomplishing and completing. We keep on learning. We keep on believing. We keep on hoping. We keep on being sincere. We keep on thanking. Most of all, we keep on loving one another.

Angayuqaq Oscar
Kawagley and Dixie
Dayo

Revitalizing Harmony in Village and School Relationships

Sharing Our Pathways, Vol. 4, Issue 5, Nov/Dec 1999

The relationships between Alaska Native people and the schools have often been adversarial. This may be due to Alaska Natives' mistrust of the outside educational system and its practitioners. For too many years the schools did not acknowledge the different ways of knowing and ways of making sense of this world extant in the villages. Instead, another way of making a life and living was espoused by the newcomers.

After making a visit to Alaska in the 1880s, Sheldon Jackson approached the United States Congress for money to educate Alaska Native people. The money he received for this purpose was very limited so he approached religious organizations to establish schools, many of which were associated with the church-run orphanages that sprung up after the viral epidemics. In their minds they were doing God's work, with the very best of intentions. However, they were also carrying out the assimilation policies of the times, in which Alaska Native students were to lose their Native language and ways of making a living. After many years of experiencing this type of education (under both church- and government-run schools), Alaska Native people began to recognize that schooling in pursuit of the American Dream was a largely unattainable goal made up of empty promises. As a result of this bifurcation of purpose, many of the teachers who served as the purveyors of the new knowledge through the schools never became a part of the community in which they taught. This split has contributed to the debilitation of the villages to the point where many villagers have abdicated their educational responsibilities with an attitude of "Let's leave things alone, they know better." In this way, the educational system has failed Alaska Natives and, in turn, Alaska Native people have contributed to that failure. So, what can be done to overcome this legacy of adversarial relations between school and community?

In the not-too-distant past, when newcomers came into Alaska Native communities, they were welcomed as visitors and made comfortable. The Alaska Native people shared their food, homes and knowledge about the surrounding flora and fauna. They shared the arts and skills of hunting, trapping and survival in a sometimes harsh environment. They found some of the early newcomers had left behind their individualistic and competitive world in search of another way of making a life and a living—one compatible with Alaska Native peoples' inclinations. These newcomers grafted themselves to the lifeways of the community in which they settled and became a part of it. They allowed any feelings of superiority to dissipate in the wind. However, they were followed by another group of people, some of whose goals and motivation were driven by a different mindset—that of ambition and greed to gain land and take natural resources for attaining riches.

The original host-visitor relationship was broken asunder and the Alaska Native people found themselves thrust into smaller and smaller pockets of land differentiated by artificial boundaries and restrictions. This was now a conqueror and conquered relationship. The Native people found themselves struggling for survival in their own land. They found themselves subjected to new laws, values and institutions. They experienced new diseases and poverty, as well as the language, arts and skills that were now being taught to them. The Native peoples' perception of harmony in life practices which upheld the recognition that the whole can be greater than the sum of its parts was disrupted. This is a sad commentary for a people who were once self-sufficient and practiced a spirituality that edified this harmonious way of life and making a living.

More than a century has elapsed and it is time to reexamine the relationship between community and school in rural Alaska. This recognition was brought about by a recent trip to New Zealand of Alaska Native educators and our subsequent participation in the World Indigenous Peoples Conference on Education (WIPCE) held in Hilo, Hawaii. At every Maori *marae* (meeting house) that we visited in New Zealand, the protocol of welcoming the visitors was performed. On the first day of WIPCE, the Hawaiian people performed a traditional welcoming ceremony for the 2000 guests who came to the Islands to attend the conference. All of these were awe-inspiring experiences that engendered a feeling of being a part of the host community and confidence in knowing what would be expected of you as a visitor.

The Maori *marae* and many of the Hawaiian settlements have become bastions of indigenous spirituality, philosophy, identity, language and values. Because these ceremonies are so steeped in spirituality, there is a feeling of respect for place, people and all that they have and stand for. These are places where real teaching and learning can take place because they are working for the good of the community with spirit and feeling.

Why don't Alaska's villages do the same for incoming administrators and teachers? It is time we take the initiative and get involved in providing a more holistic education for our children. This can only happen when we change the adversarial relationship between the village and school. We must realize that we cannot expect the school to raise our children. This has been happening for too long and the result has been a school that is too often a battleground between teachers and students, as well as with the parents and villagers. The time is ripe for putting the statement, "It takes a whole village to raise a child" into practice. Let us briefly suggest how a process like this might begin. It is up to each of you to do the rest.

No matter where Alaska Native people come from, they have had a way of welcoming the *allanret*—the visitors. We should revive these practices, starting with welcoming the principals and teachers who come to the village to help in the education of the children. They are with us the greater part of the year and spend much of their waking hours with our children. So it is only fair that we make them feel welcome. These welcoming ceremonies must include local speech makers. The Alaska Native speakers should include (in general terms) what is expected of the administrators and the teachers. The principal and teachers can respond by briefly stating what their philosophy of education is, what and how they meet the expectations of the villagers and to ask where they may need help themselves. It is important that everyone come to mutual terms on what can be done to improve the education of the village children.

The same appreciation should be accorded those Native educators who have chosen to obtain a higher education to acquire a teaching certificate. Those who return to the village should be treated with a similar welcome, in a manner that is well endowed with love, care and nurturing to help them become successful teachers. There should be no expressions of jealousy or alienation shown toward these individuals. Villagers should allow the spirit to act as the mediator to elevate these Alaska Native people who have taken the risk of failure, suffered through times of depression or bewilderment, confronted insensitive administrators and faculty and experienced financial hardship to gain access to the profession of teaching. Alaska Native educators have a willingness to excel and they know the village situation well—thereby earning our support.

These acts of harmony and compassion contribute to the healing process on all sides. Villagers need to participate in board meetings to clarify any questions that arise, let the participants know what is being accomplished to meet village expectations and what needs further work. This must be done with honesty and in accord with Alaska Native values. Compassion, cooperation and teamwork have always been the hallmark of Alaska Native hospitality. This must be resurrected to function as an organism with all its parts working together for the good of the whole village. It is admirable to note that this is already being done in some villages. This is where synergy really begins to kick in with each part working for the good of the community and thus making it stronger than its individual parts. The ways of Alaska Native people may become the model for the future. *Tuaii, piurci.*

Nita Rearden,
Lower Kuskokwim
School District

Gathering the Resources

Sharing Our Pathways, Vol. 5, Issue 1, Jan/Feb 2000

The following is a speech that was given during the Alaska Native Education Council (ANEC) conference in Anchorage on Oct. 18, 1999. Certain areas were revised for the reader to understand from a readers point of view. This speech was made for a listener. Quyana naaqluqu.

Some of you will remember when our parents, grandparents or great grandparents saved practically everything. They saved items like canvas, flour and sugar sacks, Crisco and coffee cans, Blazo boxes and kerosene cans, and different types of glass bottles. Each item was recycled in such a way that nothing was wasted. For instance, Blazo boxes were used for cupboards or storage containers; flour and sugar sacks were used for dish towels, diapers or even undergarments if mothers sewed; empty cans were used for kitchen and tool containers or dog dishes; gallon Blazo cans were used for seal-oil containers or other purposes.

I remember one time I was traveling to Fairbanks after the holidays with a Blazo can full of seal oil in my hand. My mother recycled every resource material she could. At the Anchorage airport, when I walked through the line to get on the jet, a security officer stopped me and told me I could not take the Blazo on board. I answered her that it wasn't Blazo, but the content was seal oil. She didn't believe me and said she would have to check it. Oh boy! I mentioned to her the contents would make the airport smell. She went ahead and opened it anyway. The truth did come; she wrinkled her nose and the people behind me smiled and my friends laughed.

Do you remember as a child all of the materials we collected that were considered trash but we used as toys? We gathered cans for our play dishes or parts of clothing. We put cans on our shoes to look like we were wearing high heels. We used grass and wooden sticks for dolls because we could not take our nice homemade dolls outside. We used willow branches for bows, slings and arrows to hunt pretend grass seals. We collected pebbles for play bullets, marbles or food. We used sticks for storyknifes when we were not allowed to take out the beautiful decorated, ivory storyknifes. We made do with whatever we could create in order to play and pretend. All of what we did was good! We were using hands-on experiences in the content areas of science, social studies and language arts. Today we find our own little people would rather watch TV, play Nintendo or sports instead of utilizing natural resources. Parents found out that these distractions are convenient for babysitting but don't realize the harmful effects.

Our respectful ancestors taught us to collect resources from nature such as animal skins for clothing, plants for food and medicine and grass, tree barks and roots used for dishes or for water and berry buckets. When we collected these items, we learned skills such as sewing, taking care of animals, hunting and more. Our background dealing with these resources has made us strong Alaska Native people! Our resources are real! When a person is connected to either land, religion, home, culture or school, the person has an anchor to their identity. Today we gather some of these same materials for beautiful Native arts and crafts to sell or make gifts for someone special. Money has become an important part of our gathering. So many resources are available from the stores, we see many items wasted whether it is food, household items or other materials. Most everything ends up in the dump!

As an educator we still gather resources. They aren't necessarily the resources our ancestors taught us about but they are necessities for classroom use as books, textbooks and writing supplies. Teachers gather resource materials to help them become better teachers in order to meet the needs of their students. Many educators today are researchers. We search to gather information especially if we believe what we worked for is the right thing. For instance, in my job, I look for research on bilingual materials in order for parents in our district to understand that speaking two languages is better than being able to communicate in only one. Research shows that as adults, being able to communicate in two languages helps us to be better problem solvers.

When I was thinking about what topics I could talk about for this conference, I thought of many issues, issues such as the English-only law, the new bilingual law, subsistence, loss of languages, benchmark testing, high school graduation qualifying exams and quality schools—all of which are issues that affect us. I thought of how I could discuss these matters, but you know what? Without the background knowledge we have gained from a resourceful childhood, we would not be able to deal with any of these issues.

Just recently a teacher from Atmautluak and I were discussing how children learn. She told me about an interesting moment she had with her father when she became a teacher. He told her that a child is like a tree acquiring many branches. The branches of the child increase as he learns new concepts. New branches continue to grow when they are utilized well. Sometimes branches stop growing when a person drops his cultural background. From this I learned we can discuss issues and link them to our cultural background. It is important that our children know how to utilize their cultural resources!

This year it seems like we have very strong issues to deal with. I think the Alaska Native Educators' Conference is an important place to begin. Communication and understanding of the issues is important to allow us all to grow another branch. Let's continue to gather our resources to help one another and our children. *Quyana qanemcivqarlua.*

Angayuqaq Oscar
Kawagley | # Identity Creating Camps

Sharing Our Pathways, Vol. 5, Issue 2, Mar/Apr 2000

There is a crying need for healing among Alaska Native people and an essential element of the healing process is the need to retain our unique Alaska Native identities. This is best done through the use of the Native language because it thrusts us into the thought world of our ancestors and their ways of comprehending the world. With the use of the Native language, we begin to appreciate the richness and complexity of our traditional philosophical and spiritual world views. It is for these reasons that we need to pay more attention to how we can draw upon our Alaska Native languages to serve as the foundation for the various science and cultural camps that we sponsor. To gain the full expression of our languages, identity and way of life, the camps must also take place in all the seasons of the year with the Elders being the prime movers. Their description of traditional activities through the local language best conveys the relationships between a Alaska Native concept and its practice.

The following are a few suggestions on how we might approach and design camps for different purposes. Three types of Native cultural camps are described and each may be revised and adapted to suit the local situation and needs.

Cultural Immersion Camp

These camps are for students who have a good command of the Native language or dialect in a particular region and thus can be immersed on all aspects of the local culture.

1. All activities are done utilizing the Native language only and the focus is on in-depth learning of the things one needs to know to make a life and a living.

2. All planning and implementation includes local Native Elders and other knowledgeable Native people explaining what and why things are done the way they are for cultural adaptability and survival. This can include the following topics:

   a. Use of and relationship to plants and animals: times for harvesting; how and why certain rules are followed to ensure continuation of species; explain the traditional preparation and preservation techniques; how does the process contribute to natural diversity and cultural adaptability?

   b. Medicinal plants: their use and how they have been preordained by Ellam Yua (Spirit of the Universe) to have power to heal certain diseases; harvesting process-preparation and preservation; how to use them, being mindful of the physical, mental, emotional and spiritual inclinations of the person being treated; how do they contribute to natural diversity and cultural adaptability?

   c. Explore the nature-mediated technology of the Alaska Native people: materials; preparation methods; explanations of why certain parts of materials are used; how the idea for the technology came about; functioning of the various parts; use and care of the item; does it utilize refined or unrefined natural resources and why; is it biodegradable; what are its spiritual aspects; how does it contribute to natural diversity and cultural sustainability and adaptability?

   d. Explore the natural sense-makers of nature for weather, seasons, flora and fauna.

   e. Discuss time and its measurement.

   f. Navigation techniques: finding direction using nature and celestial objects.

3. Use song, dance and drumming for transmission of culture, especially its spiritual aspect; develop a realization that everything a Native person does is a form of prayer and paying

homage to Ellam Yua (or whatever name a tribe has for the Creator.)

4. Use mythology and stories for value-creation and teaching what it means to be human; the entire experience should be value-creating and give a cultural orientation, an identity.
5. Live off the land as much as possible, using traditional techniques and technology.
6. The scheduling must be flexible and determined by the Elders to do things when it feels right.

Language Development Camp

This camp is for students who have little or no understanding of the Native language or have little or no speaking ability. Thus the focus is on learning the language itself in a setting where it has inherent meaning.

The process is best determined on a day-by-day basis by the Elders and teachers, but it could range from full immersion as outlined above, to gradual immersion starting with the Native language being used with English interpretations, then progressing to an hour or two in which only the Native language is used. In either case, the goal would be to have the last week be all in the Native language. Otherwise, all of the suggestions outlined for immersion camps would apply.

Bridging Science Camp

Same as above but incorporating aspects of a Eurocentric viewpoint. The bridging camp should include not only the Native language and cultural practices, but also the Eurocentric scientific concepts and practices.

Most of the activities outlined above apply, but with the addition of a comparative perspective. All activities are coordinated to best achieve understanding. The traditional activities are not separate activities from Eurocentric mathematics and sciences, but are planned to be compatible and complementary with one another.

1. Identify some of the most used Eurocentric scientific terms and coin corresponding Native words with help from Elders and students.

2. When using Eurocentric science knowledge, concepts or theories, explore how they may add to or detract from one's Nativeness.

3. Examine whether the Eurocentric knowledge is useful and applicable in the place you are situated or is it extraneous knowledge in that context. When and where is it useful?

4. Use traditional estimation and intuitive measurement techniques; explore recognition of pattern and symmetry without mathematical equations to confuse the issue—the universe is not all numbers.

5. Use computers and other technological tools sparingly; explore the implications of the statement, "our memories are becoming obsolete."

6. How does adding Eurocentric knowledge to the traditional ways of knowing enhance or detract from natural diversity and cultural adaptability?

7. Examine ways in which technological tools may add to environmental and mental pollution.

8. Examine ways in which the camp activities foster values of cooperation and harmony or competition and individualism.

9. The camp planners and implementers should always have the local list of Native values in front of them for guidance in determining what to include from the modern world.

The bridging science camps are intended to incorporate the Eurocentric mathematics and scientific concepts along with the local knowledge base of the Elders. All daily activities should be coordinated to effectively and efficiently teach and validate both thought worlds. The students should gain a keen understanding of Eurocentric scientific research since many of the findings corroborate Native observations and have helped to identify globally-stressed arenas that explain why Mother Earth is suffering. This makes it absolutely necessary that students learn Eurocentric concepts as well as their own ways of recognizing patterns, utilizing symbols, employing estimation and intuitive measurement and developing a keen observation of place.

The Native students have to realize that our ways of knowing are identity-building processes. They can then pursue careers in mathematics and the sciences buttressed with a nature-mediated world view giving them a kind and polite disposition to the world in which they live.

Esther Arnaq Ilutsik

Developing Culturally-Responsive Curriculum

Sharing Our Pathways, Vol. 5, Issue 3, Summer 2000

Keynote address presented at the Bilingual/Multicultural Education Conference February 4, 2000

Greetings to the first Bilingual/Multicultural Education/ Equity Conference of the 21st century. I am honored and humbled to be standing before you—honored that I have been asked to speak and bring forth issues that need to be addressed by all of us as we enter the 21st century, and humbled by the great expertise that is assembled in this room. I will begin with an oral story, as is the tradition of the Yup'ik people, told and shared by my late mother Lena P. Ilutsik. She begins:

> And then there was this blackfish swimming up the river, maybe he was heading down the river. As he was going along he came to this fish trap. Well, he got inside and he probably had others with him. While they were trapped inside of the fish trap, they heard a person coming up on top. Well, when he got to them he pulled them up. Well, he poured those blackfish into his pack. Then that person said, "Oh my, one of these blackfish is so big! What a big blackfish." Well, he brought them home. He packed them and brought them home. When he got home he told his wife to cook the blackfish. He wanted to eat that big blackfish. Well, she cooked and she cooked them. When they were cooked that man apparently

ate that blackfish, the one he was praising. Well, he (the blackfish) got inside of that man, he was still conscious even if he was cooked. Well, he was inside the man, and when he got tired of being in there he went out of the man. Well, that man passed him. It was during the time when outhouses had not been introduced to the people yet. And people just used to go on the ground. Well, that man passed him and the blackfish who was still conscious just stayed in the man's feces. Then as he was staying there this dog started coming toward him. Well, that dog ate him. Well, he stayed inside of that dog. Then by and by when he wanted to go out that blackfish went out. Well, when he went out he stayed there in the dog's feces. As he was laying there he saw a person walking toward him. Well, when that person got to him and when he stepped on him he lost consciousness, Well, this is as far as the story I heard went.

(translated by Virginia Andrew, 4/16/97)

Why do I begin with a story? As a Yup'ik, as an educator, as a parent and as a lifelong learner, I find myself a part of a cultural group and a world in transition. Some of us have found ways to retain some of our oral stories and we do this by providing a theme story for the curriculum units that are developed and integrated into the school system. We, as educators, need to demonstrate by example. If we believe in something we need to demonstrate that we can also utilize the model and method of approach in our own teaching method. Addressing a group of people and sharing our knowledge and ideas is a method of teaching. Too often we hear potentially unique and aspiring methods but they are not utilized by the messenger.

We need to share the approach that we are using within the classrooms. This is the theme of my presentation to you. I will be referring to it during the remainder of my talk. In the meantime, think about why would a mother share the blackfish story with her children? Remember, within the Yup'ik culture, as with many other indigenous cultures, stories were told without being analyzed. They were told so that the listener would have his or her own interpretations, so that at some point in his or her life the story would surface and meaning would become clear—that is why the story was shared with me.

One of the blessings of parenthood is that it makes us reflect back on our own educational experiences, both at home and in the school setting. We, as parents, are concerned about the education that our children will receive. We want the best for our children. We want to make sure that they have a good foundation—a good understanding of who they are and where they fit into this world that is being presented to them. Far too many of us remember ourselves as the "invisible" people with an aspiration to adopt the dominant culture's model.

Remember the reading series, Dick and Jane and their dog Spot? What did it show us? It provided an ideal American, Caucasian family living in suburban America—a mind set laid down subtly showing us that our little humble dwellings did not fit the ideal that American education was after. It brings to mind the man who desired the largest blackfish in the fish trap. The desire was so great that all the other blackfish were invisible. We too have looked at the ideals that were portrayed in the schools, in the textbooks, and other materials as the big blackfish and all other aspects of our life became invisible—our traditional foods, our stories, our dances, etc. Our desire was to consume and become like the big blackfish. Fortunately at some point in our life, we expelled the big blackfish. We became disillusioned,

Left: Michael Filipek listens to his heart as part of the Heartbeat unit. Right: Alex Lopez practices his storyknife skills. Photos by Esther Arnaq Ilutsik.

confused and disoriented with what we had desired. Like the man in the story, we expelled this blackfish from our body and mind, but unfortunately the blackfish still did not lose consciousness. We still find ourselves being drawn everyday to adopt another life form.

Parenthood makes us bold and inquiring of what is being taught and emphasized in the school setting. We begin some innocent investigating. On the surface, the curriculum looks promising, but investigating further we find that certain textbooks, including the ones for the "core" curriculum adopted by the district and used by the teachers, haven't really changed that much since the Dick and Jane series. Now, instead of a dog named Spot, we have a dog named Bingo. Although animals from our environment may be portrayed, they are often presented with misleading information. One can wonder how our Elders would have presented this information. What would be their focus and would the information be presented in a culturally and locally relevant way? Actually, I was shocked to find that none of the stories contained in one of the current reading series portrayed any of the North American indigenous peoples. There were tales from Japan, China and even Africa, but nothing from the indigenous peoples of North America. Again, we have become the invisible people.

Our children can be portrayed as the dog desiring the feces of the man (the fantasy culture), with their own cultural identity again being invisible. Sure, the bilingual education and other federal programs that are offered are supposed to address this need for identity and equity, but they do so at a cost. Our children often go to these classes with reluctance, and the teachers that are hired for these positions are often paraprofessionals who are allowed only 30 minutes or less for instruction. Many of these teachers have very little training, if any, and most have to create their own materials that are often looked upon as second-rate in comparison to the flashy, colorful textbooks and materials that are being used by the primarily non-Native certified teachers. We, as the parents, want these types of attitudes expelled, much like the blackfish expelled by the dog, so that we can stamp out the undesirable and give our children the opportunity to start afresh with a new consciousness and a positive attitude about themselves.

Some of us parents have taken it upon ourselves to make those changes. After attempting to go through the administration to make changes, we realized that this would require many, many years of re-education and re-direction, while our children are in school now and need that foundation to set the stage for their future education. How do I as a parent make sure that my child receives the strong foundation that I so desire? As an educator, I always welcomed parent involvement, so that would be the key to getting into the classroom and influencing the teacher. I was in a fortunate stage in my life when I was between jobs and had time to enter the classroom. I was also fortunate to have been able to select the teacher that I wanted for my child. This teacher, Ina Bouker, happened to be a colleague, a member of the Ciulistet Research Group, a friend and most importantly, a relative who shared my vision of taking the Yup'ik knowledge of our Elders and bringing it into the regular classroom. We wanted to achieve integration in the true sense, not integration with 30 minutes of Yup'ik instruction three times a week, but on a daily basis through the regular certified teacher. In this way, it could truly elevate the status of the local culture.

One of the first units we tackled was the "Heartbeat Unit." This stemmed from a Ciulistet Research Group meeting that was hosted up in Aleknagik where the discussion focused on Yup'ik dancing. How do we take this information and bring it into the regular classroom? Ina Bouker had this brilliant idea of integrating this information into the health strand of the school district curriculum. The heart would be the focal point. The heartbeat would connect well with the beat of the Yup'ik drum—the beat of life. The three main Yup'ik colors (red, black & white) naturally became a part of the study with basic patterns introduced and emphasized while the Yup'ik dancing and the stories they tell provided the natural flow. Legends of the Yup'ik people were shared and told through the Sonor games (a board game adapted from the Yakutsk-Sakha, the indigenous people of the Russian Far East). What a wonderful and truly memorable experience for my daughter and her classmates. In fact she still talks about the experience she received in second grade (she is now in the seventh grade) and it was not too long ago when I was at the local grocery store during "the rush" when I heard a voice, "Esther, where have you been?" I followed my eyes to the voice and saw one of my daughters former classmates. He continued, "Why are you not coming to our classes anymore? I really miss you."

I was fortunate to get a job with the Alaska Rural Systemic Initiative through the University of Alaska Fairbanks/Bristol Bay Campus where I have been able to continue with the curriculum process we started with the heartbeat unit. I followed my child and made sure that at least one of the units taught in her classroom focused on the local culture. In the third grade we focused on the Yup'ik fancy squirrel parka with an emphasis on patterns and the history of the Yup'ik people. At the fourth-grade level we completed the patterns on the parka integrating it into the math strand and at the fifth-grade level we looked into Yup'ik basketry.

But the most important thing is that I continued to work with Ina Bouker and her students. Here we integrated many different units of study into her classroom. All the knowledge that we shared within the classroom was information that our Elders shared with us in our Ciulislet Research meetings. It was like we were finally learning things about our culture that we had missed when we went to school and now were learning them and were able to share this information with the next generation. It reminded me of what Moses went through in the Bible. Most of you know the story about Moses, how he was found floating in a basket on the Nile River by the pharaoh's daughter and was educated in the finest institutions in the then-known world. Eventually, when he was called to take his people into the wilderness, he spent another 40 years literally uneducating himself from his previous training. So it is with many indigenous peoples around the world and in North America. We have been sent to schools and literally educated out of our culture. The results have been truly devastating to many of our people, but some have miraculously succeeded and are now realizing that the knowledge of our Elders and our people is important and that this knowledge base must be taught to the future generations.

The documentation of this knowledge base must be authored by our own people. We cannot continue to rely on outside experts—professional people with prestigious degrees—to come in and study our culture and write about how we should integrate this information into the school system (even if it is reviewed and acknowledged by indigenous educators.) We need to do it ourselves—we need to demonstrate to the world that we have come to a point where the information provided is authentic and is based on interpretations by local indigenous people. We cannot continue to accept information written by a person "looking in." We cannot continue to read information that was obviously written by a person from another cultural perspective. We cannot continue to serve in the role of providing corrections and apologies.

We are entering an era where we, as indigenous educators, have to author our own materials with confidence in our own abilities. We can strengthen our role by getting the *Alaska Standards for Culturally-Responsive Schools* to be addressed by the local schools as well as through the Alaska Department of Education and Early Development. With commitment and determination, we are able to gather the knowledge of our Elders and bring it into the classrooms. We are able to author our own materials, test them in the classrooms and develop them into resources that will be available for other educators.

In conclusion, we have arrived at a point where we are slowly beginning to expel all the misinformation that has plagued and stereotyped us in the past. We are, by demonstration, showing the world that our cultural knowledge can be portrayed in a positive light by our own people. With this foundation we will be able to enter the 21st century with confidence—confidence that our cultural identity will play an important role in laying a solid foundation down for our descendants. Our descendants will fill those leadership roles that require an understanding and respect of themselves and other cultural groups. We will once again become whole—a complete person—that is the ultimate goal of the Yup'ik people.

Angayuqaq Oscar
Kawagley

How Does the Crane Keep Its Language?

Sharing Our Pathways, Vol. 5, Issue 5, Nov/Dec 2000

When I was a little bitty baby, my momma would rock me in the cradle, in them old tundra hills back home," and as I rocked I would hear the voices of my ancestors just as the crane chicks in their nest hear the mother crane making its call.

I don't know if the crane has the DNA to make its own distinctive call or if it learns it from its mother and other members of its own kind, but it does learn to speak the crane language. Baby cranes do not make a call like that of a seagull's raucous, squalling sound or like any other member of the bird family. Each species has its own distinct call—a language readily identifiable as its own—and all those unique languages continue to be passed on from one generation to the next.

As Native people, we too have our own unique languages which have been passed on from one generation to the next for many millennia. So why are we losing our Native languages so rapidly? Could it be because we, as parents, grandparents and villagers, do not speak to our children in our own Native language anymore? Why is it that we do not speak to them in our languages? One of the reasons is that our primary language has become English, which is a voracious language that eats up our Native languages. Perhaps this is brought about as a result of the remembrance of some Elders and parents of the shaming, abuse and punishment they received in school for speaking their own Native language. We must begin to freely talk about such experiences and the hurt feelings and shame so the healing process can begin.

So what must we do to keep from losing our Native languages? For one thing, we can look at other indigenous people who have been successful in re-enlivening and revitalizing their languages. We can take a look at the Maori language nests or the Native Hawaiians' programs and then put into practice that which is proving to work. We must consult with our Elders to see what we, as Native people, need to do to save our Native languages. This is a very tough and complicated charge for those of us engaged in teaching, research and role modeling. Head Start teachers, parents, Elders and villagers have the grave responsibility of teaching our Native youngsters their Native language. After all, they are our future.

Why teach our Native languages that are often looked upon by the modern world as useless, nontechnical and incapable of conveying profound meaning and concepts? As Alaska Native people we need to convince ourselves and our young ones that our Native languages are important and can convey deep meaning and complex thinking. As I have said in the past, using our Native languages thrusts us into the thought world of our ancestors. We can talk about our traditional hunting and gathering ways and sophisticated technology by using our Native languages. For example, our Yupiaq word, *pinaa*, which means "his, her or its strength," can mean physical strength of a person, of a bow, of the *oogruk* skin covering the *qayaq* or of water. It can mean intellectual prowess of a person, place or thing. It can mean emotional or spiritual strength and stability, all depending on the context in which it is used. Or take *qalluq*, our word for rolling thunder or electrical discharge. It is now our word for electricity. Who says our Native languages are not technical? They can be very technical and profoundly spiritual at the same time. Don't ever believe anyone who puts forward such feeble reasons for encouraging us to lose our Native languages. Manu Meyer, a Native Hawaiian, puts it this way: "We practice abstract thinking, but it is tied to purpose and a meaningful existence." We—ourselves and our youngsters—need to learn and understand this important philosophical thought.

There are other reasons why we should not lose our Native languages. They allow us to articulate spiritually and emotionally and convey the deeper meanings of life. Richard Littlebear of Montana has pointed out that our languages allow our people to articulate the subtle attributes and meaning associated with self-governance, law and order, jurisprudence, literature, a land base, spirituality and sacred practices. We, as well as the rest of the world, cannot afford to diminish the diversity of cultures. To have but one language and one culture in this world would be boring indeed and would put our very existence as a species at greater risk.

The most important part of growing up is when children are developing a beginning understanding of their language, culture and place. However, human beings do not have a built-in mechanism for learning a particular language. Unlike the crane, Native children have no such genes in their genotype, so they have to listen, imitate and learn to utter the sounds found in their own languages. It is like having to learn English, German, Russian or any other language—they have to work at it. The children have to be talked to in their own language during play, so they can imitate, mimic things and ask a lot of questions. They have an acute curiosity to learn during their early lives. We must encourage this attribute by doings things that they can learn from in association with their families, friends and communities. By doing things that are important to their families and communities, their curiosity and willingness to learn will never diminish. In the school, however, they are often learning about things that are foreign to them and find no application in the surrounding community so that by the time they get into the fifth and sixth grades, their inborn curiosity to learn has been leached out of their minds. Sad, but true. We have too many dropouts from high school and others who drop out intellectually and emotionally long before they enter high school.

I have a problem when history is written by an outsider, especially when it deals with Alaska or Alaska Native history, because it is often just one interpretation, usually from a limited perspective. You know where our history is found? It is in our *quliraat* (mythology) and *qalumciit* (stories). So invite the Elders to come into the classroom to tell the stories in their own language. You will find that the values and those qualities that make us a strong people are embedded in our Native words and stories. The youngsters will begin to understand and yearn *yulunii pitallqertugluni*—being a person who is living a life that feels just right. Alaska Native mythology contains the power and wisdom for guiding us in making a life and a living that feels just right. Alaska Native languages enable us to show proper respect and express courtesy for all elements of Mother Earth.

Another important language activity is to arrange for the Elders to teach the youngsters singing, dancing and drumming. In doing so, the children will become acquainted with the technical words ascribed to rituals, ceremonies and sacred practices. By learning the songs, they will begin to cultivate an identity and connection to place. As hunter-gatherers, we had no need for written history because our history was embedded in place, stories, songs, dances and movement from place to place according to the seasons.

The youngsters should be brought outdoors to begin to appreciate and experience the beauty of nature such as the caterpillar, chamomile and tree. They must be taught that we are connected to everything. The caterpillar eats vegetation, turning it into excrement which is useful to the tree. It gives off carbon dioxide which is also used by the tree. The tree provides a home and food for the caterpillar and gives off oxygen which is used by the caterpillar. As shown by the abbreviated cycles above, everything must go somewhere. Everything that is done in nature is done for some purpose.

Human beings cannot have everything that we want. We must learn to live with limited needs. We must learn to respect and be satisfied with what we have. Life is the greatest gift that we have and we must nurture that which makes life meaningful. Most importantly in that regard, we must maintain our languages because language, more than anything else, shapes who we are, just as it does for the crane. By maintaining our languages, we are sustaining the ultimate standard of health and endurance of the human species.

Qelakun Wall' Qetegkun?

Cecilia Tacuk Martz

Sharing Our Pathways, Vol. 6, Issue 1, Jan/Feb 2001

Keynote address presented at the Bilingual/Multicultural Education Conference, February 3, 2000

This year's conference theme, "Honoring the Past, Celebrating the Present, Creating the Future," brought to mind an incident that happened at home with my children. They were pretty young and like all young Catholics, they were attending catechism classes. One night at dinner, I wanted to find out if they were learning what I had learned during my catechism days, so I asked them:

"What do you have to do to get to heaven?"

I was expecting them to answer that they had to be good, live in harmony with other people and perform Christian duties. One of my kids gave me a look that implied I should already know the answer to that question, so I asked again:

"What do you have to do to get to heaven?"

Finally, one of the kids said, "Mom, you have to die!"

Trying to hide my smile, and still trying to get the answer that I wanted, I tried again:

"But how do you get to heaven?"

The same kid, this time with a quizzical look, answered, "By heaven plane?"

Often as parents, teachers, colleagues, friends and relatives, we don't realize that what we do or say to others can have unexpected results, just as my children gave me a totally unexpected answer to my question about heaven.

Sometimes we may believe that what we are doing or saying is positive, but we need to stop and think. We need to put ourselves in other people's places and minds and ask ourselves what unanticipated consequences may come from our words, deeds or ideas.

For instance there's a phrase that, on the surface, sounds like a positive, even inspiring, slogan to guide indigenous peoples along the path to success in the modern world. To achieve success, we are encouraged to "walk in two worlds."

I've thought long and hard about that phrase, "walking in two worlds."

During the summer of 1998 I had the privilege of serving as one of the faculty for the Island Institute's Sitka Symposium. During my week there I reflected more deeply on the concept of "walking in two worlds," and since the symposium encourages writing, critical thinking and debate, I wrote down my reflections. I'd like to share those thoughts with you now.

Not In Two Worlds, But One

A number of years ago the phrase "to walk in two worlds" arrived in Alaska and took root. It was uttered in speeches, written about in books and articles, discussed at conferences and in conversations among educators, social scientists and students. It became a slogan seen and heard in classrooms, on radio and television and on posters. Who was it directed at? Mostly it was used in reference to Yup'iit/ Cupiit, Athabascan, Tlingit, Aleut, Iñupiat, Tsimshian and Haida. Many kass'aqs embraced the phrase and its seemingly positive meaning. Of course, it wasn't necessary for them to "walk in two worlds," only for Alaska's First Peoples. Oh, what a wonderful concept and everyone, it seemed, thought so.

There was a certain Yup'ik person who thought about this phrase, "walking in two worlds." She mulled it over, discussed it with trusted friends and concluded that it was physically impossible to walk in two worlds. She looked for an opportunity to share her thoughts with a few prominent First People to see if they had arrived at the same conclusion. She wanted to do this discreetly because, at the time, her conclusion seemed to be politically incorrect.

An opportunity came when this Yup'ik person was invited to speak at a Canadian conference on education. On the second day of the conference, as this Yup'ik was walking with two prominent Canadian First People educators, she hesitantly asked them, "Do you know the phrase "walking in two worlds?" When they answered yes, she carefully said, "You know, I really never liked that phrase." One of the others replied in relief, "Me, too!" The Yup'ik asked, "Would you like to see what it looks like to walk in two worlds?" The other two looked at her with puzzlement and said, "Sure." So the Yup'ik walked in front of them to demonstrate. The other two immediately burst into hearty laughter. A passerby saw the action and appeared to be thinking, "crazy Natives" (it showed on her face.)

After the laughter subsided, the Yup'ik asked, "A person who walks like that, what does it remind you of?" The other two started laughing again and after they finally quit laughing one of them said, "A person who had an accident in his/her pants."

Then their conversation turned serious as they began discussing other thoughts related to the phrase "walking in two worlds." Concepts such as schizophrenia, conflict, failure, skills, abilities and language all emerged. What about all the conflicts this slogan could raise inside a person? Why are only the Yup'iit, Athabascan, Iñupiat, Tlingit, Tsimshian, Haida and Aleut expected to walk in two worlds and not others?

The goal of the phrase is a positive one—to be successful in the *kass'aq* world and yet be a whole person in one's own culture. Yet, what is a person—an indigenous Alaskan—to do to achieve the goal that the phrase "walking in two worlds" implies? The answer that came up was this: first and foremost a person must have a solid foundation in his or her own culture and be able to walk solidly in that one world, learn all about it, believe in it and live it. Then, if a person chooses to do so, he or she can add to that one world the best from others: Japanese, Russian, German, American *kass'aq* etc. The phrase should not be "walk in two worlds" but should be "walk in your own world first" and then add to it from the worlds of others. And it should be directed to everyone, especially to those who live with people from other cultures.

Each one of us has to have an intimate knowledge of all aspects of our own world first. We have to constantly educate ourselves in our own language and culture. Even if no one is encouraging us to educate ourselves about our own language and culture, it is our duty to learn it, use it and teach it to others until the end of time. We've heard our Elders say this over and over again. Paul John from Toksook Bay says it very eloquently in the video tape *Nutemllaput: Our Very Own* (available from ANKN.)

We bemoan the loss of our Elders and wonder what we'll do without them. In our cultures' histories, when the oldest Elders passed on, others came up and took their places. Why should that stop to-day? Each generation, each of us individually, has to face the reality that we will become Elders one day and we must assume the responsibility that fact carries with it. It is our responsibility to teach our young people our traditions, our languages and everything that we've learned and continue to learn from our Elders. We can practice our traditions and languages at home, at the restaurant, at church, at the airport, at Sam's Club, even in Senator Ted Steven's office. I applaud people like Agatha John and others for teaching their children to speak our Yup'ik language in the midst of English-speaking communities. I applaud Paul John and his family in Toksook Bay, Andy Paukan of St. Mary's, Howard Luke of Fairbanks, Nora Dauenhauer of Juneau, Joe Lomack of Akiacuaq, Wassilie Berlin of Kassigluk, Louise Tall, Nita Rearden and Loddy Jones of Bethel along with the many others who take it upon themselves to teach their cultures and be positive influences in their own communities.

Before closing, I would like to do something very un-Yup'ik. Understand, the Elders are my heroes. I respect them and I learn from them practically every single day. This is very hard for me to say, but it hurts me deeply when I hear Elders say that they are not smart because they haven't attended *kass'aq* school, or because they can't speak English, implying that they are uneducated. You Elders are the most educated people I know. Most of you even surpass those who hold doctorate degrees in the Western world. You have great minds and your responsibility is to teach us, your heirs, all you can of what you know so that we can carry that knowledge and pass it on to those who follow behind us, just as we are following behind you.

One last message: when we, as Alaska's First Peoples, hold positions of power, we have to use that power wisely and in the best interests of our own people. We must be careful not to use that power to our own personal advantage, to please our administrators at the expense of our autonomy or succumb to the temptations that power carries with it.

So I challenge all of you: Yup'iit, Iñupiat, Athabascan, Tlingit, Aleut, Haida, Tsimshian to take advantage of opportunities to learn your own languages and cultures and pass them on so we can truly honor our past, celebrate our present and create our own future.

Quyana.

Theresa Arevgaq
John, Director Rural
Alaska Native Adult
Program, Alaska
Pacific University

Multicultural Education: Partners in Learning Yugtun Qaneryararput Arcaqertuq

Sharing Our Pathways, Vol. 6, Issue 2, Mar/Apr 2001

Keynote address to the 27th Annual Bilingual Multicultural Conference, February 7, 2001

Waqaa! Greetings to the bilingual conference planning committee, Elders, educators, parents, students, administrators and community members. I am honored and humbled to be the keynote speaker for the 27th annual BMEEC 2001 conference theme, "Multicultural Education: Partners in Learning." There are several key points in regards to the Yup'ik heritage language and culture I feel are important to address today. I will use English as well as Yup'ik in my presentation.

The key points that I would like to address are:

Arguments

1. Who is responsible for the language maintenance? Is it the parents? Community? Educators? Elders? Self?
2. Should we be concerned about maintaining Yup'ik Language? Why?
3. Will bilingualism affect a child's formal education? How?
4. Do children with bilingualism have better educational outcomes?
5. Will we lose our Native cultural identity along with language loss?
6. Where are the Elders?
7. Should we support Yup'ik immersion programs?

Ethnic Identity Formation and It's Implications for Yup'ik Language Development

I am fortunate to have been raised in a remote Yup'ik-speaking community on Nelson Island. This was the era when formal education was just being implemented into the community. Elders, grandparents, parents and prominent community members were the main educators who taught youth and adults the indigenous traditions and *customs-quliraat, qanruyuutet, alerquutet* and *inerqutet*. Oral traditional education passed down creation, raven stories and cultural values. Many Elders and community members truly believed and still believe in our creator, Ellam Yua. We are taught that Ellam Yua granted us our indigenous language, culture, history and spiritual world for us to keep and maintain. The ancestors' innovative and effective traditional teaching methods are integrated and effective multicultural education materials.

The Yup'ik pledge (below) is recited in some Kuskokwim Delta villages like Toksook Bay. When I attended Calista Elder's Conference last November, I had an opportunity to visit the school and participate at the school assembly. There I requested the students to recite the pledge which I've attempted to translate.

Wangkuta yupigni qanruyutet aturluki anglituukut. Ilakuyulluta, ukvertarluta, pingnatuuluta.
We, the Yup'ik people, grow up following the traditional values and principles. We live in harmony, we have faith and also strive for prosperity.

Nallunrilamta yuuyaramteni piciryarangqerngamta nutemllamtenek.
This is because we have wisdom and knowledge of our traditional lifestyle.

Qigcikiyaram aturtai taringumaut ellam iluanelnguut elpengqellrit nunuliutengqellrit-llu.
Those who hold and respect the traditional knowledge and laws of our spiritual worldview know that they will be rewarded for their proper behavior.

Qanruyutem aturtai umyuartululuteng, elluatuuluteng, nuuqitevkenateng yuuluaqerciqut.
Those who follow the traditional values, laws and principles will become wise, knowledgeable and live to be prosperous and wealthy.

I specifically wanted to share this with you because it's written in Yup'ik. The words in this pledge remind me of late Elders like Billy Lincoln, Sr. and my grandmother, *Al'aq* (respected leaders) who spent endless hours teaching us kids using these exact words. The important messages reflect cultural integrity, accountability, self-determination and encourage a foundation for youths' achievement.

At this time I would like to take a moment to recognize and thank the Yup'ik associate professor Cecilia Martz, former Kuskokwim Campus faculty member, who developed the Y/Cuuyaraq poster containing these words. Our students will learn and live as the key holders of our Elders words.

With fluent indigenous languages, youth can have strong cultural and traditional knowledge, spirituality, communication skills and self-esteem. It is also evident as time goes on that it will only become more difficult for youth to maintain their first language. The English language world surrounds us and is slowly eroding our languages away, which is our power base with each generation. The lack of indigenous language brings suffering for youth and adults. For example, language barriers make it difficult for new generations to learn about traditional family ties and clans, ancient stories and songs, leadership skills, ceremonials, hunting and gathering skills and traditional laws.

We have learned from the research presented by the Alaska Native Language Center at the University of Alaska Fairbanks regarding language loss among our Native groups. In some cases, like the Eyak and a few others, the only speakers are dying off. We must make an effort to ensure that the remaining indigenous languages are enhanced and taught to all ages. Our language and cultures are greatly affected and impacted by the daily use of English. On the other hand, we have community members who cannot speak their language yet have an understanding and sense of their culture. I would like to share with you two heartbreaking encounters I had with two elderly women who expressed their pain and sorrow with me. Both events happened in Bethel around the mid-1980s.

The first person was an Elder woman in her sixties from a coastal village, waiting for a flight at the airport. While we waited, sitting on benches across from each other, a young lady came to her and asked her a question in English and grandmother responded back in broken English. Her voice was quivering when she told me that she could not communicate effectively with her own grandchild that she was raising. She was unable to teach her and other children the Yup'ik traditions and values because they did not have a common nor efficient communication tool. The grandmother looked very sad at that moment, which made me feel sorry for her. She was sad to see the passing of her heritage language, including her culture, as the students used only English at school and watch television after school. There is an argument that we face daily regarding language use responsibility. Who is responsible for resolving situations like this? Are we as parents and families responsible or are the schools? I think we are all responsible—as parents, relatives, community members and educational employees—we must not let this continue.

The second Elder shared a similar situation with me. In her case, the teacher advised her to speak to her children in English because that would benefit their education. About twelve years later, another teacher approached her and said, "Why didn't you teach your children Yup'ik?" At this point, she felt confused by two educators approaching her with opposing advice. She admitted it was too late now for children to learn Yup'ik who are older and will have a hard time learning the new language. She sat silently and cried. This is a national controversial issue with schools, governments and leaders who all struggle to deal with the question of if/how we should include indigenous languages in our schools. Like our ancestors, let us unite and make a commitment to incorporate indigenous languages into all aspects of our villages so we can have societies with common languages.

These two women were willing to share their painful family crisis for a reason. They are not alone in this situation, many of our people are going through the same crisis. We cannot continue to hurt the hearts of our Elders, the holders of our cultural wisdom and knowledge. They are the backbone of our families and deserve the utmost respect. As Native speakers who are also educators and administrators, we can enhance language use in schools and at home and provide efficient communication tools for the students without endangering their scholastic achievement.

To encourage Native heritage language development, the parents, school board members, educators and prominent leaders all need to get involved in planning the annual academic curriculum. We must become proactive members by joining local and district school boards that guide and work with school administrators. We can and must identify quality Native educators and administrators with expertise and proficiency in Native languages and let them control the schools. Native educators should promote and provide local knowledge, wisdom and innovation through developing a dynamic curriculum. These steps will provide positive consequences for our Yup'ik heritage language.

We have our own Native immersion programs in place, like the ones in Bethel and Kotzebue, that develop and implement community-based, culturally-relevant curriculum. They have dedicated Native educators, staff and teacher aides who work diligently to ensure indigenous education through first languages. When I visited the immersion school in Kotzebue, I was impressed with little kids speaking Iñupiaq only. Shortly after I arrived, their teacher informed me that I could not speak English beyond the entrance area. I spoke to them in Yup'ik because my Iñupiaq language is limited. Disciplinary rules like these will enforce indigenous language use.

Theresa Arevgaq John instructing a class at the University of Alaska Fairbanks. Photo courtesy of Rural Student Services, UAF.

Naluk, my niece, has gone through the Yup'ik Immersion Program in Bethel since it was implemented a few years ago. She is now in the fifth grade, with fluent Yup'ik speech and grammar. Her mother, Agatha John-Shields, has been an influential educator and proactive parent of the program. Thank you for your persistence, Gus, in teaching all your children and other's Yup'ik at home and school. There is fear that some parents feel in giving their children an opportunity to learn the indigenous language. I was shocked and horrified that some Yup'ik parents in Bethel were resistant to enrolling their children into the immersion program. They believe their children will have a hard time adjusting to a standard English classroom after Yup'ik immersion classes. They simply don't see the need and are eager to have their kids become like everybody else. Today my sister's children can communicate with their grandparents in their first language. This proves that indigenous languages can be taught at home and school. It takes dedication, determination and persistence to make this happen. These students are the future leaders of our languages.

I applaud the efforts of all immersion teachers who provide essential lifelong cultural foundations for youth and serve as role models for students and educators. I used these two examples of what I consider to be an ideal and effective immersion program with a community-based curriculum. There are challenges from opposing parents, school board and community members who feel that Native education is not essential to our youth. Please don't let them stop you from doing your job. Through programs like these, our descendents will learn and live Native ways of knowing without endangering their future success in an integrated society.

The Impact of Yup'ik Language Programs on Student Attitudes

The Yup'ik language programs influence student attitudes in ways that make them feel proud of their heritage language and culture and will have a long-lasting positive impact on their attitudes. Harold Napoleon, in his book *Yuuyaraq*, states "Many villages have expressed interest in reviving cultural heritage activities and Native language use in their schools, because it has become evident that practicing one's cultural heritage and speaking one's heritage language promotes self-esteem in young people."

The Alaska Standards for Culturally Responsive Schools says "Culturally-knowledgeable students are well grounded in the cultural heritage and traditions of their community." One of the objectives of this standard states, "Students will be able to reflect through their own actions the critical role that the local heritage language plays in fostering a sense of who they are and how they understand the world around them."

When the youth learn to speak their heritage language fluently, they will be able to hear and learn many of our traditional *qanruyutet* and *alerqutet* that will give them guidance for healthy and prosperous lifestyles. Knowing one's language is interlinked with learning one's culture.

When I was doing my student teaching at Bethel High School in the early eighties, I had an opportunity to form a cultural club that met weekly. I formed this club because I had heard that there was a problem with cultural diversity in school. The Native students were criticized for speaking Yup'ik or for wearing Native clothing. The goal of the cultural group was to develop and encourage cultural identity among students through traditional activities. They learned the history and meanings of traditional Yup'ik songs. During our sessions they viewed videos of dancers, learned about masks, mukluks, *qaspeqs* and headdresses. After a few gatherings, students began to show up in their *qaspeqs* and mukluks and were no longer ashamed of themselves. The parents of my students approached me in local stores and asked what I was doing to their kids. They informed me that their childrens' attitudes improved at home and they were anxious to attend school. We, as educators, can inspire our youth to become proud owners of their language and traditions.

My late grandmother, Anna Kungurkak, like many Elders, was my best educator allowing me to benefit by maintaining the advanced first language that belongs to our people. Elders in her generation who were raised through oral history have a solid personal and educational foundation. She once said *"Ilaten kenkekuvki elitnaurciqaten"*: "If you love your family and community members, you will educate them." The true meaning of love is to make time to educate the young future leaders using the integrated teaching methods of our Native ways of knowing.

Our ancestors also teach us the importance of knowing who we are and that we should know our cultural values. The Yup'ik term *aciriyaraq*, refers to acquiring a Native name. It is an honor and comes with responsibilities. Through the naming system, we keep our ancestral spirits alive and we must carry that name with respect. The

Elders stress traditional values like *naklekiyaraq-caring* for others, *kenkiyaraq*—love for all, and *ilangqersarag*—having friends and associates. These are integral parts of our societies that we must revere and nurture.

In reference to our traditional spirituality, we must revisit our traditional ceremonies and rituals that meant so much to our ancestors. Yuraryarat, the various dance ceremonials including *kevgiq, ineqsukiyaraq, kelgiq, kegginaquryaraq* and *nangerciciyaraq* are diverse forms of prayer. The *angalkuut* (shamans), both men and women, played very important roles in these communities. The *angalkuut* are gifted with powers to heal, interact with animal spirits and serve as composers and choreographers. I am not promoting shamanism—I'm just informing you about the past. Elders inform us that our Native spirituality was forced aside or put under the table when newcomers arrived, with the expectation that ancestral powers will revive again when the time is right. I feel that the time is right now to empower ourselves to bring back our traditional forms of prayer through multicultural education. In the southwestern region of Alaska, young people are bringing back the drums and forming school dance groups. With formations of local dance groups, we are bringing back language and Native spirituality. This is possible with Native educators who organize and teach with the help of local Elders. I recommend books like *Cauyarnariuq* and *Agayuliyararput* for teachers to use that describe various ancient ceremonies told and described by the Elders.

In the past, I had several opportunities to work with and learn from respected Elders who live in various parts of our state. First, the Bilingual and Cultural Institutes in Bethel brought in Elders to assist Native educators for four intensive weeks. They collected materials and developed community-based resources for K–12 books. The Elders-in-Residence program at UAF allowed me to work and teach with Elders from all over the state as well. These Elders taught college students for five intensive weeks. The students recorded, cataloged and archived videos and audiotapes at the local library. I would recommend all educators to utilize these resources of Elders sharing their biographies and life stories as cultural teaching tools.

I would like to take this time to recognize some of these Elders who took time to provide invaluable knowledge and wisdom in the past: Frank Andrew, Chief Paul John, Susie and Mike Angaiak, Teddy and Maryann Sundown of Southwestern; Austin Hammond of Southeast; Catherine Attla, Chief Peter John and Moses Johnson of the Interior;

Mary Bourdokofsky of the Aleutians; and Jimmie Toolie and his wife and Mr. and Mrs. Issac Akootchook of the North. I salute all the Native Elders who have contributed to the education of our Alaska schools. Without them we would not have quality resources for our cultural curriculum. They are truly our Native professors.

Strategies to Strengthen Communities and Families

The following are strategies I feel will assist in strengthening our communities and families for our children's education. For parents, the caretakers and first educators, please make time to teach your heritage language at home. Start with simple words like *kenkamken*—I love you. If you don't know the language, learn it with your children. Use note pads to write down Native words and post them all over the house. For example, post them in living rooms and kitchen areas and use them as visual reminders. Make time to talk with your children. It is best to teach them early in the morning when their minds are fresh, and repeat them again later that evening. I would suggest a few words at a time so they don't get confused.

For communities, make a conscious effort to use the indigenous language daily. We need to become proactive and encourage members to become fluent speakers. I encourage you to invite Elders to use their first language to address the public in schools, churches, local events or on radio and television. Build a team of local education and community organizations to collaborate in efforts to incorporate and implement the use of indigenous language in social functions.

Academic institutions and administrators should become friends and supporters of immersion schools as well as bilingual and cultural education centers. Incorporate and implement culturally-relevant orientations for school board members, administrators, staff and educators on local language, history, culture and seasonal lifestyles. It is essential for all academic employees to understand and incorporate traditional ways of living. Partner with local Elders, prominent community members and agencies to assist in developing community-based academic curriculum. Utilize the *Guidelines for Strengthening Indigenous Languages* in conjunction with the *Alaska Standards for Culturally Responsive Schools*. Encourage and sponsor bilingual educators to get certified and hire them. This will have a positive impact on our student retention rate.

Tamalkurpeci cingamci mary-agcisqelluci yugtun qaneryararput nutemllarput-llu ciumurucesqellukek elitnauruteklukek-llu. I just summoned you to fight to keep our indigenous languages and cultures alive. It's going to be an uphill battle. Let's stand up together as one team to enhance multicultural education.

Tuaingunrituq Quyana.

John P. Angaiak

Alaska Native Village Education

Sharing Our Pathways, Vol. 6, Issue 2, Mar/Apr 2001

John's article was first published in Tundra Drums, *October 19, 2000, vol 28 number 31.*

When and where do we begin? On education, I think we know when to start—at the birth of a child and it does not matter where on earth you live. The philosophy of education is highly politicized and emotional today. Along the way, parents learn that the way a child views education early on is a mirror image of the way his parents look at it. The child's attitude toward education is reflective of the attitude of his/her parents.

There is more than one way to look at education. It is a personalized, family affair. Some parents sacrifice their time and effort for the education of their children. Others may look at it only as an alternative option to subsistence, or enough to get by. It seems that we develop a better perception of education when we get older. Adults have a better understanding of how it was then and how it is now.

I grew up with a strong subsistence-oriented education, though I entered Western schooling before 1950. The first school in my village was a BIA school. Our parents only had what they learned from their own hands and subsistence experience. Their kind of education was learning skills for survival. For boys, it was knowledge of a vast area of terrain, hunting skills, the sea and weather. To know these skills meant being a good provider for their family. The girls mastered skills from their mothers on how to make mukluks and parkas, to sew, prepare food and take care of hunting needs. The girls knew how to complement what their husbands provided. They were partners for life.

All this was obtained by hands-on experience from their parents and Elders, so clear that their children knew what they would become in the next decade.

When Western education arrived, it did not change who I was as a person. It created an opportunity to expand my subsistence education. It meant that I could strive to master a subsistence education and master Western education too—to survive in a different lifestyle. We will always be Alaska Natives and speak more than one language, regardless of where we are living. We will always be attached to a subsistence lifestyle. In fact, modern education helps you better understand subsistence, to appreciate it, to understand its weaknesses and strengths and, above all, how it defines who you are.

Our attitude toward Western education should not be different from subsistence education. We should treat them both equally as important to our survival. They should complement each other. It is here that I want to make my point. Western education is here to stay. We should make the best of it and take advantage of it. There is no way getting around it.

The facts, figures and politics of education are not what I want to talk about. It is about our general attitude. I believe we need not fear for the future of our children anymore. Sometimes what we say at statewide gatherings on education is not what we say about education at home. We pass resolutions directing our leaders to solve our Native education problems. We seem to blame the system for our weaknesses.

Somewhere in the corner of each village, silent parents reside whose children are known to be above the norm in school. The parents never seem to do anything different, but they make sure their children are dressed well for winter, eat well, do their homework and are in bed by nine o'clock. They don't blame the system.

What makes the silent parents different? They truly give attention to their children. They talk to them freely, all in their Yup'ik language, because they never went to school. They encourage their children to excel in school, listen to the teachers, do homework and go to bed on time. Such parents believe education starts at home. They want their children to have better opportunities. The children feel comfortable. The children are encouraged to feel that they could go far with a good education. Parents are right there with them. Education is fun. Parents give their children the right attitude and the freedom to be educated in subsistence and beyond. The children feel they can now return all the love and care their parents gave. It is about respect between parents and children.

These parents have never been to the Alaska Federation of Natives Convention. They were too poor and could not afford all the conveniences of the modern life. They only knew how to provide for their children the best they could. Their reward was that most of their children graduated from the universities and all have jobs now. These traditional parents never liked to be confused with the philosophies of education. They would lose their sense of direction when people of high thinking started talking about the best way to educate children. Their rules were simple: to read, write and excel in mathematics and science. Beyond that, it was elective.

To read, write and excel in mathematics and science are the core of a universal education. All the children of the world are being drawn to the core, down to the smallest village. Education is here to stay.

Our ancestors were committed to making sure their children knew how to provide for their own so that they would survive in their time. We should have the same grasp about survival today as our ancestors did about surviving in their time. This century belongs to our children. They should fit well in this century. As parents, our time was yesterday.

What about the changing world all around us? We may someday need two earths to sustain the world population with its staggering growth rate. The explosive world population is now on the move everywhere. Most often its masses are highly educated. They can take jobs in our villages while we can't make up our minds about educating our children for future jobs. Everywhere around the world people are talking about survival, at any cost.

If we don't change our attitudes toward education now, we cannot be partners with the rest of the changing world. Education will not change our status as Alaska Natives, but it will gain us respect for our unique culture as an educated society and help us to be partners in the changing world. We have to make a move on education. We should not corner ourselves in our own villages. The world has nothing for us unless we take education seriously. We should not lose our language, the way we do things and who we are. Such an education is not for the privileged few. It's okay to be educated twice.

Angayuqaq Oscar Kawagley

Nurturing Native Languages

Sharing Our Pathways, Vol. 7, Issue 1, Jan/Feb 2002

We know ourselves to be made from this earth.
We know this earth is made from our bodies.
For we see ourselves. And we are nature.
We are nature seeing nature.
We are nature with a concept of nature.
Nature weeping. Nature speaking of nature to nature.
                    —Susan Griffin, *Woman and Nature*

Many Americans are intolerant of diversity, be it cultural with its concomitant languages, or biodiversity in an ecological system. Instead, we see notions of human and cultural superiority with designs for a monolingual and monocultural society in which the English language and its associated culture presumes to become the language and culture of the world. Thus indigenous cultures have to contend with a language and its ways that has a very "voracious appetite," as phrased by Richard Little Bear. We, indeed, have a formidable enemy which absorbs our Native languages and cultures very readily, unless we are cognizant of its hunger and take protective steps. This mass culture can be most appealing to young people. Its behaviorisms, codes of dress, languages and sometimes destructive proclivities inveigle young people to its world.

Griffin's observations ring true to me because my Yupiaq language is nature-mediated, and thus it is wholesome and healing. It contains the creatures, plants and elements of nature that have named and defined themselves to my ancestors and are naming and defining themselves to me. My ancestors made my language from nature. When I speak Yupiaq, I am thrust into the thought world of my ancestors.

Let me cite two examples of the elements of nature naming and defining themselves. The first is *anuqa*—the wind. It is telling its name and telling me what it is. It is the moving air which is needed for life. The other is *lagiq*—the Canadian goose. It's call is "lak, lak, lak" giving its name to us and by its behavior telling us its habitat and its niche in the ecological system. "We are nature with a concept of nature." Truly!

We, as Native people, have seen our languages become impoverished in the last several centuries. Many of us now speak our Native languages at the fourth and fifth grade levels (if such a grading system existed for us). We look at the wounds in our minds and we see that the wounds also exist in nature itself. "We know ourselves to be made from this earth" and it makes us weep when we see the destruction and pollution around us. We realize that the relationship between ourselves and our places is a "unity of process" (Joan Halifax). We know that there cannot be a separation between the two.

As we lose our Native languages, more and more of us begin to take part in the misuse and abuse of nature. We use English predominately in our everyday lives today. We don't realize that English is a language contrived by the clever rational mind of the human being. The letters were derived by the human mind. The words are a product of a mindset that is given to individualism and materialism in a techno-mechanistic world. For us to think that we can reconstruct a new world by using English and its ways will not work. We need to return to a language that is given to health and healing. To try to make a paradigmatic shift by using the consciousness that constructed this modern world is bound for failure. Albert Einstein stated something to the effect that "you cannot make change in a system using the same consciousness used to construct it." This should be very clear to us as a Native people.

In my Yupiaq ancestral world egalitarianism was practiced. In this form of governance no creature, plant or element becomes more important than another. All are equal. In the great state of Alaska, I can incontrovertibly state that racism is alive and seems to be gaining strength. This is a circumstance which is unconscionable and reflects a very destructive and alienated stance in the larger society.

How is it that we "stabilize indigenous languages"? I think that we must once again speak the Native languages in the home a majority of the time. If we expect only the school to do it, it will surely fail. The school must become a reflection of a Native speaking family, home and community. During the waking hours of the day, the children must hear the Native language being spoken—in the home and in school. The one-to-one and family conversation in the local language must be the standard of the day. The community, family, parents and especially the children must begin to know place. How is this to be done? By the Elders, parents and community members speaking to one another in their own language and from the Yupiaq perspective.

To know self, one must learn of place. How does one learn of place? You begin by telling *quliraat*, the mythology, stories of distant time, which are powerful teaching tools still applicable to the present. You learn of the times when our ancestors were truly shape-shifters. It was easy to change from one form to another, and one was in control of self. Values and traditions are taught by these stories which are so ancient that we call them myths. From these you can tease out problem-solving tools and discern characteristics that make for a healthy and stable person living in a healthy and sustainable place. Told by an Elder whose inflections, facial and body language add to the words, these myths teach not only discipline for the members but more importantly self-discipline. We must re-inculcate self-discipline in our people as a matter of survival.

The *qalumcit* must be told, as they are the stories of us as a Native peoples. They tell us how we got to be at this place, our movements, problems encountered and resolved, years of plenty and scarcity and how to read the signs foretelling events, how we made sense of time and space, how trade and exchange of goods and services was accomplished and how genetic diversity in the community was maintained.

The rituals and ceremonies must be relearned and practiced. The loss of these have developed schisms in our lives. We have become fractured people. These rituals represent revival, regeneration and revitalization of our Native people.

The *yuyaryarat*—the art and skills of singing, dancing and drumming—brings one to a spiritual level. Our word, *yuyaq*, means to emerge into a higher plain, a higher consciousness through concentration on the movements when singing and drumming.

We must also seek to relearn the Native names of places. It is incomplete knowledge for us to know the distance between two places in miles. It is also important to be able to "guesstimate" the time it will take to go from point A to point B and to know the history and place names between the two points. Then it becomes whole and useful knowledge.

I just recently returned from Hilo, Hawaii where I was a participant in a planning meeting for revitalizing the Hawaiian language
and culture. One interesting side trip was a visit to a Native Hawaiian
charter school a few minutes from Hilo. I learned that the local Native
people had begun landscaping unkempt property and refurbishing
dilapidated buildings. This was initiated even before grant funds
were made available for the project. This is true determination and
motivation to reconstruct education which is meaningful and effective for the Native people. When my hosts and I arrived, we were met
by the students at the entrance to their school. They sang in their
own language and several students made welcoming remarks again
in their own language. When protocol called for my response, I responded in my Yupiaq language. To see and hear the protocol that had
been practiced for millennia by their people made my heart feel good.
This happening after hundreds of years of barrage to change their
language and culture gave me hope that we, too, can save our Alaska
Native languages.

It was refreshing and energizing of spirit to look at the landscape
and see the work that had been done. The best part was a plot of land
where only the original flora of Hawaii had been planted—a very
ambitious endeavor which required research and feedback from the
few Elders still with them to determine which plants are native to the
land. One building had photovoltaic panels on its roof to power some
of their computers and filter pumps for their fish hatchery tanks. At
another location, young men were preparing food in the traditional
manner of heating rocks with the ingredients placed in baskets on top
and covered over with banana leaves and canvas. The food was eaten
prior to the graduation exercises.

If you find yourself in a situation where there is a minimal number
of myths, stories, rituals and ceremonies available, then I would suggest that you find sources that are well written and your Elders deem
to be true. Translate these into your own language with the help of
Elders and knowledgeable community members that may be familiar
with the technical language contained in that treatise. When satisfied
with the final translation, read it to the group for approval. Then it
would behoove us to read it to the youngsters who will become the
historians of the community—the future keepers and practitioners of
sacred knowledge.

To bring the above back into practice is to know who you are and
where you are. This would contribute broadly to the important notion

that it is alright to be Native, to speak the Native language and to use Native tools and implements in play and work. After all, our technology was made by our ancestors to edify our Native worldviews. Please, what ever you do, do NOT give to the youngsters the idea that modern technology has an answer for everything. It does not. Use it merely as a tool and use it minimally and judiciously. Remind the students that technological tools are intensive in the use of natural resources and energy. To accept technology blindly is to negate the painful works to revitalize our Native languages and cultures. I wish you all the wisdom of the Ellam Yua, the Great Mystery in your continuing efforts. "We are nature." *Quyana*

References

Russell, Peter. *The White Hole In Time: Our future evolution and the meaning of the now*. Harper: San Francisco. 1992.

Halifax, Joan. *The Fruitful Darkness: Reconnecting with the body of the earth*. Harper: San Francisco. 1993.

Griffin, Susan. *Woman and Nature*. Harper Collins Publishers. San Francisco. 1978.

Richard Littlebear speech delivered to the Fourth Annual Stabilizing Indigenous Languages Symposium. Flagstaff, Arizona, May 1997.

Esther A. Ilutsik,
Ciulistet Research
Association

Oral Traditional Knowledge: Does It Belong in the Classroom?

Sharing Our Pathways, Vol. 7, Issue 3, Summer 2002

As local educators who are documenting the oral traditional knowledge of our ancestors and developing methods and means of bringing this information to our descendents through the public educational system, we are faced with many decisions that drastically affect the validity of this knowledge base that was once so fluid. Public schools represent a system that is foreign to the methods and means of transmitting this information in the past. We are constantly faced with decisions that affect how this knowledge will be passed on to our future descendents.

Many of us local educators have been through the Western educational system and have been taught the pedagogy of that system. Many of us have taken this very method of instruction and infused our local traditional knowledge as a means of educating our own people about our traditional culture. But we continue to ask ourselves, "Is this the proper way to get our oral traditional knowledge passed on to our descendents?"

With questions like these always at the forefront of our minds we continue to document and develop materials for integration into the public educational system. With the adoption of the *Alaska Standards for Culturally Responsive Schools*, we need to begin making critical decisions that will affect the types of oral traditional knowledge that can be integrated into the public school system and how this information will be taught. As educators we are always looking at how other local cultural groups are addressing these very difficult issues.

On March 26–28, 2002, I had an opportunity to attend the Third Annual Native Hawaiian Education Association Convention at the Leeward Community College in Hawaii and present a workshop titled

"Oral Traditional Knowledge: Does It Belong In The Classroom?" The session began with a brief introduction to Alaska with a special emphasis on the Yup'ik people of Bristol Bay, followed by a brief presentation on how traditional Yup'ik oral knowledge is documented and then presented within the classroom. This was followed with Michelle Snyder (my daughter), a ninth-grader from the Dillingham High School, presenting a paper on "Cultural Education in the Classrooms". This set the stage for those participating in the workshop session (see below).

Oral traditional knowledge—what is meant by that? Within the oral traditions knowledge was sacred. This knowledge encompassed all aspects of life from birth to death, including the natural world and environment. This knowledge in the past was forever flowing to fit the needs of that age and time. It was so fluid that it could be defined in regional and subregional terms. As N. Scott Momaday put it:

Oral tradition stands in a different relationship to language. Words are rare and therefore dear. They are jealously preserved in the ear and in the mind. Words are spoken with great care, and they are heard. They matter, and they must not be taken for granted; they must be taken seriously and they must be remembered. Thus in the oral tradition, language bears the burden of the sacred, the burden of belief. In a written tradition, the place of language is not so certain.

So the oral traditional knowledge of our people was sacred knowledge that was not passed down freely. It was passed down as the need arose with all the special circumstances in life that was lived and continues to be lived. In the past, the oral traditions of our people were not passed down to be documented and questioned, but rather it was passed down as the need arose and was practiced without question.

In this Western-influenced world we are constantly asked to categorize, so that we cannot simply say that the oral traditions encompassed LIFE, instead we need to be specific about the areas. The oral traditional knowledge that is collected and documented are the songs, dances, prayers, rituals, stories, limericks, medicinal plants, ceremonies, music, games, chants, relationship to animals, plants, water, fire and all living things and virtually everything that affects all aspects of the living. All this knowledge, so sacred to our ancestors' existence, is documented. Often, as local educators, we question within ourselves whether this is the proper way of preserving our knowledge. But we continue to document this knowledge and put it into the proper category for future reference.

Cultural Education in the Classrooms

by Michelle Snyder, March 21, 2002

As long as I can remember, back in my elementary school years, my mother would come into my classroom to teach about Yup'ik culture. This is important to me and other Yup'ik children. It teaches us who our ancestors were and who we are today.

Every year beginning at kindergarten through the fifth grade, my mother has been teaching about our culture in the classroom. It's hard for me to remember as far back as kindergarten; mostly I remember learning Yup'ik dances and stories. My first strong memory is when I was in the second grade and we learned about the sonar legend board games; we learned stories and morals while playing the board games. I remember in later years learning dances, Yup'ik colors, story-knifing, Yup'ik patterns and grass-mat weaving.

The dances that I remember learning were the Porcupine Dance, the Agutak Dance and some others. We even made up our own dance by learning the Yup'ik words for the different months and forming it into what we called the "Calendar Dance". All of these dances told stories. We also had to make headdresses; we learned how to beat the drum and how to bounce our knees in rhythm. We listened to our heartbeats and applied that rhythm to the drum.

We learned about Yup'ik colors. They are red, black and white and are all found on Yup'ik clothing and artwork. The color red is to honor the mother. It represents the mother's blood. It is found in many places on the parka and other clothing and beading. White represents our great Yup'ik warrior, Apanuugpuk. During one of the great wars he was captured and force-fed caribou fat by his enemies. He escaped and while he was running away he regurgitated the fat. White can also represent snow. Black represents the unknown or shamanism. It can also represent the black fly.

Yaaruin—stories told with a knife in the mud—were another thing that we learned. We learned Yup'ik legends and how to tell them in the mud with knives, as our people did for entertainment when there was no television or computers. This included Yup'ik patterns, pretend windows, pretend mountains and pretend boxes. There are different patterns for each family. My Grandmother's pattern was a salmonberry leaf, so I have now inherited that pattern.

The last year that my mother came into my classroom was fifth grade. That year we learned about grass mats. We learned to split grass into three parts and found out that the middle part that we didn't use was referred to as a male, the other two parts were referred to as the female. We learned about different dyes, natural and store bought. We experimented to see which one would have the most color and last the longest. The natural dyes were berries and some other substances that I don't remember.

Learning about all this as a girl has helped me see who my ancestors were; I have learned about my culture and my language. It has helped me form a positive image about who I am and who my people are. It has made me proud that I am a Yup'ik Eskimo. With this knowledge I don't feel lost; I know who my ancestors were and that is so important to me. My only regret is that I couldn't learn more about my culture and my language but what I have I am grateful for; it helps me form my own self-image and helps my self esteem. It has made me who I am today.

304 | SHARING OUR PATHWAYS

We document how traditional knowledge was passed down and in some cases attempt to replicate those very practices. We know that the oral traditions of our people were passed down within everyday activities. For example, they were passed down by engaging in a ceremony or participating in the evening ritual of purifying the sod homes, or doing certain rituals before the hunt or the gathering of wild edible plants. We know that many times, if our people needed to be reprimanded for an action or reminded of how one is to act, it was done through the oral stories that were shared within the sod homes or at the men's house. For there was a proper way of sharing this knowledge and passing it down. This knowledge was not studied but LIVED.

We, as local educators, now take this very sacred knowledge and attempt to bring it into the public classroom using the Western methods that are the basis for the educational system that is presented to us today. In some instances we attempt to replicate certain practices by actually participating within traditional cultural settings, but even these cultural camps can be strongly influenced by Western teaching methodology.

These circles of questions bring us again to the question, "Does oral traditional knowledge belong in the classroom?" This is what many of our local educators who are documenting the oral tradition of our people are asking themselves. Are we doing the right thing by documenting this knowledge and then making it available in written form to the general public for their use and judgment? How do we go about making sure that if this knowledge base is documented that it will be respected and understood by those of another cultural group? Whose responsibility is it to train our own local educators and those from another cultural group? How do we measure success in the understanding of the local cultural group?

We leave you all with many questions that each regional group will have to ask of themselves. We did not come up with answers, but these will have to come from within ourselves through our own local people.

[For further guidance in addressing these difficult questions, refer to the *Guidelines for Respecting Cultural Knowledge* available through the Alaska Native Knowledge Network]

In The Maelstrom of Confusion, a Stilling Voice

Angayuqaq Oscar Kawagley

Sharing Our Pathways, Vol. 7, Issue 3, Summer 2002

The spirit and pride of Native being has been struggling in a maelstrom of confusion due to the many people living with homeless minds, destitution, poverty, pestilence, war and dereliction of being, even as we live in the wealthiest nation in the world. You see, we have tried to comply with the wishes and dreamworks of a narcissistic society, but we have not been able to progress from the doldrums of uncertainty and hopelessness. However, a few of our American Indian and Alaska Native people have begun to see through the small channels in the blizzard and once we are able to see more clearly again, we will have something very important to share with the world.

We, as Native peoples, have always known that genotypes of all living things have micro-consciousness or micro-intelligence that enables them to communicate with one another and to work together for the good of the whole. Let me tell you why I think this is so. As a Yupiat, we have many rituals and ceremonies, some of which require special masks. Some of the masks are human masks. A few of these will have a third eye painted on the forehead. This eye we call Ellam iina, the eye of the universe, the eye of consciousness, the eye of awareness, thus intelligence. This says to me that the Great Consciousness, God if you wish, resides in my mind, and my consciousness is in the Great Consciousness. It is there that we find our collective memories and the power of our collective mindfulness. These essences of memory are imbued into the creatures, plants and elements of nature to remind and teach us how to be people that live lives that feel just right.

Nature is our textbook as a Native people. In it we find wisdom to make a life and a living. In order to have dialogue with it we must listen for the still small voice within. To ensure growth of wisdom, we recognize that we need to be with those that we consider wise, most often the Elders. We know that we become that which we hold up and respect. How many times have you heard this truth! You and I, as educators, seek through dialogue with those we admire, through reading all sorts of written media, through seeing videotaped media and through learning to read and communicate directly with nature. The information we gather requires that we sift through it to remove the chaff in the form of misdirected, misinformed and useless information which we or others may have interpreted wrongly. Knowledge is merely information, but wisdom requires that we understand, become enlightened or aware and, as we grow, live what we know! This is what we learn from our wise Elders—this is wisdom.

This wisdom cannot be separated from the sacred—our Native spirituality. Wisdom is embedded in the sacred, thus we live it. Remember that wisdom also resides in you—look for it. As a Native person, you need your Native language to commune with nature and to describe it in its own terms. A Native friend of mine from the village of Minto told me that our Native languages are living languages and that if you don't use it, you are giving yourself away—relinquishing your identity. As a Yupiaq man, I have to draw on my Yupiaq language and mindset to feel the crispness of the snow, the balminess of a warm wind. I have to draw on my language to fully experience the mountains, the moon, the sun, the river, the spruce tree, the taste of Hudson's Bay tea, the wolf, the eagle and the paramecium—it is a living language! All these experiences with the language, along with the five senses and intuition, are necessary for my growth and my spirituality.

Barriers have to be removed for my continued growth, otherwise staleness follows. This is another reason why we must get the children out of the classrooms as much as possible to be with and in nature. Ralph Waldo Emerson wrote: "Nature becomes (to man) the measure of his attainments. So much of nature as he is ignorant of, so much of his own mind does he not yet possess. And, in fine, the ancient precept 'know thyself' and the modern precept, 'study nature' become at last one maxim." Get the children to see beauty in the flower, tree, butterfly, grass, stream, fish and, yes, the slug. These living things interact and cooperate. This process does not leave out the rocks and other elements of Mother Earth—they are all an integral part it. Let them begin to understand that we are here for a purpose, to contribute to the good of the tribe and be of service to others. This involves goodness of self, morality, joy, cooperation and happiness. We have Christ, Dalai Lama, Ghandi, Chief Peter John, Lyons and others who have the selfless love which is the stabilizer, the balancer of life. They are our role models.

Let the children think of all the good traits and skills that they possess. Someone has called these the "inner assets". They have talents and skills inherited from their ancestors with the Great Mystery working the genotypes to fit the place and conditions. This process needs our continued meditation and prayers for the still, small voice to let us know what else needs to be done. *Ellanginginartuqut*—we are becoming more aware!

The inner assets might include ability to interact effectively with others, intuitive perception, athletic skill, ability to observe and make sense of what is being seen, ability for abstract thinking, dexterity combined with mind, leadership skills, mindfulness of place, cooperation, showing love and humility and all the many other positive traits that children may possess. Not only must the children be guided to making a worthwhile living but to making a life that feels good to them as well. This is done through the mythology, stories, singing, dancing, drumming, place names and all the other rituals and ceremonies that have been handed down to us through many thousands of years. They must be guided to living life to the fullest—a good and responsible life working to become the very best they possibly can while making a contribution to their community. Children who want to live a healthy and stable life will be contributors to a healthy, stable and sustainable community.

These inner assets of children have to be capitalized on for them to become the very best that they are capable of. They can become the very best hunter, medical doctor, electrician, artist, craftsperson or medicine person, but this has to be infused with liberal amounts of love, humility, compassion and open-mindedness. This means that love has balanced the outer and inner ecologies of the young person. They work and experience place for the good of the community. We have to know place in order to know self, for place is our identity.

The last 500 years or so we have seen a maelstrom of confusion, a perfect storm! It is destructive because it is based on self-love, greed, hate and anger, which are in direct conflict with what nature teaches us. We must avoid personal narcissism just as we must avoid spiritual narcissism. We have to work for a balance. Some American Indian people refer to this as "Walking the Red Road", a very narrow path which guides us on that thin line between good and evil. We are gradually emerging from this maelstrom of confusion and getting on a pathway that feels just right!

We, as teachers, are not just repositories of knowledge, but serve as a role model and guide for the physical, intellectual, emotional and spiritual development of these children, our future. May the Ellam Yua, the Spirit of the Universe, give us guidance and direction in this most important role.

Ac'arralek Lolly
Sheppard Carpluk | # Who is this Child Named WIPCE?

Sharing Our Pathways, Vol. 7, Issue 4, Sept/Oct 2002

Who is this child named WIPCE (pronounced wip-see)? It is the coming together of the youth, youthless (in-betweens) and Elders of the world's indigenous peoples, according to its founder, Dr. Verna J. Kirkness. The very first World Indigenous Peoples Conference on Education (WIPCE) was held in North Vancouver, British Columbia, Canada in 1987. The 1987 conference theme was

Workshops and presentations were held in over 60 teepees sprawled out over a field at WIPCE 2002 in Calgary, Alberta, Canada.

"Tradition, Change and Survival." Tradition represented by the past and the Elders; Change represented by the present and the youthless and Survival represented by the future and the youth. There were participants from 17 countries, with a total of 1,500 people attending the 1987 WIPCE.

Dr. Verna J. Kirkness equated WIPCE to being a child who was born in Xwmelch'sten, North Vancouver, Canada—a difficult and laborious birth, she recalls. From there WIPCE was nurtured and suckled at Turangawaewae Marae, Aotearoa (New Zealand) in 1990 on its third birthday and then on to Wollongong, Australia for its sixth birthday in 1993. WIPCE's ninth birthday was spent in arid Albuquerque, New Mexico in 1996 and in 1999 WIPCE was really happy to spend its twelfth birthday in Hilo, Hawai'i. This year's host for WIPCE's fifteenth birthday was the First Nations Adult and Higher Education Consortium (FNAHEC). The conference drew 2500 people to the beautiful site of Stoney Park on the Nakoda Nation Reserve near Morley, Alberta, Canada.

I had no idea what to expect when I attended my first WIPCE in Albuquerque in 1996. I had no clue that I would share similar struggles in education with like-minded indigenous peoples who soon became friends from across the world. Little did I expect to network with indigenous people who had developed models of education and a way of thinking that were the beginnings of turning indigenous education around. Little did I expect to participate in celebrations of who we are as indigenous peoples with dancing, singing and, most important of all, the sense of humor that pulls us through all of life and its challenges. All this happened and more.

The sharing of models and ideas flourished with the attendance of over 5000 people at the Fifth World Indigenous Peoples Conference on Education hosted by the Hawaiians in Hilo, Hawaii in 1999. So, too, the networking and connections continued with the Sixth World Indigenous Conference on Education in Stoney Park. The WIPCE 2002 mission statement stated that we would celebrate "the sharing and promoting of indigenous-based initiatives by featuring holistic educational efforts to maintain and perpetuate our ways of knowing and to actualize the positive development of indigenous communities."

The conference objectives supported the mission statement by providing a means for indigenous nations to honor their cultures and traditions by recognizing, respecting and taking pride in respective unique practices. The conference opening and closing ceremonies, the daily sunrise ceremony, the evening cultural exchanges and performances and the many workshops provided the means to achieve these valuable experiences. In addition, the conference provided a continuation of dialogue and action around educational issues that indigenous nations face, as well as a forum for international exchanges and the promotion of experiential teachings that actively involved all conference participants.

We honored and recognized the teachings of our Elders by incorporating their experiences in the various workshops and activities. The conference organizers sought to strengthen and continue the WIPCE legacy that indigenous peoples gain greater autonomy over their everyday lives and strive to overcome the effects of colonialism. Presenters were encouraged to share how they are implementing the provisions articulated in the Coolongata Statement on Indigenous Rights in Education that was adopted at the 1999 WIPCE in Hilo.

FNAHEC was founded on the belief that the realization of cultural identity is essential to the development of the self-actualized person. So it was their intention that hosting the world conference would enable them to "bring about greater unity and co-operative action to make our world the place that our creator intended it to be." The conference brought educators together from around the world to provide

Elder Julie Kanagin giving her presentation at the "virtual teepee". WIPCE 2002, Stoney Park, Calgary, Alberta.

opportunities for collaborative initiatives. A challenge in hosting the conference was to make the circle larger by bringing representatives from countries that had not previously participated. Thus the conference included people from Central America and Samiiland.

The WIPCE 2002 logo was drawn by Allen B. Wells from the Kainai Blood Nation in Alberta. His logo captured the proud spirit of First Nations heritage and the attainment of education. The peace pipe stood as a spiritual symbol of our cultural beliefs, a gift from the Great Spirit. Within the circle was a teepee, the meeting and learning place from which emanates the knowledge for living that is passed on from generation to generation. The mountains in the background represented the spiritual essence of our culture. They also formed the beautiful backdrop for the chosen venue of WIPCE 2002—the land of the Nakoda Nation. The feathers represented the four seasons flowing in perpetual motion—the Circle of Life. Also, embodied within the meaning of the feathers is the Great Spirit above whom has blessed us with spiritual, mental, physical and emotional balance to live in harmony within His creation.

WIPCE 2002 began on a cold, gray day nestled in a clearing surrounded by poplar and pine trees, with the majestic Rocky Mountains in the background and the beginnings of the Bow River as it flowed from the mountain range out into the prairie lands that surround Calgary. We, from many international indigenous nations, huddled together for warmth on bleachers as we listened to the opening ceremonies. The largest contingencies came from Hawai'i and Aotearoa, with more than 100 from each nation. There were about 30 people from Alaska, a majority of whom are involved with the Alaska Rural Systemic Initiative, either as employees or memorandum-of-agreement (MOA) partners.

On Monday, Tuesday and Friday, workshops and presentations were held in over 60 teepees sprawled out over a field that is also gopher and grasshopper habitat. We either walked or rode on golf carts from the entrance to our destinations. Most of the teepees had no electrical outlets which presented a challenge for those who came with PowerPoint presentations or had planned to use transparencies. As a result, we truly relied on traditional methods of sharing through our oral tradition. It made for a startling jolt from the taken-for-granted modern technology that we have become accustomed to. But by the end of the week everyone was comfortable with this type of presenting, because it seemed to encourage more interaction. We were taken to a time where we had to listen with our ears, eyes, minds, hearts and souls.

The Alaska Rural Systemic Initiative representatives and MOA partners put on a joint presentation with a delegation of Native Hawaiians from the Kahuawaiola Teacher Education Program in Hilo. This presentation was held in a virtual teepee (outdoors on the ground), and it was appropriate since it accommodated a large audience. Part of the Alaskan group held a dance practice in one of the teepees before the joint presentation, as we didn't want to be out-done by the Hawaiians with traditional dances. Yaayuk Alvanna-Stimpfle and Nita Rearden each lead an Iñupiaq and a Yup'ik dance, respectively. Over the last two years there has been an intense exchange and networking between the Alaskan and Hawaiian Native education groups around the development of cultural standards, which was the theme of our three-hour presentation. This is a great partnership that is sure to continue with the development and exchange of models and ideas to improve education.

A group of us attended a workshop presented by Graham Smith of the University of Auckland in which he shared recent developments among the Maori in Aotearoa (New Zealand). He discussed at length a theory of transformative action during which he shared that the *te Kohanga Reo* (language nests) served as a flagship for a new mindset of indigenous peoples realizing that the movement to integrate indigenous language and culture was an affirmation of self-determination. As indigenous peoples we are cognizant that our languages and cultures are parallel to and on par with those of the colonizers and thus we do not need external endorsement that our culture is valid and something we should be proud of. This realization has now reached to all levels of education and is having an impact on everything from infant to tertiary (postsecondary) institutions.

Another presentation that we attended was lead by Pita Sharples of Auckland, Aotearoa. He presented a rationale and strategy for the development of a Maori Education Authority, where there would be a Maori education minister with joint responsibility for the coordination of all Maori education programs. He wanted feedback from the audience on this concept as a way to exercise greater self-determination and to increase Maori control over Maori education.

Virginia Ned and I led a workshop on "Promoting an Indigenous Perspective in Research." I discussed my personal journey in becoming an indigenous researcher, with help from the timely work

314 | SHARING OUR PATHWAYS

and publications by Linda Smith of Auckland, Aotearoa and Marie Battiste of Saskatoon, Saskatchewan. I discussed the benefits of doing a community research assessment and how I would like to go about it. I believe each Native community is at a different level in their journey to accepting research from an indigenous perspective. Virginia presented her preliminary study of research that has been conducted in the Interior Athabascan region. The results from her study are extensive and very interesting and should be shared with Native peoples throughout Alaska. All the participants were interested in finding out more about further work on indigenous perspectives in research.

On Wednesday and Thursday, we had the opportunity to participate in cultural and educational tours. A group of us went on the Siksika (Blackfoot) Nation tour. We went onto a reserve that was 20 by 80 miles in size. Our tour was opened with a prayer before we visited historic sites, including a memorable visit to the site where Treaty Number 7 was signed. The significance of the setting was felt spiritually and moved a group of Maori who were on the same tour to lead a prayer and blessing. We were treated to a wonderful feast and powwow.

WIPCE 2002 gave birth to a new organization, the World Indigenous Nations Higher Education Consortium (WINHEC). The declaration establishing WINHEC states that, "as indigenous peoples of the world, we recognize and reaffirm the educational rights of all indigenous peoples, and we share the vision, united in the collective synergy of self-determination through control of higher education" (see sidebar at right). The members of the consortium are also committed to building partnerships to pursue common goals through higher education. This was a historic moment, bringing together indigenous higher education representatives from all the indigenous regions represented at the conference to support the creation of this new organization.

The concluding comments by the five representatives of past WIPCE organizing committees gave us a clearer picture of what WIPCE has been and will continue to be—the rebirth of indigenous peoples realization that our language and culture will always define who we are, and it is our right and responsibility to make sure this is passed on to future generations. Thus it was appropriate that Dr. Verna Kirkness equated WIPCE with a child, for the rebirth of indigenous peoples education began with the infant in the language nest and has grown to nurture the full potential of our children and their parents as we move through the different stages of development and grow into those who will become our future Elders. For that child, it has been a time of celebrating learning, celebrating cultures, celebrating our ancestors, celebrating who we are and celebrating our goals and aspirations. As Verna pointed out, it has also been a time to share our knowledge, a time to give thanks to the Creator and even a time of romance, not only among the young but among the old(er) as well.

That child's image has been molded by each nation that has hosted the conference, helping us to continually discover new ways to move beyond being merely guests in someone else's educational system. We need to better define who we are and continue to highlight what is indigenous about WIPCE. As the Elders have taught us, it is important to take good thoughts with you and leave the bad thoughts in the snow, so that come springtime they may be reborn into good thoughts. Dr. Bob Morgan of Australia pointed out that Elders are our pathway to the past and the youth are the custodians of the future. As the WIPCE child has grown, there have been themes of cultural affirmation by performances and ceremonies; exchange of ideas and materials where we learn from each other and develop connections between and among nations, strengthening and reinvigorating ourselves in an open forum, networking and sharing so that the whole

WIPCE 2002 Alaska participants peek out the door of a teepee after dance practice. Top L to R: Olga Pestrikoff, Lolly Carpluk, Virginia Ned, Bernice Tetpon, Caroline Tritt-Frank. Bottom L to R: Florence Newman, Yaayuk Alvanna-Stimpfle, Nita Rearden, Cecilia Martz, Julie Kanagin.

becomes greater than the sum of its parts, celebration and renewal for all to love being indigenous and thankfulness that we are going home with full hearts to take the learning and growth to our families.

In looking to the future of the WIPCE child, Verna Kirkness encouraged holding youth forums, emphasizing that we need to do more for our youth so they know that we now have new instruments by which we can reinvigorate our educational agenda. We can create a path of harmony for our young people and we can create institutions that celebrate our advocacy for indigenous education. We are fortunate to have our Elders who can guide us in our return to our traditional language, laws, values, beliefs and rituals that will be at the center of the rebirth, rebuilding and recreating of our institutions for tomorrow.

As this year's theme stated, the answers are going to have to come from within us. Our traditions will show us how to cleanse our souls and our minds to deal with finding the answers. Harold Cardinal reminded us that we have to look deep within ourselves as we revisit our past to create the most successful institutions for our future, so they will bring harmony to our nations, as well as to the rest of the world.

The Maori of Aotearoa were selected to host the 2005 WIPCE. There was an eruption of celebrations as this news was shared. It is appropriate that the WIPCE child return to Aotearoa, since the Maori have created models of education for the whole child. We will try our very best to be patient for the year 2005 to arrive, when we can all join in another open forum of renewal and celebrations.

I would like to thank the Nakoda Nation and FNAHEC, on behalf of the Alaska contingency, for the wonderful and loving care you shared with us in hosting WIPCE 2002. As I was leaving the bus that took a small group of us to the Calgary airport, the nine year old girl that accompanied her mom (who was the bus driver) gave me a pin that said, "Make the Circle Stronger." So, as the WIPCE logo incorporates the Circle of Life, may we continue to be blessed with spiritual, mental, physical and emotional balance as we live in harmony with all creation.

Angayuqaq Oscar
Kawagley

Revisiting Action-Oriented, Multi-Reality Research

Sharing Our Pathways, Vol. 7, Issue 4, Sept/Oct 2002

Alaska Native people have often thought of the white man as having capabilities that go far beyond our own abilities as creators and inventors, forgetting to consider some of the long-term side-effects of our infatuation with the Eurocentric ways. That feeling of awe and wonder is fast changing as we see our world deteriorate, driving us to action for a change in consciousness and returning to our own eco-centric worldview.

For the last several centuries, native/tribal people have been inundated with the products of a materialistic and techno-mechanistic society. We have marveled at the power of the rational mind and ingenuity at producing many and varied gadgets that are getting more complex and thus more difficult to understand and operate. The Euro-Americans have used the scientific method, objectivity and reductionism to produce these wonders. They have made gadgets galore and produced boundless knowledge of the physical universe. But we should pay heed to the words of Gregory Peck in the movie, The Snows of Kilimanjaro, when he said, "Just because the airplane goes faster than the horse does not mean that we are better off now than we were then." We now suffer from overpopulation, erosion of natural resources, violence and a loss of faith and trust in our clergymen, politicians and other institutional leaders.

The Euro-American scientists are coming to the North in droves to do research in places that they know little or nothing about, and often fumble around in the dark, almost blindly. Yet the indigenous people who have lived on this land for millennia are left out of the research projects in many instances. These original people who know the history and how to keep their place sustainable are ignored and seen as being primitive, having only anecdotal and place-specific knowledge. Native people are led to believe that they will find the problem and fix it with some form of new technology. However, there are seldom technological solutions to biological, mental or spiritual problems.

Western science seeks to identify symptoms of problems and then develop treatments, whether it involves physical, intellectual, emotional or spiritual phenomena. This is well and good to a limited extent, but it has a obvious weakness. These generalized inclinations have thrust insights drawn from the physical world into a world of abstractions[2] . The phenomena studied becomes absorbed by the generalized approach to solving problems. This outmoded notion of reductionism and objectivity gets in the way of compassion and cooperation and denies emotional and spiritual connection between the human, other creatures, plants and elements of Mother Earth. However, indigenous people can only be understood as part of their environment, part of their place.

Early in our heritage as we experienced change, our Elders recognized that this technical world produced much to purportedly make life easier, but they also warned that there is a danger in this trend. Too much of the resources are being used and wasted and the refining and manufacturing processes involved require excessive use of energy. In extracting minerals and timber, much land is laid to waste and it takes a long time for it to recover. These processes do not take into consideration the needs of the seventh generation. Will our descendants be able to enjoy the resources in a similar state of abundance and savor the beauty of Mother Earth as our ancestors did?

Psychologist Carl Jung has written of the "collective consciousness" and other scientists have used a holographic metaphor to convey the complexity of our relationship to our past and to each other. I can readily appreciate this as it lends itself to explaining our ancestral memory and ways of knowing. During gestation in the mother's womb, a chord is struck which resonates in the universal holographic mind. Early in life, certain notes in this chord vibrate stronger than others, such as for suckling, crying when hungry or hurting, smiling to show love and joy and so forth. As the child gets older these early notes become weaker as others become stronger, from which emerges an outgoing personality, a spiritual attitude, a love of music,

2. Berry, Wendell. (2000) *Life is a Miracle: An essay against modern superstition*. Washington, D. C.: Counterpoint

a mathematical or scientific interest and so forth. These will continue to grow while others begin to shrink as we mature.

There is a story of a hunter about to cross a newly frozen body of water. He remembers his Elders telling him that he should test the strength of the newly formed ice by dropping his ice pick. If it penetrates and does not stop, don't try crossing because the ice will be too weak. If the pick stops where the wooden handle and bone point intersect, the hunter can try to cross. To do so, he has to gather energy by looking at the sky, the sun, currents, wind, moon and stars from which he gains a feeling of lightness in his mind. He starts across the ice establishing a rhythmic gait, and he makes it to the other side. The energy chord produced from his observations has struck a resonant chord in the holographic mind bringing his body in rhythm with the surrounding environment.

It behooves us, as Native researchers, to redesign research methodologies that go beyond those we have learned in the Euro-American universities. We must first try to find balance in our own lives before we attempt to establish a meaningful and dynamic relationship with those we are seeking to understand. In some instances we may have to rely on spiritual methods altogether. This will allow us to truly interpret data that we have gathered by asking questions, observing and directly participating in an experience. We, as Native people, thrive on first-hand experience as the primary source of knowledge.

We have heard stories about tuberculosis being healed by drinking juice of the spruce needle, or the remission of cancer by drinking stinkweed juice. These treatments require belief and faith from one's own worldview, using the whole mind and body to try to explain and understand. If no rational explanation is found, then one has to accept this on belief and faith of something greater than you and I. In using this method of knowing it presents a new frontier of research methods using the whole self. The self is consciousness without knowing. It has been said that mysticism is a dialectic of feeling, while science is a dialectic of reason. We must work toward the integration of the intellectual with the mystical for the healing process to be complete. Albert Einstein noted that spirituality is the strongest and noblest motive for scientific research and as such is a philosophical/psychological prerequisite for research.

Most research methodologies in vogue today require that we only use a part of our self. However, the modern scientific method combined with Native ways has the potential to produce a new breed of scientists and engineers who are able to exercise all their capabilities with compassion and a sense of greater purpose as they strive to build a technology kinder to the human, the environment and the spirit that resides within all of us. These scientists will work for restoring balance, healing and living a life that feels just right. This is action-oriented, multi-reality research which will put Alaska Native people on a pathway to greater control of our past, present and future.

Reviving Our Cultures and Languages: A Cup'ik Perspective

John F. Pingayak

Sharing Our Pathways, Vol. 8, Issue 1, Jan/Feb 2003

The anchor for any healthy society is culture: it determines behavior through traditional beliefs and observances; it also governs the life of the people. The foundation for any culture is language, the means of communication which ties the society together. For Alaska Natives, the last 95 years have been such an erosion of culture, cultural institutions and languages that the basis for Alaska Native societies has been undermined resulting in confusion, especially among the young.

Simplicity vs. Complexity

Our ancestors knew exactly what they wanted because they formed and communicated around the circle of life. This is why our Elders are knowledgeable in survival today. They acquired the knowledge by starving and experiencing hunger when the food was scarce. For us to analyze our cultures and our languages, whether they may be simple or complex, will open a thought system that will require high-level cognitive thinking skills. The documentation of our way of life has primarily been written by the outside educators and anthropologists. Where are the Cup'ik interpretations of what has been going on with our people? With that in mind, I will explain my concerns and aspirations for our own Native people of Alaska.

We usually try to make our immediate tasks simple so we can complete our goals one step at a time. We do not try to take on too many objectives at once that will lead to failure. In our Native ways we try to make things as simple as possible which may be why we do less talking and more nonverbal communications. Our way of life may look simple, but it is really complicated within our own philosophies of living.

Following our traditional values is simple when they are reinforced based on the training we have received at a very young age. Our language is simple when we are talked to in the same language from the time we're born. Our Elders practice repeating lessons and stories over and over again, yet they never say "It's boring." It is very important that we develop an outlook on life based on learning about our own ways and traditions. Respect and honor are used to acquire knowledge and wisdom. Nothing comes to us free—we have to work hard for everything. Just as our Elders tell us, laziness and sleepiness will become a poor way of living.

Influence of Dominant Society

I remember when I was a boy, I only knew Cup'ik and heard about all that my parents went through. My parents and their extended family used to spend all of their time trying to survive. The families spent their time in spring, summer and fall camps. I have experienced everything they went through, especially their subsistence way of life. Although men went to canneries in Bristol Bay, the influence of Western culture was not too great in those days. As a boy I used to wonder if we were the only race in the whole world. I would look to the horizon and wonder who would be alive, like me, beyond that horizon. Of course, I did not have aspirations like Columbus, but my frame of thought was on the same track. Since then, I have seen many

John Pingayak plays the drum in a classroom.

other cultures way beyond my expectations. I have traveled to the Soviet Union twice, Brisbane, Australia, New Zealand and Fiji.

Today, my saddest experience is seeing my culture dying without enough effort and adequate solutions to revive it. I'm sorry to say, but most of the programs that deal with our own Native people are not working. Please let me explain. I have been like a broken record, telling everyone that programs are not working because we, the real people, are being overlooked to plan, administer and teach in those programs. Too many of our people are relying on state and federal government for welfare, health care, food stamps and energy assistance. Because of these kinds of outside assistance, our people are forgetting how to work for their own needs.

Self-Determination and Governance

We have not been allowed the chance to determine our own destiny. Most often, when self-determination and self-governance comes into play for our people, many of the federal and state leaders become uptight and do everything they can to block the efforts of our people through courts and legislation. We have not been allowed full power to take care of our own needs. When will that time come? Many of our problems exist because we appear helpless in acquiring the funds to run the programs. In order to run these programs that are vital to the existence of our people we need funding, but when we ask for funds we have to categorize our people as "high risk." How can our people heal if we are not considered fit to live and be like everybody else and have control over our own destiny?

Many years ago we never knew how to be business or corporate leaders or that we could be legislators, teachers, doctors and managers. Now we have awakened from a deep sleep and are beginning to realize that we can take care of it all. We have learned that we can determine our own way of life. We learned we can take over our schools. We learned we can govern ourselves without influence from the outside world. It is up to us to take our future into our own hands.

In this journey of our lives, we all need to start learning from each other. I have given you some of the negative aspects of our Cup'ik lives. Our way of life was a subsistence economy and now much of it has changed to a cash economy. Although our way of life has been influenced by the Western world, we still possess our traditional values, many of which are intended for all races. My Grandpa told me that no matter where we are, we are talking about the same concerns.

We still teach about our traditional tools and some of the traditional clothing in our schools. We are maintaining some of our physical cultural elements but the losing battle in maintaining our language. The only way it's going to survive is for our families to start speaking Cup'ik in our homes. The school can only provide supplementary support for language retention but it alone cannot take on the task to retain our language. Some villages are not too late to save their languages, though others have lost it completely. Our hope lies in those villages with strong Native languages that are being practiced by the young. It is up to us to take over some of these programs and practice being providers for our own people. We are slowly taking responsibility for our mistakes and reshaping the future for our younger generation.

I feel we have a lot to offer to the Western world—all we need is recognition that we are existing and struggling to survive as Cup'ik people in this modern era. I thank you for your support and may the force be with you!

Navigating Across the Tundra with Fred George

Claudette
Engblom-Bradley

Sharing Our Pathways, Vol. 8, Issue 4, Sept/Oct 2003

In Alaska villages along the Kuskokwim River, Yup'ik hunters follow a rigorous schedule for subsistence hunting and trapping of animals, gathering of herbs and berries and ice fishing. Between October freeze-up and April break-up, they travel by snowmachine long distances across the tundra to hunt, trap and gather berries. Snow covers the tundra with a white blanket that is continually stirred up by the strong winds. During long winter nights they navigate across the tundra using stars, frozen grass, tree growth and snow waves to guide their way (Bradley, 2002).

Trained by his father since he was a young boy, Fred George has become a highly skilled navigator of the tundra with 60 years of experience. Currently an Elder of 68 years, he lived with his wife Mary in Akiachak until she passed away in November of 2000. Fred and Mary have eight children and many grandchildren. Nearly everyday Fred leaves to attend to his subsistence responsibilities and returns home with lots of fish and sometimes caribou or ptarmigan. His subsistence activities feed not just his family, but his extended family and sometimes friends.

The following is an interpretation of how Fred George manages to navigate 90 miles across the tundra at night. It is based on the many discussions shared by Fred George and other Elders, Yup'ik teachers and UAF faculty together with the author's experiences on the tundra and investigations of star behavior.

On November 10 at 10 p.m. Fred George begins his first trip of the season across the tundra. At that moment Tunturyuk (Big Dipper) hovers 30 degrees above the northern horizon, like a giant spoon sitting on a table. Scientists have identified the seven stars in the Big

Dipper (from right to left) as alpha, beta, gamma, delta, epsilon, zeta and eta star. The Gamma Star sits directly over due north on the horizon in Akiachak on November 10 at 10 p.m. This position of the dipper is a reference position for Fred George.

Before leaving Akiachak Fred carefully checks his snowmachine for gas and working parts. He loads his machine with hunting equipment, dresses warmly and starts his snowmachine shortly before 10 p.m. He heads out of the village using snowmachine trails heading north. About five miles away from the village at 10 p.m. Fred stops his snowmachine to check the time on his watch and the position of Tunturyuk (Big Dipper).

Fred George checks the position of the third star, Gamma, in the Tunturyuk with a sequence of hand measurements. He uses his right "hand span" with the tip of his thumb at Gamma Star and his pinky pointing down to the horizon. Fred keeps the tip of the pinky in stable position while closing his fingers and rotating his hand downward using "four-finger measurement." He keeps the index finger in stable position and rotates his hand downward using "three-finger measurement" which puts the ring finger at the horizon. The tip of his ring finger locates true north on the horizon.

Fred chooses one of two routes, which lead to his fish camps. If the weather has little or no snow falling or strong winds blowing, he will choose to travel to the northwest fish camp by heading in the direction under the Dipper handle on November 10 at 10 p.m. This direction turns out to be just less than 30 degrees west of north.

If the weather is moderate with some snowfall, clouds and wind (but not completely overcast), Fred will choose his second route and travel due north for two hours and turn northeast under the dipper handle, towards his other fish camp on the Yukon River. By 12 midnight the Dipper has moved to the right and the Dipper handle is over true north on the horizon. His watch tells the direction he needs to turn, which is 30 degrees west of due north.

If the weather is very bad, Fred waits until the storm is over. The Elders do not travel in stormy weather. If a storm comes when they are out on the tundra, they build a snow cave to wait out the storm. This is one reason why weather prediction skills are so important to develop starting at the young age of eight years old. Young boys are told to observe the weather at sunrise and sunset every day. A skilled Elder can predict the weather for the next 12 months.

The tundra has a countless number of lakes between the Kuskokwim and the Yukon Rivers. Every lake has been given a Yup'ik name. The lake names are family names given to the lake for the family's historic use of the lake for fishing and camping. The northeast winds make waves in every lake. The waves freeze in position. The October snow falls over the frozen waves and becomes hard snow; making snow waves rolling in the southwest direction over the lakes. Fred George travels on his snowmachine at 15–20 miles per hour and uses the snow waves to find his direction. He feels the waves kinesthetically with the movement of his snowmachine traveling over the waves. If the snowmachine changes its direction Fred can feel a change in the rhythmic motion. He has learned to maintain the rhythmic motion to retain his course. Fred relies heavily on the snow waves when the sky becomes overcast or the weather is somewhat stormy. However, if the weather is too stormy, he stops, and waits for the storm to pass.

When he exits a lake and travels on tundra, Fred must use the frozen grass and wind-blown trees as compasses. The prevailing northeast winds cause the long blades of grass to lean over in the southwest direction; snow freezes the grass leaning in the southwest direction. The few trees are generally in isolated spots. The heavy winds cause the trees to also lean in the southwest direction and to grow most of their branches and leaves on the southwest side of the tree, leaving the northeast side of the tree barren, which creates a natural compass.

Fred also recognizes landmarks. Landmarks are rivulets, streams and small structures or tiny log houses. During my first trip out on the tundra, Fred identified a partially fallen 10' by 10' log cabin used in the old days by Yup'ik hunters. Such landmarks appear occasionally along his pathway to fish camp. Mary George, Fred's wife, said that the location of landmarks are essential to navigating across the tundra. They reinforce the navigators understanding of his position on his journey.

By now its midnight and Tunturyuk has moved to the left, i.e., counterclockwise 30 degrees. The end of the Dipper handle is directly over true north. The Dipper appears to be turning upward towards east. After riding the tundra for two hours, Fred stops his snowmachine to check his watch and the Tunturyuk. Fred places his watch in front of his chest with the 12 in the north direction and the 6 in the south direction. Fred checks his snowmachine which is heading 5 minutes (11 on his watch) to the left of north (12 on his watch), i.e. 30

degrees west of north. With the 12 heading toward the dipper handle hovering over true north his snowmachine must head in the direction of 11 on his watch, or 5 minutes to the left 12, which is 30 degrees west of north.

He checks the landmarks recognizing the frozen streams and distant mountains. The strongest winds come from the northeast direction. On the first day of snow the wind blows the grass in one direction. Generally the grass is blown to the southwest. The weight of the snow holds the grass in the direction of the wind and the cold temperatures freeze the grass. Frozen grass becomes a natural compass on the tundra. Fred can use the grass to determine his direction.

Another two hours has passed and it's time for Fred to check his watch and the Big Dipper. The Dipper handle has moved upward and east. It appears parallel to a north direction. Fred will hold his hands up so that one is in the north direction and the other is in the direction of the dipper handle. By 4:00 a.m. Fred has reached his fish camp. He needs to build a fire, eat, set up his tent and go to sleep.

On clear or even partially cloudy nights Fred navigates with the Tunturyuk in the late evening and Venus, the morning star, in the morning. In February and March Fred navigates with Venus, the evening star in the evening and in the morning. Fred generally remains home in Akiachak during the coldest month, January.

On his return home in the morning Venus is east and on his left when he faces south. Facing south he places his watch in front of his chest, so that 9 marks the east direction, 12 marks the south and 3 marks the west. Fred knows that Akiachak would be 5 minutes (30 degrees) east of south, i.e., in the direction of 11 on his watch.

Heading 5 minutes to east of south, Fred feels the motion of his snowmachine over the snow waves. He maintains the motion to keep in the direction of Akiachak. The snow waves are perpendicular to the southwest direction. Since his snowmachine is traveling southeast. The left side of the front end rises up first, tilting the snowmachine down on the right side. As the snowmachine goes over the top, the tilt reverses. This motion simulates a boat rocking in the ocean.

Elders say young people are not spending time and listening to Elders as they did in the past to learn their cultural ways and stories. Yet they drive snowmachines out on the tundra and many get lost, run out of gas and cannot find their way home. Fred's knowledge of the stars and the tundra environment would give them a chance to survive.

Preserving Fred's knowledge of navigating across the tundra is important to the self-esteem and cultural identity of Yup'ik people. A study of Fred's ways of navigating across the tundra uncovers the wisdom, courage and ingenuity of his Yup'ik ancestors.

For the rest of our society, Fred's knowledge will enhance any person's library of way-finding or orienteering, plus his knowledge of the stars helps us understand how they move in relation to time. We can use the stars to find our way and tell what time it is.

References

Bradley, C. E., (2002). "Traveling with Fred George: The Changing Ways of Yup'ik Star Navigation in Akiachak, Western Alaska," I. Krupnik & D. Jolly (Eds.), In *The Earth is Faster Now: Indigenous Observations of Arctic Environmental Change*, Fairbanks, AK: Arctic Research Consortium of the United States in cooperation with the Arctic Studies Center, Smithsonian Institution.

Angayuqaq Oscar
Kawagley | # Blowing in the Wind

Sharing Our Pathways, Vol. 9, Issue 2, Mar/Apr 2004

There are messages for us, as a Native people, blowing in the wind
that are older than any of our Native languages. I think one message is telling us that we can make change for the better in our lives
through dedication, motivation, tenacity and traditional creativity to
overcome the limitations of the current education system. This means
that we educate our Native people in their Native languages and

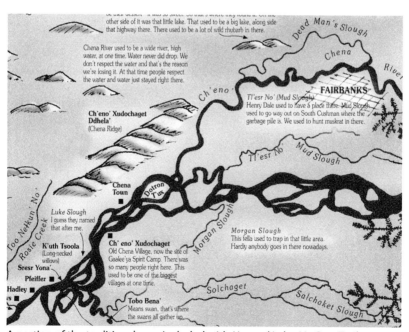

A portion of the traditional map included with *Howard Luke: My Own Trail*.

English to become articulate in both. This will enable them to think in their own worldviews for answers to their problems and exercise the means of control of the modern world to clearly and effectively articulate demands for change.

I use the tetrahedral metaphor as a way of trying to explain the synergistic process of keeping balance in ones life. The base is a triangle with the human, natural and spiritual worlds as the foundation of the worldview. I have read a book which analyzes the number three as a "breaking through to a world of infinite possibilities" (Brailsford, 1999). He further points out that three symbolizes creation and that one and two are the parents of number 3, the first born. If I think of it in this manner then the triune God of the Bible comes into mind. For the tetrahedral, it is the spiritual power that is eternal and omnipresent. Mother Earth is created and from its rocks comes all life, including the human being, thus serving as the basis of all life. This process presents infinite possibilities of solutions for overcoming a mechanical worldview that is so destructive to life, liberty and the pursuit of happiness. It then behooves the Native people to pursue education diligently in their own thought world as well as in the disciplines of the modern world. This enables Native people to use their own problem-solving tools as well as those of the mechanical world to effect change.

I have often said and heard that sense of place serves as the basis for identity and a home for the mind and heart. In some schools, students have been engaged in cultural mapping activities to identify the Native geographic names associated with the features of a particular place. This gives a cultural grid to place over the land, that provides order, meaning and stability to those who live on that land. To know place is to know oneself, which empowers us to do things with courage and determination.

I have experienced a process in New Zealand whereby Maori Elders were taken to landmarks of the Waikato traditional lands. They were reviewing a booklet that had been prepared citing important places, what had transpired there and myths associated with that place. A guide was appointed who gave a running dialogue of points of interest and what was known about them, which the Elders then critiqued. The process was very constructive as it entailed correction of pronunciation of place names and added information to what was already known that sometimes led to significant revisions to the name and what actually happened there. This authentication process is needed as the Maori want to rewrite their history, not from the point of view of an outsider, but from within.

Wouldn't it be advisable for Alaska Native people to engage in a similar process? For urban areas such as Fairbanks, a group of knowledgeable Native Elders could be taken to various historical sites whereby the traditional Native name is given and the story told as to its use, occupancy, burial places of leaders, old migration trails, battle skirmishes, peacemaking, kinship, alliances, particular resources and so forth. All this information would be recorded by video and audio tape, transcribed and edited and later the Elders would again gather to piece together a story acceptable to all. Some beginning examples of this are already available, such as the Minto Mapping Project (ankn.uaf.edu/chei/mapproj.html), the Angoon Cultural Atlas (www.ankn.uaf.edu) and the traditional map and book assembled by Howard Luke (Luke, 1999).

I can foresee a caravan of snow machines transporting Elders to different areas such as camp sites, places of warrior skirmishes, hunting grounds and burial places where the correct name and what transpired there would be clarified. In the summer, boats loaded with Elders could be taken to significant sites agreed upon to tell their stories. I can envision a bus full of Elders slowly going around Bethel recounting the old sites of fish camps, the kasegiq, the original location of Mamtellrilleq south of the Kuskokwim River by the old Air Force airport, and the island that once was in front of the present site. They could explain why the original Yupiat did not settle in the present site, the history of Kepenkuk (now Brown Slough) and *orutsaraq* (place for gathering sphagnum moss for caulking), the location of old reindeer corrals and so forth. This would give our Yupiat a sense of kinship and belonging to a place that one could call home and mean it, because it has a well-documented story from the perspective of the Yupiat people.

I would encourage teachers to take their students out into nature whenever possible, where the local language and culture can come alive in natural ways. By doing this, you are not limiting what is taught to knowledge alone, as the school typically does, but paying attention to the deeper needs of the student and the community. Within the classroom, the natural rhythms of life can be tapped into through singing, dancing and drumming, as well as other traditional activities that are acceptable to Elders and parents. The essential balance that is represented in the tetrahedral metaphor requires attention to all the realms of life, including the human, natural and spiritual. This message is blowing in the wind—a message older than our Native ways.

References

Brailsford, Barry. *Wisdom of the Four Winds*. Stoneprint Press: Christchurch, NZ, 1999.

Luke, Howard. *Howard Luke: My Own Trail*. Fairbanks: Alaska Native Knowledge Network. 1999.

Ray Barnhardt,
Angayuqaq Oscar
Kawagley and
Frank Hill

Cultural Standards and Test Scores

Sharing Our Pathways, Vol. 5, Issue 4, Sept/Oct 2000

With the release of the first Benchmark and High School Graduation Qualifying Exam scores this fall, educators throughout Alaska have been convening to address the many issues that are raised by these new checkpoints on the educational landscape.

Debates are already underway on ways to interpret the results and develop appropriate responses, given the predictable differences in

Harriet Nungasak, Alicia Kanayurak, George Olanna (instructor), Kimberly Rychnovsky and Donald Tritt work on their science projects at the ANSES Science-Culture Camp held at Gaaleeya Spirit Camp July 11–25, 2000. Skills gained at science and cultural camps are brought into the classroom and utilized throughout the school year.

performance among various students and schools. At the heart of these debates are concerns over the use (or misuse) of the test results to make critical judgments about students, teachers and schools in ways that attempt to reduce complex school performance issues down to a few simplistic variables.

We need look no further than the latest editions of Education Week, Phi Delta Kappan or Educational Researcher to see that these debates are occurring on a national scale and that Alaska is not alone in venturing out into uncharted waters in the name of school accountability. Hopefully we can learn from other peoples mistakes, and by doing a few things right, maybe others can learn from our successes. However, this will require taking a long-term perspective on the many issues involved and not expecting to find a silver bullet that will produce instant solutions to long-standing complex problems.

First of all, we must recognize the practical limits of the tests themselves. As diagnostic tools coupled with other related indicators of ability and performance, tests that are properly designed, flexibly administered and judiciously interpreted can provide valuable information to guide educational decision-making. However, there are two features of these legislatively mandated high-stakes tests that inhibit their educational value and thus make it necessary to exercise considerable caution in their use as accountability tools in the current standards-driven environment.

Since the tests are mandated for all students at four grade levels, the sheer number and frequency of the testing introduces a major time and cost factor. As a result, the design of the tests tends to rely on approaches that are simpler and cheaper to administer and score (i.e., multiple choice and short-answer questions) with only minimal use of the more costly, but flexible, culturally adaptable and educationally useful performance-based approaches to assessment. Unfortunately, this emphasis on ease of administration has also narrowed the selection of which content standards count and which ones don't, leaving the harder-to-measure aspects of the standards in the background.

As a result, teachers (and districts) are caught in the dilemma of aligning their teaching and curriculum with the full range of learning outcomes outlined in the standards or narrowing their lessons down to that which is measured on the tests. In this regard, the current testing system can be seen as working against the implementation of the standards-based school reform efforts with which it was originally associated. A true standards-based educational system requires a much broader approach to assessment than current resources allow.

The second feature that reduces the educational value of high-stakes testing is its intended use in making critical decisions that can adversely impact people's lives and careers (e.g., grade-level promotion, eligibility for graduation, teacher reward/punishment and school rating/ranking.) When used for such purposes, the tests themselves tend to revert to those measures that the test-makers (in Alaska's case, CBT/McGraw-Hill) can defend in court when challenged by those affected. Consequently, we see a heavy emphasis on standardization (in both content and administration), whereby many important aspects of the content standards that require local adaptation or are not easily measured are set aside in favor of those items and testing practices that meet the test of "legal defensibility." So we should not be surprised when we run into problems with a testing system that has been constructed around legal and political, rather than educational considerations.

What are the Options?

For better or worse, the Alaska Benchmark and High School Graduation Qualifying Exams are a reality and it is our professional responsibility to do what we can to minimize their negative effects and to maximize their potential benefits. Most critical in that regard is the need to examine the issues that emerge in the broadest context available to us and not to use the results to promote simplistic, short-term solutions to long-term, complex problems. Nor should we fall into the trap of "blaming the victim" (i.e., the student) when there are significant group variations in academic performance. This is especially true in a cross-cultural setting such as rural Alaska, where we have a long history of repetitious unsuccessful educational experimentation on students while ignoring the well-documented source of many of the problems—that is the persistent cultural gulf between teachers and students, school and community.

Based on the experiences in other states and the rife speculation underway here in Alaska, we can expect several things to happen over the next few months. The initial responses to the release of the test results are likely to point to two factors to explain differential performance between students and schools—low teacher expectations and lack of opportunity to learn—each of which will lead to predictable forms of remediation.

Under the banner of "all students can learn to high standards," teachers will be admonished to teach harder and more of whatever it is that students are determined by the tests as lacking. While this may seem logical on the surface, it ignores the possibility that the real issue may not be low expectations at all (though certainly that does exist) and that "more of the same" may exacerbate the problem by producing higher dropout rates rather than addressing the more fundamental issue of lack-of-fit between what we teach, how we teach it and the context in which it is taught. Intensifying the current curriculum and extending schooling into the weekend or summer also ignores the inherent limitations to school improvement in rural Alaska that result from having to import teachers and administrators from outside for whom the village setting is a foreign and inevitably temporary home.

The second issue of making sure students have had the opportunity to learn the subject matter on which they are being tested is more readily identifiable as a problem, but no less complicated (and expensive) in producing a solution. If a small rural school is not offering the level of mathematics instruction that students need to pass the exam, the solution is not to send the students elsewhere for schooling. To assume that a boarding school (as some legislators are suggesting) can make up for the limitations of a village high school ignores the fact that a well-rounded education consists of much more than just the subject matter that is taught in school. It also ignores the negative impact that taking students out of their home has on the family, the community and the student's own future role as a parent and contributing member of society. There is nothing taught in a boarding school that can't be taught cheaper and more effectively in a village school linked together with other village schools in a web of rich and extensive learning opportunities. Furthermore, there are many important things that are learned at home in a village setting that cannot be taught in a boarding school. Boarding schools may be justified as an optional alternative program for selected students, but not as a substitute for village schools.

When providing "opportunities to learn," we need to consider all aspects of a child's upbringing and prepare them in such a way that they can "become responsible, capable and whole human beings in the process" (see Alaska Standards for Culturally Responsive Schools). When we do so, the issues associated with benchmark and qualifying exams will take care of themselves. How then do we go about this with some degree of confidence that we will achieve the outcome we seek—graduates capable of functioning as responsible adults, including passing state exams?

Impact of Cultural Standards on Standardized Test Scores

For the past five years, the Alaska Rural Systemic Initiative has been working intensively with 20 of the 48 rural school districts in the state to implement a series of initiatives that are intended to "systematically document the indigenous knowledge systems of Alaska Native people and develop educational policies and practices that effectively integrate indigenous and western knowledge through a renewed educational system." The assumption behind the AKRSI reform strategy is that if we coordinate our efforts and resources across all aspects of the education system and address the issues in a focused, statewide manner, perhaps better headway will be realized. Two outcomes of this work are worthy of consideration as schools review the results of the state tests and ponder their next steps.

First of all, building an education system with a strong foundation in the local culture appears to produce positive effects in all indicators of school success, including dropout rates, college attendance, parent involvement, grade-point averages and standardized achievement test scores. With regard to student achievement, using the eighth-grade CAT-5 math test scores as an impact indicator for the first four years of implementation of the AKRSI school reform initiatives in the 20 participating school districts (which have historically had the lowest student achievement levels in the state), there has been a differential gain of 5.9% points in the number of students who are performing in the top quartile for AKRSI partner schools over non-AKRSI rural schools. AKRSI schools gained 6.9% points in the upper quartile compared to a 1.0% point gain for non-AKRSI schools, with a corresponding decrease in the lower quartile. With AKRSI districts now producing 24.3% of their students testing in the upper quartile, they are only 0.7% point below the national average. In other words, through strong place-based education initiatives, the AKRSI schools are closing the achievement gap with the non-AKRSI schools. The following graph illustrates the gains on a year-by-year basis:

Eighth Grade Mathematics Performance
Percentage of Students on Top Quartile on CAT-5, 1996–1999

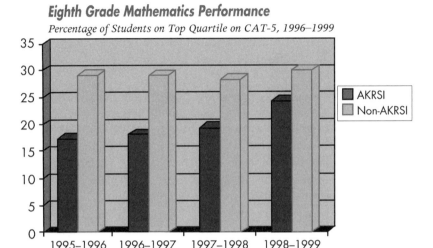

In reviewing this data (drawn from the state summary of the school district report cards), it is clear that something has been going on in the 20 AKRSI school districts that is producing a slow but steady gain in the standardized test scores (along with all the other indicators we have been tracking.) So just what is it that is producing these results? Since the gains are widespread across all cultural regions and the scores show consistent improvement over each of the four years, they clearly are not a function of one particular curricular or pedagogical initiative, nor are they limited to AKRSI-sponsored activities. The best summary of what it is that has produced these results can be found in the *Alaska Standards for Culturally Responsive Schools*.

These "cultural standards" were compiled by educators from throughout the state as an outgrowth of the work that was initiated through the Alaska Rural Systemic Initiative and implemented in varying degrees by the participating schools. As such, when coupled with the impact data summarized here, they provide some concrete guidelines for schools and communities to consider as they construct school improvement plans aimed at producing more effective educational programs for the students in their care. We now have strong evidence that when we make a diligent and persistent effort to forge a strong cultural fit between what we teach, how we teach and the context in which we teach, we can produce successful, well-rounded graduates who are also capable of producing satisfactory test scores.

The AKRSI staff are currently working with the Alaska Department of Education and Early Development to provide assistance to schools for whom cultural considerations play an important part in the design of their educational programs. Alaska Native educators, including Elders, are an important resource that all schools need to draw upon to make sure that our responses to the results of the Alaska Benchmark and High School Graduation Qualifying Exams go beyond Band-Aid solutions and lead to long-term improvement of our education systems. The future of our state depends on it. Curricular resources and technical assistance for such efforts are available through the regional Native Educator Associations, as well as the Alaska Native Knowledge Network web site at www.ankn.uaf.edu.

.

Appendices

Alaska Standards for Culturally Responsive Schools

Adopted by the Assembly of Alaska Native Educators Anchorage, Alaska, February 3, 1998. Published by the Alaska Native Knowledge Network, 1998.

Alaska Standards for Culturally-Responsive Schools are endorsed by:

Alaska Federation of Natives
Association of Northwest Native Educators
Alaska Rural Systemic Initiative
Alaska Native Education Student Association
Alaska Rural Challenge
Alutiiq Native Educator Association
Alaska Native Knowledge Network
Unangan Educator Association
Ciulistet Research Association
Alaska Native Education Council
Association of Interior Native Educators
Alaska Native Teachers for Excellence/Anchorage
Southeast Native Educators Association
Consortium for Alaska Native Higher Education
North Slope Inupiaq Educators Association
Alaska First Nations Research Network
Association of Native Educators of the Lower
    Kuskokwim
Center For Cross-Cultural Studies
Alaska State Board of Education

Preface

The following standards have been developed by Alaska Native educators to provide a way for schools and communities to examine the extent to which they are attending to the educational and cultural well being of the students in their care. These "cultural standards" are predicated on the belief that a firm grounding in the heritage language and culture indigenous to a particular place is a fundamental prerequisite for the development of culturally-healthy students and communities associated with that place, and thus is an essential ingredient for identifying the appropriate qualities and practices associated with culturally- responsive educators, curriculum and schools.

For several years, Alaska has been developing "content standards" to define what students should know and be able to do as they go through school. In addition, "performance standards" are being developed for teachers and administrators, and a set of "quality school standards" have been put forward by the Alaska Department of Education to serve as a basis for accrediting schools in Alaska. To the extent that these state standards are written for general use throughout Alaska, they don't always address some of the special issues that are of critical importance to schools in rural Alaska, particularly those serving Alaska Native communities and students.

Through a series of regional and statewide meetings associated with the Alaska Rural Systemic Initiative (with funding provided by the National Science Foundation and the Annenberg Rural Challenge, and administrative support from the Alaska Federation of Natives in collaboration with the University of Alaska), Alaska Native educators have developed the following *Alaska Standards for Culturally-Responsive Schools* for consideration by educators serving Native students around the state. Though the emphasis is on rural schools serving Native communities, many of the standards are applicable to all students and communities because they focus curricular attention on in-depth study of the surrounding physical and cultural environment in which the school is situated, while recognizing the unique contribution that indigenous people can make to such study as long-term inhabitants who have accumulated extensive specialized knowledge related to that environment.

Standards have been drawn up in five areas, including those for students, educators, curriculum, schools, and communities. These "cultural standards" provide guidelines or touchstones against which schools and communities can examine what they are doing to attend to the cultural well-being of the young people they are responsible for nurturing to adulthood. The standards included here serve as a complement to, not as a replacement for, those adopted by the State of Alaska. While the state standards stipulate what students should know and be able to do, the cultural standards are oriented more toward providing guidance on how to get them there in such a way that they become responsible, capable and whole human beings in the process. The emphasis is on fostering a strong connection between what students experience in school and their lives out of school by providing opportunities for students to engage in in-depth experiential learning in real-world contexts. By shifting the focus in the curriculum from teaching/ learning about cultural heritage as another subject to teaching/learning through the local culture as a foundation for all education, it is intended that all forms of knowledge, ways of knowing and world views be recognized as equally valid, adaptable and complementary to one another in mutually beneficial ways.

The cultural standards outlined in this document are not intended to be inclusive, exclusive or conclusive, and thus should be reviewed and adapted to fit local needs. Each school, community and related organization should consider which of these standards are appropriate and which are not, and when necessary, develop additional cultural standards to accommodate local circumstances. Terms should be interpreted to fit local conventions, especially with reference to meanings associated with the definition of Elder, tradition, spirituality, or anything relating to the use of the local language. Where differences of interpretation exist, they should be respected and accommodated to the maximum extent possible. The cultural standards are not intended to produce standardization, but rather to encourage schools to nurture and build upon the rich and varied cultural traditions that continue to be practiced in communities throughout Alaska.

Some of the multiple uses to which these cultural standards may be put are as follows:

1. They may be used as a basis for reviewing school or district-level goals, policies and practices with regard to the curriculum and pedagogy being implemented in each community or cultural area.

2. They may be used by a local community to examine the kind of home/family environment and parenting support systems that are provided for the upbringing of its children.

3. They may be used to devise locally appropriate ways to review student and teacher performance as it relates to nurturing and practicing culturally-healthy behavior, including serving as potential graduation requirements for students.

4. They may be used to strengthen the commitment to revitalizing the local language and culture and fostering the involvement of Elders as an educational resource.

5. They may be used to help teachers identify teaching practices that are adaptable to the cultural context in which they are teaching.

6. They may be used to guide the preparation and orientation of teachers in ways that help them attend to the cultural well-being of their students.

7. They may serve as criteria against which to evaluate educational programs intended to address the cultural needs of students.

8. They may be used to guide the formation of state-level policies and regulations and the allocation of resources in support of equal educational opportunities for all children in Alaska.

Curriculum resources and technical support to implement the kind of learning experiences encouraged by the enclosed cultural standards may be found through the Alaska Native Knowledge Network web site located at http://www.ankn.uaf.edu, or call (907) 474-5897.

Cultural Standards for Students

A. Culturally-knowledgeable students are well grounded in the cultural heritage and traditions of their community.

Students who meet this cultural standard are able to:

1. assume responsibility for their role in relation to the well-being of the cultural community and their life-long obligations as a community member;

2. recount their own genealogy and family history;
3. acquire and pass on the traditions of their community through oral and written history;
4. practice their traditional responsibilities to the surrounding environment;
5. reflect through their own actions the critical role that the local heritage language plays in fostering a sense of who they are and how they understand the world around them;
6. live a life in accordance with the cultural values and traditions of the local community and integrate them into their everyday behavior.
7. determine the place of their cultural community in the regional, state, national and international political and economic systems;

B. **Culturally-knowledgeable students are able to build on the knowledge and skills of the local cultural community as a foundation from which to achieve personal and academic success throughout life.**

Students who meet this cultural standard are able to:

1. acquire insights from other cultures without diminishing the integrity of their own;
2. make effective use of the knowledge, skills and ways of knowing from their own cultural traditions to learn about the larger world in which they live;
3. make appropriate choices regarding the long-term consequences of their actions;
4. identify appropriate forms of technology and anticipate the consequences of their use for improving the quality of life in the community.

C. **Culturally-knowledgeable students are able to actively participate in various cultural environments.**

Students who meet this cultural standard are able to:

1. perform subsistence activities in ways that are appropriate to local cultural traditions;

2. make constructive contributions to the governance of their community and the well-being of their family;

3. attain a healthy lifestyle through which they are able to maintain their own social, emotional, physical, intellectual and spiritual well-being;

4. enter into and function effectively in a variety of cultural settings.

D. **Culturally-knowledgeable students are able to engage effectively in learning activities that are based on traditional ways of knowing and learning.**

Students who meet this cultural standard are able to:

1. acquire in-depth cultural knowledge through active participation and meaningful interaction with Elders;

2. participate in and make constructive contributions to the learning activities associated with a traditional camp environment;

3. interact with Elders in a loving and respectful way that demonstrates an appreciation of their role as culture-bearers and educators in the community;

4. gather oral and written history information from the local community and provide an appropriate interpretation of its cultural meaning and significance;

5. identify and utilize appropriate sources of cultural knowledge to find solutions to everyday problems;

6. engage in a realistic self-assessment to identify strengths and needs and make appropriate decisions to enhance life skills.

E. **Culturally-knowledgeable students demonstrate an awareness and appreciation of the relationships and processes of interaction of all elements in the world around them.**

Students who meet this cultural standard are able to:

1. recognize and build upon the inter-relationships that exist among the spiritual, natural and human realms in the world around them, as reflected in their own cultural traditions and beliefs as well as those of others;

2. understand the ecology and geography of the bioregion they inhabit;
3. demonstrate an understanding of the relationship between world view and the way knowledge is formed and used;
4. determine how ideas and concepts from one knowledge system relate to those derived from other knowledge systems;
5. recognize how and why cultures change over time;
6. anticipate the changes that occur when different cultural systems come in contact with one another;
7. determine how cultural values and beliefs influence the interaction of people from different cultural backgrounds;
8. identify and appreciate who they are and their place in the world.

Cultural Standards for Educators

A. **Culturally-responsive educators incorporate local ways of knowing and teaching in their work.**

Educators who meet this cultural standard:

1. recognize the validity and integrity of the traditional knowledge system;
2. utilize Elders' expertise in multiple ways in their teaching;
3. provide opportunities and time for students to learn in settings where local cultural knowledge and skills are naturally relevant;
4. provide opportunities for students to learn through observation and hands-on demonstration of cultural knowledge and skills;
5. adhere to the cultural and intellectual property rights that pertain to all aspects of the local knowledge they are addressing;
6. continually involve themselves in learning about the local culture.

B. **Culturally-responsive educators use the local environment and community resources on a regular basis to link what they are teaching to the everyday lives of the students.**

Educators who meet this cultural standard:

1. regularly engage students in appropriate projects and experiential learning activities in the surrounding environment;
2. utilize traditional settings such as camps as learning environments for transmitting both cultural and academic knowledge and skills;
3. provide integrated learning activities organized around themes of local significance and across subject areas;
4. are knowledgeable in all the areas of local history and cultural tradition that may have bearing on their work as a teacher, including the appropriate times for certain knowledge to be taught;
5. seek to ground all teaching in a constructive process built on a local cultural foundation.

C. **Culturally-responsive educators participate in community events and activities in an appropriate and supportive way.**

Educators who meet this cultural standard:

1. become active members of the community in which they teach and make positive and culturally-appropriate contributions to the well being of that community;
2. exercise professional responsibilities in the context of local cultural traditions and expectations;
3. maintain a close working relationship with and make appropriate use of the cultural and professional expertise of their co-workers from the local community.

D. **Culturally-responsive educators work closely with parents to achieve a high level of complementary educational expectations between home and school.**

Educators who meet this cultural standard:

1. promote extensive community and parental interaction and involvement in their children's education;
2. involve Elders, parents and local leaders in all aspects of instructional planning and implementation;

3. seek to continually learn about and build upon the cultural knowledge that students bring with them from their homes and community;
4. seek to learn the local heritage language and promote its use in their teaching.

E. **Culturally-responsive educators recognize the full educational potential of each student and provide the challenges necessary for them to achieve that potential.**

Educators who meet this cultural standard:

1. recognize cultural differences as positive attributes around which to build appropriate educational experiences;
2. provide learning opportunities that help students recognize the integrity of the knowledge they bring with them and use that knowledge as a springboard to new understandings;
3. reinforce the student's sense of cultural identity and place in the world;
4. acquaint students with the world beyond their home community in ways that expand their horizons while strengthening their own identities;
5. recognize the need for all people to understand the importance of learning about other cultures and appreciating what each has to offer.

Cultural Standards for Curriculum

A. **A culturally-responsive curriculum reinforces the integrity of the cultural knowledge that students bring with them.**

A curriculum that meets this cultural standard:

1. recognizes that all knowledge is imbedded in a larger system of cultural beliefs, values and practices, each with its own integrity and interconnectedness;

2. insures that students acquire not only the surface knowledge of their culture, but are also well grounded in the deeper aspects of the associated beliefs and practices;
3. incorporates contemporary adaptations along with the historical and traditional aspects of the local culture;
4. respects and validates knowledge that has been derived from a variety of cultural traditions;
5. provides opportunities for students to study all subjects starting from a base in the local knowledge system.

B. **A culturally-responsive curriculum recognizes cultural knowledge as part of a living and constantly adapting system that is grounded in the past, but continues to grow through the present and into the future.**

A curriculum that meets this cultural standard:

1. recognizes the contemporary validity of much of the traditional cultural knowledge, values and beliefs, and grounds students learning in the principles and practices associated with that knowledge;
2. provides students with an understanding of the dynamics of cultural systems as they change over time, and as they are impacted by external forces;
3. incorporates the in-depth study of unique elements of contemporary life in Native communities in Alaska, such as the Alaska Native Claims Settlement Act, subsistence, sovereignty and self-determination.

C. **A culturally-responsive curriculum uses the local language and cultural knowledge as a foundation for the rest of the curriculum.**

A curriculum that meets this cultural standard:

1. utilizes the local language as a base from which to learn the deeper meanings of the local cultural knowledge, values, beliefs and practices;
2. recognizes the depth of knowledge that is associated with the long inhabitation of a particular place and utilizes the study

of "place" as a basis for the comparative analysis of contemporary social, political and economic systems;

3. incorporates language and cultural immersion experiences wherever in-depth cultural understanding is necessary;
4. views all community members as potential teachers and all events in the community as potential learning opportunities;
5. treats local cultural knowledge as a means to acquire the conventional curriculum content as outlined in state standards, as well as an end in itself;
6. makes appropriate use of modern tools and technology to help document and transmit traditional cultural knowledge;
7. is sensitive to traditional cultural protocol, including role of spirituality, as it relates to appropriate uses of local knowledge.

D. **A culturally-responsive curriculum fosters a complementary relationship across knowledge derived from diverse knowledge systems.**

A curriculum that meets this cultural standard:

1. draws parallels between knowledge derived from oral tradition and that derived from books;
2. engages students in the construction of new knowledge and understandings that contribute to an ever-expanding view of the world.

E. **A culturally-responsive curriculum situates local knowledge and actions in a global context.**

A curriculum that meets this cultural standard:

1. encourages students to consider the inter-relationship between their local circumstances and the global community;
2. conveys to students that every culture and community contributes to, at the same time that it receives from the global knowledge base;
3. prepares students to "think globally, act locally."

Cultural Standards for Schools

A. A culturally-responsive school fosters the on-going participation of Elders in all aspects of the schooling process.

A school that meets this cultural standard:

1. maintains multiple avenues for Elders to interact formally and informally with students at all times;
2. provides opportunities for students to regularly engage in the documenting of Elders' cultural knowledge and produce appropriate print and multimedia materials that share this knowledge with others;
3. includes explicit statements regarding the cultural values that are fostered in the community and integrates those values in all aspects of the school program and operation;
4. utilizes educational models that are grounded in the traditional world view and ways of knowing associated with the cultural knowledge system reflected in the community.

B. A culturally-responsive school provides multiple avenues for students to access the learning that is offered, as well as multiple forms of assessment for students to demonstrate what they have learned.

A school that meets this cultural standard:

1. utilizes a broad range of culturally-appropriate performance standards to assess student knowledge and skills;
2. encourages and supports experientially oriented approaches to education that makes extensive use of community-based resources and expertise;
3. provides cultural and language immersion programs in which student acquire in-depth understanding of the culture of which they are members;
4. helps students develop the capacity to assess their own strengths and weaknesses and make appropriate decisions based on such a self-assessment.

C. A culturally-responsive school provides opportunities for students to learn in and/or about their heritage language.

A school that meets this cultural standard:

1. provides language immersion opportunities for students who wish to learn in their heritage language;
2. offers courses that acquaint all students with the heritage language of the local community;
3. makes available reading materials and courses through which students can acquire literacy in the heritage language;
4. provides opportunities for teachers to gain familiarity with the heritage language of the students they teach through summer immersion experiences.

D. A culturally-responsive school has a high level of involvement of professional staff who are of the same cultural background as the students with whom they are working.

A school that meets this cultural standard:

1. encourages and supports the professional development of local personnel to assume teaching and administrative roles in the school;
2. recruits and hires teachers whose background is similar to that of the students they will be teaching;
3. provides a cultural orientation camp and mentoring program for new teachers to learn about and adjust to the cultural expectations and practices of the community and school;
4. fosters and supports opportunities for teachers to participate in professional activities and associations that help them expand their repertoire of cultural knowledge and pedagogical skills.

E. A culturally-responsive school consists of facilities that are compatible with the community environment in which they are situated.

A school that meets this cultural standard:

1. provides a physical environment that is inviting and readily accessible for local people to enter and utilize;
2. makes use of facilities throughout the community to demonstrate that education is a community-wide process involving everyone as teachers;
3. utilizes local expertise, including students, to provide culturally-appropriate displays of arts, crafts and other forms of decoration and space design.

F. **A culturally-responsive school fosters extensive on-going participation, communication and interaction between school and community personnel.**

A school that meets this cultural standard:

1. holds regular formal and informal events bringing together students, parents, teachers and other school and community personnel to review, evaluate and plan the educational program that is being offered;
2. provides regular opportunities for local and regional board deliberations and decision-making on policy, program and personnel issues related to the school;
3. sponsors on-going activities and events in the school and community that celebrate and provide opportunities for students to put into practice and display their knowledge of local cultural traditions.

Cultural Standards for Communities

A. **A culturally-supportive community incorporates the practice of local cultural traditions in its everyday affairs.**

A community that meets this cultural standard:

1. provides respected Elders with a place of honor in community functions;
2. models culturally-appropriate behavior in the day-to-day life of the community;

3. utilizes traditional child-rearing and parenting practices that reinforce a sense of identity and belonging;
4. organizes and encourages participation of members from all ages in regular community-wide, family-oriented events;
5. incorporates and reinforces traditional cultural values and beliefs in all formal and informal community functions.

B. **A culturally-supportive community nurtures the use of the local heritage language.**

A community that meets this cultural standard:

1. recognizes the role that language plays in conveying the deeper aspects of cultural knowledge and traditions;
2. sponsors local heritage language immersion opportunities for young children when they are at the critical age for language learning;
3. encourages the use of the local heritage language whenever possible in the everyday affairs of the community, including meetings, cultural events, print materials and broadcast media;
4. assists in the preparation of curriculum resource material in the local heritage language for use in the school;
5. provides simultaneous translation services for public meetings where persons unfamiliar with the local heritage language are participants.

C. **A culturally-supportive community takes an active role in the education of all its members.**

A community that meets this cultural standard:

1. encourages broad-based participation of parents in all aspects of their children's education, both in and out of school;
2. insures active participation by community members in reviewing all local, regional and state initiatives that have bearing on the education of their children;
3. encourages and supports members of the local community who wish to pursue further education to assume teaching and administrative roles in the school;

4. engages in subsistence activities, sponsors cultural camps and hosts community events that provide an opportunity for children to actively participate in and learn appropriate cultural values and behavior;

5. provides opportunities for all community members to acquire and practice the appropriate knowledge and skills associated with local cultural traditions.

D. **A culturally-supportive community nurtures family responsibility, sense of belonging and cultural identity.**

A community that meets this cultural standard:

1. fosters cross-generational sharing of parenting and child-rearing practices;

2. creates a supportive environment for youth to participate in local affairs and acquire the skills to be contributing members of the community;

3. adopts the adage, "It takes the whole village to raise a child."

E. **A culturally-supportive community assists teachers in learning and utilizing local cultural traditions and practices.**

A community that meets this cultural standard:

1. sponsors a cultural orientation camp and community mentoring program for new teachers to learn about and adjust to the cultural expectations and practices of the community;

2. encourages teachers to make use of facilities and expertise in the community to demonstrate that education is a community-wide process involving everyone as teachers;

3. sponsors regular community/school potlucks to celebrate the work of students and teachers and to promote ongoing interaction and communication between teachers and parents;

4. attempts to articulate the cultural knowledge, values and beliefs that it wishes teachers to incorporate into the school curriculum;

5. establishes a program to insure the availability of Elders' expertise in all aspects of the educational program in the school.

F. A culturally-supportive community contributes to all aspects of curriculum design and implementation in the local school.

A community that meets this cultural standard:

1. takes an active part in the development of the mission, goals and content of the local educational program;
2. promotes the active involvement of students with Elders in the documentation and preservation of traditional knowledge through a variety of print and multimedia formats;
3. facilitates teacher involvement in community activities and encourages the use of the local environment as a curricular resource;
4. promotes parental involvement in all aspects of their children's educational experience.

Southwest

Bristol Bay Yup'ik Values

Have respect for our land and its resources at all times
Be helpful to one another
Share with others whenever possible
Respect and care for other's property
Respect spiritual values
Learn hunting and outdoor survival skills
Provide for and take good care of your family
Through love, respect your children
Respect your elders
Work hard and don't be lazy
Refrain from alcohol and drug use
Learn, preserve, and be proud of the Native
    way of life

Cup'ik Values

Help other people.
Help with family chores and needs.
Early to bed and early to rise.
Provide time to see how your life is going.
There's always time to play AFTER your work is
    done.
Pingnatugyaraq: learn to do things yourself.
Respect and honor your elders
Always show good behavior
Listen to all advice given to you.
Remember what you are taught and told.

Respect other peoples belongings.
Respect the animals you catch for food.
Gather knowledge and wisdom from the elders.
Never give up in trying to do what you set your mind on.

Unangan Values

Life is gifted to you. What you make of it is your gift in return.
Know your family tree, relations and people's history.
Live with and respect the land, sea, and all nature.
Respect and be aware of the creator in all living things.
Always learn and maintain a balance.
Subsistence is sustenance for the life.
Our language defines who we are and lets us communicate with one another.

Southcentral

Kodiak Alutiiq Cultural Values

Our Elders
Our heritage language
Family and the kinship of our ancestors and living relatives
Ties to our homeland
A subsistence lifestyle, respectful of and sustained by the natural world
Traditional arts, skills and ingenuity
Faith and a spiritual life, from ancestral beliefs to the diverse faiths of today
Sharing: we welcome everyone
Sense of humor
Learning by doing, observing and listening
Stewardship of the animals, land, sky and waters
Trust

Our people: we are responsible for each other and
ourselves
Respect for self, others and our environment is
inherent in all of these values.

Southeast

Southeast Traditional Tribal Values

Discipline and obedience to the traditions of our
ancestors
Respect for self, Elders, and others
Respect for nature and property
Patience
Pride in family, clan and traditions is found in love,
loyalty and generosity
Be strong in mind, body and spirit
Humor
Hold each other up
Listen well and with respect
Speak with care
We are stewards of the air, land and sea
Reverence for our creator
Live in peace and harmony
Be strong and have courage

Far North

Iñupiaq Values

Knowledge of Language
Sharing
Respect for Others
Cooperation
Respect for Elders
Love for Children
Hard Work
Knowledge of Family Tree

Avoidance of Conflict
Respect for Nature
Spirituality
Humor
Family Roles
Hunter Success
Domestic Skills
Humility
Responsibility to Tribe

Interior

Athabascan Values

Self-sufficiency
Hard Work
Care and Provision for the Family
Family Relations
Unity
Honor
Honesty
Love for Children
Sharing
Caring
Village Cooperation and Responsibility to Village
Respect for Elders and Others
Respect for Knowledge
Wisdom from Life Experiences
Respect for the Land
Respect for Nature
Practice of Traditions
Honoring Ancestors
Spirituality